FIVE KEY CONCEPTS IN ANTHROPOLOGICAL THINKING

Richard J. Perry

St. Lawrence University

Upper Saddle River, NJ 07458

Library of Congress Cataloging-in-Publication Data

Perry, Richard John
    Five key concepts in anthropological thinking / Richard J. Perry—1st ed.
        p. cm.
    Includes bibliographical references and index.
    ISBN 0-13-097140-5 (pbk.)
    1. Anthropology. 2. Anthropology—History. 3. Anthropology—Philosophy. I. Title: 5
key concepts in anthropological thinking. II. Title.

GN25 .P39 2003
301—dc21

2002025815

AVP, Publisher: Nancy Roberts
Editorial Assistant: Lee Peterson
Editorial/production supervision and interior design: Mary Araneo
Marketing Manager: Amy Speckman
Prepress and Manufacturing Buyer: Ben Smith
Cover Art Director: Jayne Conte
Cover Designer: Bruce Kenselaar
Director, Image Resource Center: Melinda Reo
Manager, Image Rights and Permissions: Zina Arabia
Interior Image Specialist: Beth Boyd-Brenzel
Image Researcher: Beaura Kathy Ringwold
Image Permission Coordinator: Joanne Dippel

This book was set in 10/12 Palatino by Interactive Composition Corporation
and was printed and bound by Courier Companies, Inc. The cover was
printed by Phoenix Color Corp.

© 2003 by Pearson Education, Inc.
Upper Saddle River, New Jersey 07458

Printed in the United States of America

10 9 8 7 6 5 4 3 2 1

ISBN 0-13-097140-5

Pearson Education LTD., London
Pearson Education Australia PTY, Limited, Sydney
Pearson Education Singapore, Pte. Ltd
Pearson Education North Asia Ltd, Hong Kong
Pearson Education Canada, Ltd., Toronto
Pearson Educación de Mexico, S.A. de C.V.
Pearson Education—Japan, Tokyo
Pearson Education Malaysia, Pte. Ltd
Pearson Education, Upper Saddle River, New Jersey

To Ali and Grego,

with love

CONTENTS

Chapter 3
THE IDEA OF CULTURE   55

Chapter 4
THE IDEA OF STRUCTURE   95

PREFACE

For many students the most intriguing aspects of anthropology are descriptions of various cultures, explorations of prehistoric civilizations, or the mysteries of the human fossil record. When it comes to theory, intrigue is not quite the right term. Apprehension and aversion might be more accurate.

Much of this attitude no doubt arises from a sense that theoretical issues are arid and abstract at best, and perhaps still worse, that they have little to do with "reality." It may not be evident that even the most engaging narratives of cultural descriptions, reconstructions of prehistory, or interpretations of the fossil record present reality from one or another theoretical perspective, whether that perspective is explicit or not.

As the elders among the anthropology faculty know, any serious student of anthropology needs to have a good grasp of the history of the discipline and the development of its central ideas. This is especially so nowadays when sociocultural anthropology, in particular, has come under serious criticism—much of it based on erroneous perceptions of what anthropology is. Anthropology students need to know what anthropology is about, how it came to be that way, and why. They need to have a good sense of current perspectives, including the self-doubts and internal critiques that have always characterized anthropology and continue to do so. They should also have a good familiarity with the mistakes of the past and why we now consider them to be mistakes.

Students need to be conversant with the faltering and often unsuccessful attempts to account for the human experience—not only to avoid covering old ground and repeating past errors, but to develop a clear distinction between the past and present states of their field. They need, in other words, to be able to distinguish valid critiques of present theory from specious claims that confuse outmoded assumptions with current anthropological thinking.

This is not all drudge-work and duty. Faculty old timers are aware that theory has been among the most contentious, and therefore among the most interesting, aspects of the anthropological enterprise. Anthropologists have always loved a good debate.

After more years than I care to disclose of teaching undergraduate courses ranging from the introduction to cultural anthropology to a senior-level seminar on the history of anthropological theory, it has long been apparent to me and my students that we need more texts on theory that they find accessible. Marvin Harris's *Rise of Anthropological Theory*, a theoretical landmark in its own right, is now over three decades old and presents a massive challenge for undergraduate students, though it is well worth their efforts (Harris 1968). Other texts less comprehensive than Harris's have come and gone, many of them now out of print.

What most of these books have in common is an emphasis on "great names" in anthropological theory. Although this has been useful for certain purposes, this book takes a somewhat different tack. We will pay due attention to our theoretical ancestors, but we will start from the premise that as great as many of these names may be, the most valuable focus for students is the flow and development of *ideas*. Ideas and their implications, over and above their authors, will receive the major focus here.

On the other hand, this book is certainly not intended to be an alternative to reading the original works of theorists. The purpose here is to discuss their ideas in the context of other ideas—to juxtapose, compare, and contrast. But the fact remains that to develop a full understanding of what various people have had to say, there is no substitute for reading what they wrote. The idea of this book is to complement readings of major theorists, which are available in excerpted form in such collections as Bohannan's and Glazer's *High Points in Anthropology* (1988), and McGee's and Warms's *Anthropological Theory* (2000), or in the original works of the theorists themselves.

It has been a characteristic of anthropology that many of its important ideas have persisted, some of them altering in the process, some returning as old hardware with new polish, influencing and competing with one another throughout the past two centuries. This peculiar nonlinear interweaving of ideas and concepts has made the history of the discipline difficult to teach and all the more important to understand.

To grapple with this tangle of ideas, assumptions, assertions, and questions, this book focuses on five concepts that have constituted major strands in the fabric of the discipline. These concepts are *evolution, culture, structure, function*, and *relativism*. Each of them touches to some extent on others—sometimes with considerable sparks—and each leads into a range of tangential issues. Together, they offer a substantial framework for comprehending the nature of current anthropological thinking and exploring how it has reached its present state.

I happily acknowledge that this book is the product of many people's efforts. Most profound, perhaps, is the debt to the many anthropologists of the past who devoted their lives to shaping and debating an understanding of what it means to be human. I owe many thanks to the following reviewers for their careful and thoughtful reading of the manuscript: Michael Angrosino, University of South Florida; E. Paul Durrenberger, The Pennsylvania State University; Mark Moberg, University of South Alabama; Ratimaya S. Bush, Wright State University; Kelly D. Alley, Auburn University; Geraldine Gamburd, University of Massachusetts, Dartmouth. They offered some excellent criticisms and extraordinarily useful advice. I am grateful as well to my dad who, though not an anthropologist, seemed to feel that some of the book, at least, made sense. I also thank Nancy Roberts and Lee Peterson of Prentice Hall for their congenial encouragement and Mary Araneo for her production work.

Most immediately, however, I express gratitude to Alice Pomponio, my wife, department chair, and professor of anthropology at St. Lawrence University, who was willing to read through this manuscript more than once and make some excellent suggestions for revision. Inspired by our time in Kenya a few years ago, I have promised to roast a goat in her honor.

I seize this rare opportunity also to thank others in Kenya: Mike and Judy Rainy; Ngangan Lesorogol ("Pakuo"), who made us at home in his boma in Samburu District and brought us into the house of his wife Mama Lalasi; and David Kitawi and his brother Christopher Fumbu, whose homes were warm and welcoming and whose companionship made hiking the trails of the Taita Hills a pleasure.

In closing, finally, I cannot fail to thank the St. Lawrence anthropology majors of my senior seminar in 2000 and 2001. They allowed me to "field test" earlier drafts of this book on them, and they devised the discussion questions that appear at the end of each chapter. Specifically, thanks and best wishes to Ross Ackley, Jon Ainslie, Jeff Arango, McKenzie Barnes, Leah Barth, Megan Bronson, Katie Ciuffo, Rhianna Cohen, Erin Dennison, Kelli Ehrensbeck, Victoria Engel, Jen Fonda, Shannon Glazer, Zach Green, Andy Grossman, Tanya Justham, Shara Korn, Renee Koster, Jake Lamarine, Chris Little, Sarah Lott, Matt Marshall, Brynn Martusiewicz, Johanna Miller, Rob Murano, Owen Murphy, Jessica Niven, Corey Null, Matt O'Brien, Margaret Sandrof, Andrew Solod, Matt Sukeforth, Andy Tefft, Kelly Thayer, and Hope Thornton.

Richard J. Perry

Chapter 1

INTRODUCTION

The desire to understand other people is probably as old as humankind itself. The formalization of this quest as an academic discipline that defines itself as "the study of humanity"—anthropology—is considerably younger. But whatever birth date we care to assign the discipline of anthropology, its earliest thinkers drew on a repertoire of previously existing ideas, some of them ancient. They reformulated some, challenged others, tried to refute or refine still others, and many times resurrected old concepts. At times they mistook old, half-forgotten ideas for new insights. In a sense, the development of anthropological thought has not so much resembled a smoothly flowing river as a complex delta, with some currents forging ahead for a time, others meandering back on themselves, and a few reaching dead-end pools.

Fredrik Barth asserts:

> Any careful reading of the anthropological literature of the last hundred years suggests that social and cultural anthropologists have expended much effort in rediscovering old thoughts and repeating old mistakes. (2001:435)

Perhaps only a bit more kindly, Jack Goody notes:

> The history of anthropology does not offer much firm ground to tread upon . . . it is often characterized by a series of paradigm reversals at the higher level which resemble changes in clothing fashions. (1995:80)

1

These allegations may seem to be an odd way to begin a book on anthropological theory, but they warrant serious attention. Among other things, they demonstrate that historically, anthropologists have been among the severest critics of their own discipline—a tradition that has gone on with undiminished energy to the present. Yet these are also statements of people who have expressed their sense of the value and importance of anthropology by devoting their lives to it.

Few of even the most vehement critics, though, would deny that anthropology has progressed over the past century or so. We now have a vastly greater bank of information. Thousands of painstaking descriptions of hundreds of human populations—much of this information acquired at great personal risk or cost—rest on library shelves awaiting the interested reader or the student working on a research paper (who, one hopes, is also an interested reader). We have lots of facts, although we shall have occasion throughout the book to discuss just what "having lots of facts" may mean.

In any case, facts do not speak for themselves. They acquire meaning only in the context of some explanatory framework. We can recognize a small concave item, white underneath with a smooth orange pebbled surface on top, as an orange peel only because we have a general concept of what an *orange* is, and we have an idea of what part that scrap must have played in its original context. And having developed a general sense of human behavior, we might even develop a theory about how the peel came to end up on the sidewalk.

The tenuous relationship between fact and theory has much to do with the persistence or the demise of various concepts in anthropology, and for that matter, in the other social sciences. More facts and new information often call some particular theoretical assumption into question. On the other hand, challenged assumptions might just as well persist in revised form, altered to accommodate the new information, rather than being abandoned altogether. At times better information has indicated that earlier theoretical constructs were basically wrong. More often, however, it has shown that although old ideas were deeply inadequate and perhaps misleading, major revisions could give them new life.

The danger of repeating mistakes of the past is reason enough to study the history of theory. It is just as important to understand what was wrong in the development of theories and why, as it is to know what, for the time being anyway, seems to be about right.

WHAT IS THEORY?

We might begin by discussing just what we mean by *theory*. The term is capable of impressing, intimidating, irritating, and all too often, mystifying. At a basic level, though, a theory is just a version of some aspect of reality. Often this version posits causal factors to account for observed phenomena. Alternatively, it may point out correlations *without* asserting a causal relationship. Or it might merely offer a descriptive account of some occurrence or event.

Some theories account for repetitive events rather than a single incident and offer the prediction that such events will occur again, given the necessary conditions. We sometimes refer to such theories as "laws." The "law" of gravity is probably the most familiar example of this type.

A descriptive theory is the sort a prosecutor in a courtroom presents to the jury regarding who did what, and why. Like other theories, a good descriptive theory rests on *evidence*. It is also true of the defense attorney's theory, which may present a version intended to show why the defendant could not, or did not, do what the prosecutor said he or she did. If the evidence to support the allegation is overwhelming, the defense attorney may offer an alternative theory to show extenuating circumstances.

These aspects of theory are fundamentally similar, whether we refer to quantum mechanics, the theory of relativity, the "Big Bang" theory of the origin of the universe, or the theory of business cycles. For some of these cases, the evidence may give strong support to the theory. For others, such as "string theory" in physics, the evidence may be suggestive but inconclusive. A key aspect of theory, as most people use the term, is that somehow it should be subject to evidence. On this basis it is possible (theoretically) to sustain, revise, or refute a theory.

This approach is quite different from beliefs about reality that are *not* subject to testing against evidence. For some people, for example, religious beliefs are matters of faith and are not easily refuted by data. In contrasting these two modes of thought, the theorist Emile Durkheim noted early in the twentieth century that by its very nature,

> Science is fragmentary and incomplete. It advances but slowly and is never finished; but life cannot wait. The theories which are destined to make men live and act are therefore obliged to pass science and complete it prematurely. (1915:479)

The dichotomy between theory and belief is not absolute, of course. Many of us tend to cling tightly to pet "theories" even when the evidence would seem to contradict them. Some would say that this is especially prevalent in the realm of politics.

With regard to formal *scientific* theory, though, the process of testing needs to be more rigorous. As Roy D'Andrade puts it, "Science works not because it produces unbiased accounts, but because its accounts are objective enough to be proved or disproved no matter what anyone wants to be true" (2000:560).

Theory building and testing can involve two major approaches. An **inductive** approach places a priority on the gathering of evidence. As we shall see below, some early anthropologists believed that theory should arise from an extensive and thorough examination of the available information. Sufficient data, in other words, should make relationships and principles evident, and data should therefore *generate* theory. Such theories would, of course, still be subject to continued evaluation in light of further information.

A **deductive** approach, on the other hand, gives priority to the development of **hypotheses** that we can test against the data. The strategy here is not to seek support for the hypothesis but to see if we can *disprove* it. Failure to disprove a hypothesis means that it can survive, at least for the time being.

These approaches are not entirely inconsistent. Theories that arise from an inductive approach are still subject to refutation on the basis of new information. In that sense they resemble hypotheses. And with a deductive approach, hypotheses clearly do not arise from thin air. They develop because of previous information.

As to how scientific understanding progresses over the long term, the debates have been a bit more complicated. According to one view, scientific knowledge progresses as new information reveals the inadequacy of existing assumptions. The philosopher Karl Popper has been a major proponent of this "gradualist" view of science (see, for example, Popper 1957, 1966).

Others, following the arguments of Thomas Kuhn, maintain that scientific advance is far less orderly in its progress, and for that matter, far less objective in the short run. Kuhn argued that scientific research and interpretations at any point in time operate within a generally shared set of assumptions—a style of thinking that he refers to as a *paradigm*. Periodically, according to this view, dominant paradigms reach a point at which it is no longer possible to reconcile them with new data. At this point a significant number of researchers may vehemently reject the old paradigm, rather than simply modifying it to accommodate new information, and erect a new one in its place. Kuhn refers to these moments as "scientific revolutions" (Kuhn 1962). For more discussion of this debate, see also Lakatos and Musgrave (1970).

In either case—whether scientific understanding progresses gradually with the accumulation of data, or resistant paradigms periodically shatter under the increasing pressure of information they cannot accommodate—scientific theory is subject to its relationship with "reality," as people understand it.

The issue of theory testing has further complications, though. Ideally, we should apply all relevant data objectively in order to discover whether a hypothesis stands the test. But how do we determine which data are relevant? Inevitably, some information might appear to bear directly on the problem. But sometimes such data lie immersed or embedded in what appear to be extraneous phenomena. Which information counts?

One example might be the problem of the sickle cell trait, an abnormal hemoglobin that causes a severe disease in individuals who possess two recessive alleles for the trait (who are homozygous for it). At one time researchers considered this to be a genetic disease peculiar to Africans and people of African descent. Later research, however, revealed that individuals who are heterozygous for the sickle cell (they have one sickle cell and one normal allele) enjoy greater resistance to falciparum malaria. This led to the finding that the distribution of this trait closely corresponds to tropical regions throughout the Eastern Hemisphere where malaria is endemic.

Rather than being a specifically African disease, the sickle cell trait turns out to be an adaptive response among many populations well beyond Africa to a highly specific environmental factor. At a time when the scientific consensus defined the sickle cell trait as an unfortunate disease of Africans, the presence of malaria in such places as Greece and India was not considered relevant. What importance could findings in Southern India have for what everyone considered to be an African phenomenon?

Hypothesis testing rests on the principle that falsification is far more powerful than verification or positive proof (see the discussion of this issue in Giddens 1995:172–173). Basically, to establish verification, it would be necessary to show repeatedly that the hypothesis applies in every case. Falsification, in principle, requires only one negative case to disprove the hypothesis. Thus, although the two procedures of proving the positive (establishing verification) and proving the negative (falsification) are opposite counterparts, they are not symmetric or equivalent. Falsification is far more powerful.

But is it, necessarily? As Thomas Kuhn pointed out, in practice it is not unusual for scientists to explain away or ignore potentially negative cases as anomalies (1972). This is especially likely when such annoying data conflict with established paradigms or with sets of broadly accepted assumptions. Such paradigms tend to have great resiliency, especially when many researchers have built long careers on the basis of them. We even have such extreme cases as paleontologists having discarded or substituted dinosaur bones to confirm the prevailing views of what the prehistoric animals had been like. In the past decade or so, the gigantic *brachyosaurus* has received a new head. Heated debate continues on whether the large olfactory cavities of the terrifying *Tyrunosaurus rex* of *Jurassic Park* fame indicate that it was actually a scavenger.

We have noted earlier that since facts do not speak for themselves, all of us employ various theoretical frameworks to help us make sense of them. But clearly this has some disadvantages if we hope to come to grips with "reality." Our pre-existing assumptions inevitably lead us to make choices at the outset as to which information we include or disregard.

This problem is serious enough for the natural sciences, where unconscious selectivity in the use of data and, for that matter, the imperfect reliability of perception, pose problems. In that case, though, the observer usually is not interacting or communicating with the subjects of study in any significant way. Physicists may give whimsical nicknames to subatomic particles, but few, if any, converse with them.

When it comes to the social sciences, which in large part amounts to people trying to understand other people, things are immensely more complicated. Some philosophers of science, in fact, argue that the theoretical methods that apply to the natural sciences do not apply to the social sciences. Hermaneutics, the interpretation of reality, is a central issue in this regard. In viewing social and cultural phenomena, we are dealing with a reality that is already a product of human interpretation. As Anthony Giddens puts it, the social sciences are "doubly hermaneutic" (1995:193). We find ourselves faced with perceptions of perceptions. We deal with many of the implications of this dilemma in later chapters. It is apparent, though, that in such a situation the issue of a theory's testability is a daunting challenge.

As one example, we might consider a situation that I happened to encounter while staying in a small rural East African community near the Kenya coast. Most of the people in that community are devout Christians, but they retain many older practices, including the practice of *brideprice*. This payment of gifts from the family of the groom to the family of the bride, generally in the form of livestock, is important to seal the marriage bond and to establish the relationship of the couple's children to their father's clan.

In 1995, two small children in the community died suddenly within a few days of one another. There had been no indication of illness, nor was there any other apparent physical cause. The grieving mother explained that a week or two earlier, she had dreamed that she saw her deceased mother standing in the house yard under a large tree. The mother spoke to her in the dream, saying, "He should have paid that cow. Now I'm going to take the children."

As the story unfolded, it turned out that years before, at the time the families discussed the marriage agreement, a brother of the groom's father had promised to contribute a cow to the brideprice. As time went by and the couple had their first two children, the uncle failed to make good on his promise. This failure undercut the validity of the claim of the groom's clan on the children. As a final resolution, the spirit of the bride's dead mother, representing her side of the marriage arrangement, renounced the agreement and took the children away with her.

What can we make of this? Certainly all observers would agree on some aspects of this event. The children died; the bride's mother had been deceased for some time; and the uncle never came up with the cow. The problem for us is whether this failure on the uncle's part led to the deceased grandmother's *causing* the death of the children.

Most of us would probably reject this explanation. But we might ask ourselves why we cannot accept it. Is it possible to test "scientifically" the premise that the deaths happened for the reason the mother said they did? Not likely. It might be possible to show that the children died of some sudden infection, but this would not address the main question. Did the deceased grandmother *cause* these tragic deaths *through infection* because she was angry over the defaulted brideprice?

The reason we have for rejecting this version, then, can only rest on the fact that our perceptions of reality—the realm of the possible and the way things work—do not coincide with the assumptions of the people in this African community regarding the nature of things. But empirical testing offers little hope of resolving that disagreement.

We might consider another example, also from East Africa. The Samburu are pastoral people who live in central Kenya. A Samburu elder told me that his mother belongs to a clan that has a special relationship with elephants. On one occasion a herd of elephants wandered toward a group of Samburu *bomas*, the complexes of dwellings and brush enclosures where the people live and shelter their livestock.

The elephants posed some danger, particularly since their venturing so close amounted to unusual, unpredictable behavior. The man's elderly mother walked out of her *boma* and spoke to the beasts. The elephants appeared to listen quietly, then turned and ponderously walked away.

Once again, any objective observer could agree that the elephants had approached, the elderly woman had spoken to them, and then they had left. But why did they go? On the basis of empirical evidence, can we falsify the view that the animals responded to the elder's mother because of her clan's relationship with them? Or are we left solely with the refuge that such happenings are not compatible with our view of the way things work?

One consequence of such dilemmas in the social sciences is that rather than attempting to account for all aspects of the human experience—especially those experiences that involve people of one culture trying to understand people of another—it may be essential to determine which sorts of theoretical questions lend themselves to testing against the data and which human issues may lend themselves to description, at best.

At the heart of the matter, sociocultural anthropology rests on two essential questions: What do people do? And why do they do it? The first of these questions has been difficult enough to get right over the years. Until anthropologists began to make first-hand observations through fieldwork than rather relying on travelers' reports, they often were wrong. Even with the best fieldwork, though, they still can never grasp all of the phenomena they see, let alone the many things observers fail to see or to notice, even in a small community. But even if total, accurate observations of what people do were possible, we would still have the question of "why."

"Why" has invited many theoretical answers. Why, for example, do the people of community X have matrilineal clans? Is it because they have become stuck at a particular stage of cultural development? Because they have not yet figured out that relationships to the mother's and the father's relatives are equivalent? Because their specific economic circumstances place greater importance on relationships through women? Because of the particular history of that group? Because of their particular system of values? All of these, and others, have had their days as explanations.

IS ANTHROPOLOGY EUROCENTRIC?

An interest in other ways of life, even at the level of simple curiosity, may not be a universal human trait, but it certainly is common. No doubt this was one driving force behind the historic development of anthropology. But anthropology has taken this interest farther. It has become institutionalized, with its own set of precepts, rules, and understandings (some shared, some contested). More important, it attempts to understand and *explain* human social behavior rather than merely to observe it.

As it happens, this enterprise developed mainly in Western Europe and the United States. In that sense it seems justified to consider it *Eurocentric*, at least with regard to its origins. (We will consider below why this occurred.) In another sense, though, the subject matter of anthropology could hardly be considered Eurocentric. If most anthropologists until recently have been Europeans or Americans, the global focus has generally been outside the researchers' own societies. Still, critics might assert with some reason that the agenda of anthropology has arisen from European centers of power.

Anthropology in the past century or so has spread into most other parts of the world. Few countries today lack indigenous anthropologists, wherever they might have received their training. It seems clear, though, that this is a secondary spread from the earlier Euroamerican sphere. Why, then, did anthropology originate in that part of the world and not elsewhere, as far as we know?

We have many cases of people in other societies manifesting great interest in other groups. Melanesian seafaring traders have been fascinated by the customs of people on other islands (Pomponio 2000 and personal communication). The Chinese admiral Cheng Ho sailed to the coast of Africa from 1415 to 1433 and returned with tales of the local inhabitants (Fernandez-Armesto 1995:142–145). The Roman historian Tacitus wrote a description of the native tribes in the British Isles (Tacitus 1948 [orig. A.D. 98]). In the tenth century, the Arab traveler Ibn Fadlan described, with manifest disapproval, the antics of Viking traders along the Volga River (1948). The Greek explorer Herodotus wrote vivid accounts of peoples around the Mediterranean Sea about two and a half millennia ago, from Egyptians along the Nile River to Scythian nomads on the steppes of Central Asia (1998).

In general, the interests of these writers centered mainly on what they saw as intriguing aspects of strange customs and exotic peoples. No doubt these accounts offered significant entertainment value to their readers. Only in rare cases did the observers attempt to explain or account for the customs they saw. One exception is the Greek scholar and physician Hypocrates, who attributed the characteristics of various groups to such factors as climate and the quality of air. Another is the Spanish Arab scholar Ibn Khaldun, who suggested that the vigor of pastoral nomads compared to urban dwellers arose from their demanding way of life (Khaldun 1958). For the most part, these cases stand out as exceptions. More to the point, they did not form the basis of any collective enterprise that one could call a version of anthropology.

Interest in other groups can have a range of nuances. It may be prag-
matic: the other groups might be potential enemies, trading partners, or even
potential victims. Other peoples might be of interest because they have some
admirable qualities or practices. They may be the object of contempt or pity.
People who fish may feel that gardeners are pathetic excuses for human beings. Nomadic livestock herders may marvel at the soft decadence of city
dwellers. Sophisticated urbanites may view nomads as unruly barbarians.
Europeans, historically, have held these sorts of views no less than other peoples. None of it, however, adds up to anthropology. As a discipline, then, it
seems that anthropology may be an unusual consequence of some rather
unique historical convergences.

Certain basic elements were necessary for anthropology to come to
fruition. For one thing, it could only have come about in a social system with
enough wealth (or wealth disparity) to permit some individuals sufficient
idle time to pursue the study of other groups in a concerted way. This means
either a high degree of occupational specialization or a sizeable leisure class,
or both. As it turns out, most of the earliest anthropologists in Western
Europe were "gentleman scholars" who pursued their interests mostly on
their own time and at their own expense. Only much later, with the establishment of anthropology in universities—mostly in the twentieth century—
did it become feasible for a few people to make a living at it.

Many state systems have had elite classes and occupational specialization. Indeed, such features are standard characteristics of states. From the
fifteenth century on, though, Europe was unique in the burgeoning of mer-
cantile exploration and conquest that took ships to the farthest points of the
globe, where Europeans confronted much of the rest of the world's population for the first time.

Still, the motivations behind most of these ventures had little to do with
learning about other ways of life, except to the extent that such knowledge
could be put to profitable use. Columbus, while he noted the gentle nature of
the inhabitants of the Caribbean islands, set about enslaving, mutilating,
massacring them, and eventually, bringing about their extinction (see
Todorov 1987). Nor were the accounts of explorers necessarily accurate. Sir
Walter Raleigh returned from South America with tales of indigenous people
who had eyes on both shoulders and mouths in the middle of their chests.

A further element was necessary for anthropology to develop as a
science—the development of science itself.

Numerous advances in science and mathematics had occurred much
earlier in the Middle East, China, Mexico, and other parts of the world.
Europe in the eighteenth century, however, experienced an important intellectual development that has become known as the **Enlightenment.**

As we shall see, the Enlightenment represented a shift away from theological explanation and emphasized the rational, empirical examination of
the world. This period raised the ideal of scientific inquiry to a place of
prominence, coupled with a sense of optimism that such inquiry was the

greatest hope for the improvement of human life. This view, coinciding with the exploding awareness of other societies on a global scale, offered fertile ground for the development of anthropology as the study of humanity in a scientific framework.

We might note that although many European states were involved in global exploration during this period, the major developments in early anthropology centered in England, France, and what is now Germany. In Spain, despite ample opportunity to observe other cultures with its vast colonial empire encompassing much of North and South America, there is little evidence of much inquiry of the sort we associate with anthropology.

One reason, perhaps, is that much of the concern, even among those in Spain who took a sympathetic view toward indigenous peoples, was with moral issues (see Pagden 1982). Did these people have souls? Were they fully human? Were they capable of conversion to Christianity? Was it permissible to make them slaves?

It seems significant that the Church dominated most of these debates (see also Bellah 1964, Berger 1969). In northwestern Europe, the Protestant Reformation had a major effect in weakening the political dominance of the Catholic Church. Spain, on the other hand, had not undergone the secularization of intellectual life associated with the Western European Enlightenment. In the north, this emphasis on secular rather than theological explanation tended to shift inquiry from questions of morality toward the ideal of objective scientific observation and analysis. We might conclude, then, that although anthropology arose during a time of expansive European colonialism, colonialism alone was not enough to produce it.

Although the Western European and American roots of anthropology are undeniable, then, it is also important to consider that its focus has been global. Whatever its shortcomings, anthropology stands alone in human history as a concerted attempt to escape the bounds of local ethnocentrism and to understand the myriad manifestations of humans on their own terms, while aspiring toward a totality of understanding of humanness itself.

THEORY AND THEORISTS

Up to this point we have discussed ideas without much reference to the people who propounded them. It goes without saying that just as facts cannot speak for themselves, ideas have no life of their own. Or do they? Certainly ideas and concepts are the creations of living persons. On the other hand, ideas also are transpersonal. They spread—if they become popular—well beyond whoever might have proposed them in the first place, and they often last far longer than their various authors.

Ideas are *supra-individual* to the extent that they go beyond merely private thoughts. As such, they operate at a different level of existence. It is safe to say that without humans there would be no ideas. But ideas certainly continue to exist even when *particular* humans do not. More than this, ideas are not usually nuggets of insight that appear from nothing. They are distillations of other shared ideas, perhaps reactions to them, elaborations on them, or combinations of them to produce some new variant.

With this in mind, we can survey the scope of anthropological thinking as it has developed up to this point and focus on a few ideas that have been important points of contention. In doing so, we shall discuss some of the people who have developed them, shaped them, and argued for them. But the ideas, rather than the people, are the major focus of our attention.

There has long been a tendency among many students, rarely expressed, to assume that thinkers of the past were not only less informed, but somehow less intelligent than modern scholars. To some extent, perhaps, this is a conflation of inadequate information with reasoning ability. The fact that thinkers of the past operated within vastly different frameworks of assumptions, often infused with supernatural forces, no doubt has exacerbated this tendency. Even brief reflection on this issue, however, is enough to dispel it. No doubt the ratio of fools to geniuses has remained comparable in most populations throughout history; but for the most part, only the finest minds of the past have continued to command our attention.

This, perhaps, is one of the main reasons for studying their ideas. Without close attention to them, we are likely to tread ground already explored and repeat many of the same old errors. Our advantage, early in the twenty-first century, is not intellectual superiority but greater information—if we choose to use it—and the opportunity to build on ideas of the past in the hopes of going beyond them.

Five ideas have had major significance in anthropological thought: evolution, culture, structure, function, and relativism. Each has led to many other avenues and issues. But together, these concepts have formed the core of anthropological thinking for the past century and a half. Rather than parallel but separate strands of thought, these five ideas have acted on and against one another. They form a tangled fabric. We begin with the idea of evolution.

FOOD FOR THOUGHT

Is it possible to understand anything without adopting some theoretical perspective?

If there are different theoretical viewpoints, are there different understandings of "reality"? If so, how can we choose among them?

If technology has advanced so much over the past few centuries, why does our social theory seem to have changed more slowly?

Can a "scientific revolution" that embraces a new paradigm actually be a step backwards?

Chapter 2

THE IDEA OF EVOLUTION

Many of us associate the term *evolution* with biology. It is worth stepping back for a moment and considering evolution in a broader sense. Just what does the term mean?

At bottom, evolution really means *change* from one form to another. It usually implies irreversible and continuing change. A light bulb turning on and off is not a case of evolution. A caterpillar becoming a butterfly is not evolution either, even though that change is irreversible. But successive generations of caterpillars and butterflies that gradually become different genetically through adaptive change—perhaps over thousands of generations—*is* evolution.

This brings up another aspect. We usually think of evolution as being fairly slow. If we apply the concept of evolution to the human social realm, we can contrast evolution with *revolution*, which is the (perhaps over-used) term for rapid change.

But there is more to concern us here. When many people think of human social or cultural evolution, they tend to associate it with *progress*. It is important to keep a few things in mind when we think in those terms. For one thing, progress is not easy to define. If we limit ourselves to thinking of technology, the problem does not seem too difficult. A new Subaru or Toyota is certainly a better piece of machinery than a 1932 Model T Ford. (We can set aside for the moment whether the environmental damage resulting from having tens of millions of cars spewing exhaust into the air every day is "progress.")

But when we look at other aspects of life, including biological evolution, things get a bit more difficult. What are the criteria for defining progress? Bigger? Is a hippopotamus therefore more highly evolved than a 150-pound professor? Or for that matter, is a football interior lineman more highly evolved than a jockey?

Perhaps evolutionary progress means greater complexity. But what about horses, which evolved from an ancestor that had three toes on each foot but that now have only one? Or whales, which evolved from ancestors with four legs?

Perhaps evolution means survivability. But if so, humans have a long way to go before they can challenge the cockroach or the mud turtle.

We can see a few problems here involved in posing questions of "more" or "less" about evolution. Implicit in much popular thinking about biological evolution is the sense that evolution has some direction, that it is headed somewhere—and that "progress" involves getting closer to that end, whatever it may be. But most biologists from Charles Darwin's time to the present would argue that biological evolution does not have any particular direction, or **teleology**. It amounts to multiple small adaptations to local, immediate circumstances. Adaptive change is *situational*, whether it be the ability of fish to survive in stagnant ponds or for moths to adapt to polluted city air.

Evolutionary change represents the cumulative effect of these myriad adaptive changes over a long span of time, not the fulfillment of an overall program or design—even though some in the past have argued otherwise. It has always been tempting to assume that modern humans represent some *purpose* of evolution rather than being an unintended consequence of numerous situational adaptations.

We confront another problem here. Up to this point we have been discussing biological and sociocultural evolution interchangeably. Are they the same in any way? Do they at least operate according to similar principles? Some differences are obvious, given our current understanding of biological evolution. If cultures evolve, they do so in Lamarkian fashion—that is, they pass on acquired characteristics. They also, unlike animal species, take on characteristics from one another. Nonetheless, cultures and societies, like biological species, do change over long periods of time.

This long-term change, with cumulative aspects, has been one of the major points of discussion in the history of anthropological thinking. In fact, ideas about social evolution appeared much earlier than the concept of biological evolution we associate with Darwin. Over two thousand years ago the Roman philosopher Lucretius suggested that humans had once lived without fire or agriculture and subsequently advanced through a series of developmental stages to what, for him, was the modern age (Lucretius 1951).

Many of the world's peoples, in fact, have constructed versions of how things have come to be the way they are, often by recounting a series of developmental stages. The Navajo story of creation, the *Dine Bahane*, describes in detail the formative process of ascent from underground through which not only people but also the earth's surface, with its plants and animals, achieved their present forms. (For a translation, see Zolbrod 1984.)

The idea of evolution never disappeared completely from European thinking, but it did suffer an eclipse during the Middle Ages. As Christian doctrines came to prevail in the first few centuries A.D., studious interpretations of the Bible preempted most questions about the human past. Concerns about humankind's fall from Grace played a large role in thinking about where humanity was headed.

In the early Middle Ages, Europe was only a few centuries away from the Roman Empire's domination of its various tribal peoples. Scholars even in the fourteenth century pondered the wisdom of the Greek scholars who had lived over a millennium and a half earlier, particularly Aristotle as interpreted through St. Thomas Aquinas. Conceptions of the past involved images of the grandeur of earlier Mediterranean civilizations. Such a world view was not especially fertile ground for assumptions of progress. To many at the time, it seemed far more obvious that humanity, as defined within the European arena, had been going downhill.

What happened to change that? How did the ideas of progress and evolutionary change come to be linked during the following centuries?

A great deal of it had to do with the globalization of commerce in the "Age of Discovery" (see Wallerstein 1974, 1984). As European ships set out to seek new trade routes and new lands for exploitation, exciting things happened at home. The Italian Renaissance, with its florescence of art, scientific curiosity, and political intrigues, drew much of its economic base from overseas commercial ventures seated in Genoa and Naples. The newly consolidated Spanish state, having reclaimed its lands on the Iberian peninsula after centuries of Moorish occupation, sought new wealth in distant regions in competition with neighboring Portugal and later, with Dutch, French, and English interests who were not far behind in exploring the world and claiming most of it (Braudel 1979:51).

These times involved a vast increase in European knowledge, much of it acquired through contacts with the great civilizations of Asia, the Middle East, Africa, and the Americas. These contacts also raised new questions about longstanding assumptions. Theological explanation was safe for the moment. The Church, in fact, was very much involved in many of these ventures. Nonetheless, doubts and contradictions appeared. Galileo and Copernicus offered versions of the cosmos and Earth's place within it that differed radically from the established theological view, notwithstanding the hostile reception they received. In northern Europe, Protestants challenged details of existing theology, setting off bloody and prolonged religious warfare. By the mid sixteenth century the Spanish Inquisition was underway in an attempt to forestall departures from Church orthodoxy.

For intellectuals in Spain, Native American populations in the regions they conquered presented extraordinary problems in reconciling reality with Church doctrine. Were these people descendants of Adam and Eve, or the spawn of a different Divine creation? Were they barbarians suited only for physical labor, or merely untutored human beings capable of salvation?

At the center of these discussions, the learned men who comprised the School of Salamanca in the 1500s ultimately concluded that these were, indeed, humans with souls. But they reached this conclusion through reasoning they continued to base on the writings of Aquinas, who, as we noted earlier, based many of his arguments on Aristotle. Rather than offering a challenge to fundamental religious doctrines, the deliberations of these Spanish scholars set a task for the Church to extend its teachings abroad. (See Pagden 1982 for a fuller discussion of these debates.)

It was late in the seventeenth century before reputable scholars felt freer to speculate that human affairs operated according to principles arising from natural law rather than direct divine oversight. In this newer, increasingly radical view, God might exist, but not necessarily as a hands-on manipulator of earthly events. An apparent increase in secular scientific curiosity was beginning to manifest itself.

In England, Francis Bacon established basic principles of empirical scientific research. The French philosopher Rene Descartes grappled with issues of reality (including his own) within a framework of secular reason and logic rather than theology. Such contrary views eventually were to develop into a range of inquiries and new perspectives, including the idea that human beings are a part of the natural world rather than separate from it. The philosopher Baruch Spinoza wrote in 1632:

> Most writers on the emotions and on human conduct seem to be treating rather of matters outside nature than of natural phenomena following nature's general laws. They appear to conceive man to be situated in nature as a kingdom within a kingdom; for they believe that he disturbs rather than follows nature's order, that he has absolute control over his actions, and that he is determined solely by himself . . . Nothing comes to pass in nature, which can be set down to a flaw therein; for nature is always the same . . . there should be one and the same method of understanding the nature of all things whatever. . . . (quoted in Nagel 1948:272)

The 1600s saw an explosion of discoveries. It was the century in which Isaac Newton had recorded his observations and conclusions about the laws of motion and gravity; Johannes Kepler had detailed the laws of planetary motion; William Harvey had discovered the circulation of blood; Blaise Pascal had developed mathematical laws of probability; Robert Boyle had analyzed the properties of gas; and Ole Romer had calculated the speed of light.

With greater freedom to explore questions of the universe from a secular perspective, scientific discoveries generated a sense of optimism about the potential benefits of increasing knowledge. The 1700s saw further inventions and discoveries, ranging from the electric battery to the lightning rod. That period also saw the florescence of the incisive, sometimes witty, and often irreverent writings of Jean-Jaques Rousseau, Adam Smith, Voltaire, David Hume, and Immanuel Kant. The idea of progress was an inherent aspect of these developments. Progress not only seemed to be possible, but almost inevitable.

And how did progress occur? Its driving engine was the force of *reason*. This was a major departure from the views of the sixteenth-century scholars of Salamanca, who equated rational thought with the revelation of "true religion" (Pagden 1982:78). It was reason that had brought about the discoveries of the age, and the discoveries themselves gave added impetus to the conviction that the further development of rational thought would continue to resolve human problems.

This reasoning led to a concept that would become a fundamental premise of the Enlightenment: the idea that the laws pertaining to nature also pertain to humanity and human society. It was not that God was no longer a factor in European thought, but many issues called for more grounded sorts of inquiry. This was an age in which scientific discoveries paralleled an increasing desire to understand the laws of nature for their own sake. Even if divine providence lay behind these laws, they still displayed interesting dynamics in their own right.

Christianity continued to play a predominant role in the lives of most Europeans throughout this era and long afterward, however. Indeed, the bulk of negative reaction to Darwin's books, centuries later, was on religious grounds.

THE NINETEENTH CENTURY

The nineteenth century inherited this celebration of progress through reason. The French scholar **Auguste Comte**—sometimes referred to as the "father of sociology"—characterized human advance in terms of what he called **positive philosophy.** A fundamental aspect of this perspective was a reasoned, scientific mode of engagement with reality that superceded metaphysical or speculative thinking. Metaphysical philosophy, in Comte's view, had replaced the theological stage of human evolution, which had been clouded by ideas of divine causation. Toward the end of his lively but troubled career, Comte proposed that positive philosophy should have the status of a new religion (Comte 1896; see also Giddens 1995:136–140).

Early in the nineteenth century, however, a number of social developments transformed the tone of these concepts. The engine of progress shifted from reason to *competition*. How did this come about?

To understand this shift in emphasis, we need to look again at the century leading up to it. For one thing, scientific inventions had played a large part in the Industrial Revolution. Technological advances, with new and more efficient ways of producing commodities, promised to meet human material needs in a fashion that had never before been possible. Although one could still see the technological achievements of the Industrial Revolution as a triumph of human reason, the developments they spawned caused major shifts in the relationships among segments of society. Among other things, these processes required a massive exploitation of human labor.

The Industrial Revolution had many repercussions. One was increased international commerce and a peculiar phenomenon that grew out of it: the Atlantic slave trade. Known as the "triangular trade," Britain's West African slave trade played a large part in financing the Industrial Revolution, generating a massive importation of raw materials from overseas. Eric Williams notes that on the walls of the Custom House in Liverpool, the departure point for many slave ships, were a series of carved heads of Africans—a tribute to England's prosperity (see Williams 1984:150).

How did the system work? In the American colonies and the Caribbean islands were plantations where slaves, as well as European convicts and indentured servants, did most of the work. The tobacco, sugar, and cotton from these plantations became commodities in England for the European market. English mills and refineries converted these raw materials to products for sale in Europe and the colonies.

England outlawed the slave trade early in the nineteenth century, but English markets continued to benefit from American slavery on which the plantations of the South depended. Southern cotton plantations in the United States continued to be the main suppliers for English textile mills until the Civil War (see, for example, Wolf 1982:195–220).

But other developments had affected life in England itself. The Enclosure Movement, which had made vast areas of formerly common pasture land unavailable to small English farmers, drove thousands of people out of the countryside and into the cities. There, landless masses with nothing to sell but their labor became an underused and often volatile work force. By the mid eighteenth century, crime in London and other large cities led to convictions on a scale that not only exceeded the capacity of prisons but led to the transport of thousands of convicts to the American colonies and later, after the American Revolution, to Australia (see Hughes 1986).

In the same era, a minority of English industrialists and financiers were doing tremendously well. A large labor force desperate for work allowed employers to demand work days of twelve to sixteen hours for low wages. Many people had no jobs at all. The disparity in wealth between social and economic classes in England grew dramatically wider. At the bottom were displaced Irish, many of them driven from the land by English occupying armies beginning with the reign of Oliver Cromwell in the 1600s. Tens of thousands of them were shipped to the West Indies to labor on plantations, as well as to Australia. (See Mill 1923:324 for a discussion of the Irish plight.)

This was the climate in which the ideas of the Enlightenment came to be transformed into nineteenth-century evolutionary theory.

"UNILINEAR" EVOLUTION

The social misery of the early nineteenth-century Industrial Revolution posed some contradictions for Enlightenment optimists. While things seemed to be progressing splendidly for some, the mass of people living in urban squalor and rural poverty did not experience many signs of improvement.

For Karl Marx and Friedrich Engels observing London through grimy windows, the social injustice seemed obvious, as it did to Charles Dickens. Marx's chapter on "The Working Day" in *Capital* (1977 [orig. 1867]:340–416) and Dickens's many novels portraying the human misery of the times offer different, but parallel, views of the period. But a concern with social injustice was not a congenial perspective for many of the elite whose comfortable positions depended on the existing arrangement.

In some ways the evident disparity in fortune between "haves" and "have nots" became a key element in the philosophical treatment of this problem. The phrase "haves and have nots" could well have been altered in the thinking of the times to "can" and "cannot." To some, the reason why many of the masses had ended up in dire straits was not that the idea of progress through reason was invalid, but that rational thought and other abilities were not distributed equally among humanity. Some were better at it than others. This disparity had a tremendous intrinsic appeal to the privileged. It affirmed that their advantages were fully warranted and well deserved. They were privileged because nature intended them to be.

The idea of superiority was not a new one, of course. Some distinctions between nobles and commoners have probably existed in every state system in human history. But in the nineteenth century, when science had become established as an intellectual icon, the rationale for class distinctions took the form of a scientific principle rather than simply a matter of noble blood or divine will. As a rationale, science had the advantage of appearing to be objective and value-free.

An important intellectual stimulus in this thinking came from the work of **Thomas Malthus** (Harris 1968:114–116). Ironically, perhaps, Malthus drew attention to an alarming fact that posed a serious challenge to those who, by now, embraced progress as an unassailable principle. That simple fact was that even though the world's food supply increases by increments (arithmetically), populations increase by multiplying every generation (geometrically). Simple mathematics made it evident that sooner or later the population would exceed the food supply necessary to sustain it. The result would not be progress but catastrophe (Malthus 1960).

This problem of food supply and demand remains a matter of concern for many today. Better data have served to make the issue more complicated but have not resolved it entirely. In the early nineteenth century, though, it stimulated several important responses.

COMPETITION

One way to pull humanity's future out of the fire, as it were, was to suggest that other factors could help control the unbridled increase of population. For one thing, the survivability of all members of the population was not equal. Some were better able to survive than others. This fact seemed to be a simple recognition of reality. It was pointless to fret over whether it was good or bad. It just *was*. It was a fact of life, a law of nature. No use fussing about it.

The underlying element of all this was *competition*. The rich might not compete directly against the poor, in the sense of deadly confrontation. But in the struggle for survival or for wealth, some were just naturally going to be more successful and acquire more than others. Those who did well were far more likely to survive than those who did poorly.

According to this reasoning, the outcome would be that surviving generations would be superior to those who had gone before. In the future, all would be better off, since the weakest or least fit would have failed to perpetuate themselves. Progress was assured.

Herbert Spencer, who was the most prominent proponent of this view and its most articulate and prolific spokesperson, managed to keep progress and natural law firmly linked. A major threat to progress, as he saw it, was human interference with inevitable natural processes. Humanitarian intervention to provide assistance to the weak might be well meaning, but it was misguided and would only slow what amounted to a force of nature. Social programs ranging from institutions to feed the needy to public libraries and schools would only prolong the painful process leading to the unavoidable end. As distressing as nature's way of weeding out the weak might be, the result was to be desired, not avoided. It would lead to a better world for all—all of the survivors, that is (Spencer 1885).

Spencer still had a problem to address, though. Even if the fittest were the only ones to enjoy that future, Malthus's dilemma remained. What was to stop the "fit" from continuing to reproduce until *they* outstripped the food supply?

Spencer's answer was rather creative. These superior individuals obviously had greater intelligence than the less fit. For that reason, he asserted, they would have fewer children. Why? Not because of birth control methods, but because, according to Spencer, a form of competition raged even within the human body between sexual energies and intelligence. The more intelligent the person, the less sexual energy she or he had to work with.

Needless to say, this was not a theory that would fare well against rigorous scientific testing, but it was easy to summon impressionistic evidence to support it. One only had to conjure the image of squalling brats in the overcrowded slums of London—a stark contrast to the stereotyped orderly upper-class homes of Victorian England with their few, well-mannered children. To many, this proposition had a ring of truth.

The modern view that higher birthrates tend to correspond with high infant mortality, among other things, rather than resulting from the poor having more sexual energy than intelligence, probably would not have occurred to Spencer. Even if it had, the higher rates of infant death among the poor of Victorian England would not have contradicted his model of differential survival as a result of competition.

This perspective had great resonance with other aspects of current affairs as well. *Laissez faire* economics, with its unregulated competition among industrial firms, displayed the principle in another arena. Large aggressive companies could, and should, eliminate their weaker rivals. Not only would that result in more efficient business, but free competition supposedly would force all to perform at the highest possible level. Such views have not, as we know, entirely disappeared at the beginning of the twenty-first century.

Beyond their own shores, England and other European nations were extending their systematic exploitation of much of the rest of the world. Although African slavery, as we noted, was no longer legal in England, the Empire had extensive colonial holdings in India, China, Africa, and other regions that often involved oppressive labor practices. In the Pacific islands, "blackbirding"—kidnapping people from one island to work as forced plantation labor on another—was a common method.

Europeans who were aware of the harshness of colonial regimes may have felt uncomfortable about these developments. But the doctrine of survival and improvement through competition served to disguise much of this troubling reality. In the minds of many, the mere fact of European exploitation of "weaker" peoples of the world amounted to *prima facie* evidence of superiority.

In this view, European domination not only was inevitable, but desirable. Some made the argument that colonialism was actually a benefit for the colonized (even if they might not appreciate it). Supposedly, it exposed them to Western civilization. A few even made the same argument for slavery.

The popular version of this point of view became known as **"social Darwinism,"** which is often associated with the phrase "survival of the fittest." As a matter of fact, **Charles Darwin** made his contributions to this intellectual arena rather late. If anyone was the prime architect of social Darwinism, it was Herbert Spencer (see, for example, Carneiro 1967; de Waal Malefijt 1974:122).

Charles Darwin (1809–1892)

Darwin himself did, however, take some inspiration from these sociopolitical views that were so much in the air at the time. Challenged by the dire Malthusian predictions, Darwin, like Spencer, developed the insight that competition reigned in the natural world. Natural selection dictated that those who were best able to survive would flourish, while those less fit would die out. In Darwin's view, rather than producing an unbridled increase of biomass, this process generated an ever-changing panorama as some species flourished and others disappeared. The future would continue on the same path as the past.

Darwin's views, although they were consistent with the political climate and, in fact, paralleled the views of other thinkers such as **Alfred Russell Wallace** (1905), stirred a great deal of controversy. To many, one of the most horrifying implications of biological evolution was its challenge to the fixity of species, an idea that many took to be consistent with the Biblical view of creation. It would be possible, of course, to reconcile the Bible with the idea that not all creatures created at the beginning had survived to the present. The story of Noah's ark and the flood, after all, allowed for the possibility of extinctions. It was a bit dicier, though, to assert that those species that *did* survive might have *changed*.

The most contentious implication by far, however, was that human beings themselves had evolved from earlier forms. Adam and Eve may have had their faults, but surely they could not have been monkeys.

Darwin himself, anticipating such a reaction when he published his *Origin of Species*, deliberately avoided extending his evolutionary model to humans (Darwin 1858). This bit of discretion did little to prevent a public outcry. His second book on the subject, *The Descent of Man* (1876), appeared when the controversy was already well underway.

Debates about human evolution versus creation were to continue in the public arena long after Darwin's death, even arising in a Kansas board of education controversy at the very end of the twentieth century, when a school board insisted that Biblical creation had equivalent, if not superior, standing with the theory of evolution. These opposing views had not been a significant part of scholarly debate for a century or more. On the other hand, the concept of *social and cultural evolution* was to follow a track of its own that involved questions of human biology in a different and largely tangential way.

RACISM IN NINETEENTH-CENTURY EVOLUTIONARY THEORY

Many proponents of social evolution held the common view that their own population—and to a lesser extent, perhaps, Europeans in general—were superior to other populations. Some of this was simple **ethnocentrism.** It is certainly a widespread opinion among populations throughout the world that their own way of life is the epitome of human development: the most rational, the most humane, the most sophisticated, or whatever. Conversely, it is just as common for people's views of other populations to be less than complementary; those others dress oddly, if at all, have low morals, talk funny, eat strange foods, and so on.

But by the nineteenth century, European thinking had taken ethnocentrism a step further. It incorporated the idea that the supposed behavioral propensities and alleged moral qualities of other populations were a result of *inherent biological* differences. In the view of social Darwinists, the idea that some populations were more fit than others went beyond the idea of technological backwardness or disadvantages of climate. So-called "savages" or "primitives" were also biologically backward—less *capable* of refinement and high achievement than Europeans.

Part of the development of biological racism, of course, depended upon the increasing popularity of biology as a science. More than an ethnocentric view of other peoples, this style of racism required the entry of biological concepts into popular thought, allowing ethnocentric ideas to be framed in biological terms. It required, in effect, the invention of the biological idea of race itself.

At the same time, European colonial expansion, which had condemned many of the world's peoples beyond Europe to exploitation, produced a strong motivation for seeing these colonized peoples as intrinsically inferior. It created an incentive for dehumanizing them. During this era the concept of *race*, which in its archaic sense had once had a meaning similar to *nationality*, acquired a sense that approached the meaning of *species*.

Some debates around the turn of the century, in fact, had to do with whether it was possible for the different human races to mate and produce viable, fertile offspring, despite the ample evidence that this had occurred countless times throughout human history. For those who remained steadfast in their adherence to the Biblical version of creation, the debates centered on whether all races had descended from Adam and Eve, or whether God had undertaken separate creations to produce different racial populations. These views became known as **monogenesis** (one origin) and **polygenesis** (multiple origins). Some also speculated whether Adam and Eve had been "black" or "white." (For a discussion of this issue, see Stanton 1960.)

The recognition that *race* as a biological category among humans has no support in genetics did not become widely accepted among professional researchers until the mid twentieth century. Despite that recognition, however, many nineteenth-century concepts regarding race persist in current popular thought. (We shall return to this issue in later chapters.) This popular concept of race has so deeply saturated Euroamerican thinking that some writers have suggested that racism is a human universal (see for example Harris [1968:81]). Ethnocentrism may well be universal. One could argue that for any society to function, its members must believe that their own ways of doing things make the most sense. But biological racism positing inherent (or "essential") differences among humans is, as we have noted, another thing altogether.

To get a deeper sense of this perspective, we might glance for a moment at some earlier manifestations of Western thinking. **Herodotus,** the Greek historian who traveled widely around the ancient Mediterranean in the fourth century B.C., had a great deal to say about the peoples he encountered. Much of it was far from complementary, although for the most part Herodotus adopted a fairly objective attitude. He generally refrained from expressing judgment about exotic practices, with a few exceptions, as when he allowed himself to comment on the immorality of temple prostitution.

Herodotus quotes the Persian king Cyrus, for example, in accounting for the Persians' military dominance by their having avoided settlement in rich lands, expressing the view that

> soft lands tend to breed soft men. It is impossible, he [Cyrus] said, for one and the same country to produce remarkable crops and good fighting men . . . and

they [the Persians] chose to live in a harsh land and rule rather than to cultivate fertile plains and be others' slaves. (Herodotus 1998:590)

The reason for people's characteristics, in other words, lay in their environment and their choices rather than in their inherent nature. Inescapably, the implication was that even Herodotus himself, had he grown up in the same circumstances, would have developed similar characteristics. There is a clear sense of external conditions operating on and molding what amounts to a common human substance.

Ibn Khaldun, the North African scholar who traveled extensively in the Mediterranean region in the fifteenth century, began to write a general treatise on humankind. In his introductory work, the *Muqaddimah*, he discussed the vitality of nomads, whose demanding way of life kept them strong, vigorous, and independent-minded (Khaldun 1958). He contrasted them with urban dwellers, who became soft and timid as a result of their luxurious mode of living. Once again, Ibn Khaldun assumed a common human material on which various conditions of life act to produce different results.

The biologization of ethnocentrism, then, seems to have been a later consequence of the peculiar conjunction of several factors in the historical moment of nineteenth-century Europe, rather than an innate and therefore "inevitable" human way of viewing others. (For more discussion, see Montagu 1997; Graves 2001).

THE SUPERORGANIC AND SOCIAL DARWINISM

As to the ways in which the ideas of evolution applied to human society in the nineteenth century, again we can see a conjunction of post-Enlightenment ideas in the work of Herbert Spencer. Among these was the notion that human social phenomena are subject to natural laws, as Spinoza and others had asserted long before. That being the case, the only appropriate method for understanding natural laws was through science. Science not only entailed the assumption that regular laws exist, but that such laws are discoverable.

For social phenomena, or society itself, to be proper subjects for scientific study, it was necessary to establish that society is *real*—not an abstraction, but a phenomenon as concrete as a clamshell. Society, in Spencer's view, is a natural phenomenon subject to the same natural laws that apply to all living forms.

Spencer not only argued that society is real, but that human society (or societies) in general have developed according to laws that he perceived as affecting the living world in a universal sense. It is important to keep in mind that Spencer was working with a pre-Darwinian model of evolution and with mid nineteenth-century biology as he understood it. It is also worth emphasizing that although Spencer has often received credit for his **"organic**

Herbert Spencer (1820–1903)

analogy" as a model of society, his biological model of social development was more than an analogy or a metaphor. Society, in his view, was not *like* a natural phenomenon. It *was* a natural phenomenon.

Although Spencer introduced the concept of society as *superorganic*— that is, as an entity existing at a higher level of complexity than biological organisms—he argued that the same laws apply broadly to *all* aspects of life. The laws of biology were also laws of society.

> The law of organic progress is the law of all progress. Whether it be in the development of the Earth, or the development of life upon its surface, in the development of Society, of Government, of Manufactures, of Commerce, of Language, Literature, Science, Art, this same evolution of the simple into the complex, through successive differentiation, holds throughout. From the earliest traceable cosmical changes down to the latest results of civilization, we shall find that the transformation of the homogeneous into the heterogeneous, is that in which Progress essentially consists. (Quoted in Peel 1972:40 [orig. 1857])

In keeping with his assumption of progress, Spencer undertook the task of explaining the ways in which progress occurs. At the time, his views of progress had several other important implications. Progress certainly meant competition, as we have noted, but it also meant betterment. It meant growth. It also meant increasing **complexity** (1988).

Spencer drew these ideas together into a model in which the laws that supposedly apply to the organic world also apply to social or superorganic phenomena. At the lowest level of the organic world were simple, single-celled organisms. These were essentially identical and interchangeable. More important, they were self-sufficient. Each of these organisms could carry out all of the functions it needed to survive: absorption of nutrients from the environment, reproduction, and so on. The latter process was simply a matter of division. One becomes two, two become four.

How do single-celled organisms develop into higher forms? Obviously it is more than a simple matter of increasing size. An amoeba was not likely to grow indefinitely into a larger and larger amoeba. At a critical point, an amoeba divides into two, each of which is similar to the parent.

The appearance of higher forms involved the development of organisms that incorporated more than one cell. Some "lower" multicelled organisms displayed only a rudimentary specialization of functions. Spencer evokes the intriguing image of a tiny polyp with small tentacles that direct floating particles of food into its vase-shaped body cavity. The cells in the cavity have the capacity to digest and absorb the nutrients. If one were to turn the hydra inside out, according to Spencer, the cells from the exterior that had now become the lining of the interior concavity would soon develop the same ability to absorb nutrients (1885:75). The tendency toward specialized cell function, in this case, was not yet irreversible.

In the human social realm, logically, small internally undifferentiated societies can become more complex in a number of ways: they might grow and develop internal divisions; they might join other groups, forming alliances; or they might grow by conquering others. Spencer, apparently with some regret, felt that the last alternative was the most likely.

Whatever the accuracy of Spencer's biological understanding of the polyp, the example clearly depicts his model of increasingly specialized functions as an aspect of progress. This **"division of labor"** among cells marks an increasing internal complexity of the organism. In a sense, internal differentiation is a matter of progress, and vice versa.

Whatever the process of growth, though, in Spencer's view societies and the people in them were better off with this increase in complexity or internal differentiation. As they advance up the scale to more complexity and greater size, according to Spencer, the quality of life improves for all, whether we consider the societal or biological versions of the process. Compared to a hydra, a horse is immeasurably more complex, and subjectively at least, is more advanced. With that sort of organism, the differentiation of cell function is essentially irreversible. A liver cell cannot function as a brain cell. Moreover, the horse as a whole is much better off if all of its specialized cells do their particular jobs efficiently, all of them mutually contributing in their own ways to the total life of the animal. If one organ fails in its task, the animal itself, which depends on a system of mutually supporting relationships, is likely to die.

The implications for society are clear. In a time when social classes, economic disparities, and a marked division of labor were aspects of the social landscape, the lesson was not one that would encourage social disruption or protest. Society would work best when its constituent units (cells or individuals) carried out their functions smoothly and cooperatively. No use having liver cells trying to function as brain cells. The social and economic hierarchy was natural and beneficial to all.

Evolution as a concept did not always carry such obvious political implications. There was a general consensus that humanity had progressed in a direction that had produced the Euroamerican social system as its highest achievement so far. But while Spencer projected this process toward the future, seeing an era in which the fittest lived a more advanced level of existence, others focused more on how things had developed up to that point.

EVOLUTIONARY STAGES

The idea of developmental **stages,** as we noted earlier, is at least as old as Lucretius. By the mid nineteenth century, other scholars had more information at their disposal, allowing them to elaborate on this concept. In keeping with the idea of growth from small to large and from simple to complex, some scholars noted the increase in scale from societies in which the family is the primary means of structuring interpersonal relationships at one end of the spectrum to state systems at the other, in which laws and governmental institutions take priority in terms of power and authority.

Sir Henry Maine, employing his familiarity with India and his knowledge of British law, developed the principle that human society had progressed from relationships based on *status*—that is, rights, obligations, and identity arising from familial relationships—to *contract*, conforming to the impersonal principles of law (Maine 1861).

The family had not, of course, disappeared in the process of time, even in Europe. In the nineteenth century the family continued to define status to a great extent in British and American society (as the "Sir" in Sir Henry Maine suggests). But it did become increasingly interesting to many scholars that the family itself had changed over the course of human history. Many scholars were aware that Greek and Roman family structures had been different from contemporary nineteenth-century forms. The development of the family became a major issue in anthropological thinking through an apparently innocuous discovery by a lawyer in Rochester, New York.

Lewis Henry Morgan, like many Americans in the northeastern United States during the mid nineteenth century, was interested in Native American cultures. During the Revolutionary War, the Hodenosauni, or "League of the Iroquois," had been formidable participants. In the aftermath of that war, however, the Hodenosauni had suffered the loss of most of their lands. Despite their misfortunes (or perhaps to some extent, because of them?), the Iroquois and other Native Americans had become the objects of romanticized fascination on the part of many Eastern intellectuals. It was during this era that Henry Wadsworth Longfellow wrote his epic poem *The Song of Hiawatha*, drawing inspiration from a range of information, including Henry Rowe Schoolcraft's accounts of Chippewa culture and the tradition of the Mohawk Hiawatha, one of the legendary founders of the Iroquois League.

Morgan belonged to a local social club whose members were interested in learning more about the historic ways of the Iroquois. Through this club he made the acquaintance of the prominent Seneca Ely Parker. Parker later became a general in the Civil War, an aide to Ulysses S. Grant, and eventually Commissioner of Indian Affairs. In the 1840s, he and other prominent Senecas helped Morgan learn about their people.

One of the more important lessons Morgan learned had to do with the differences between Iroquois and Angloamerican family structure. The English terms "brother" and "sister" had no exact equivalents in Iroquois terminology (Morgan 1851). The Iroquois counterpart of "brother" meant more than the male children of one's own parents. It also meant the male children of the father's brothers and of the mother's sisters. Morgan was on to something. Terms for family members were not just recognitions of biology, as most Angloamericans understood them. They were variable across cultures.

Morgan undertook a cross-cultural survey, sending questionnaires about kinship systems to missionaries, government officials, and anyone else in various parts of the world who might have access to local kin terms. He discovered that many other peoples made the same kinds of distinctions the Iroquois did, grouping relatives into the same kinds of categories. Morgan had discovered **classificatory kinship systems:** that is, systems that group **lineal relatives** (such as parents) with **collateral relatives** (such as parents' brothers and sisters) (1870). But there was more.

Some groups had different terms for almost every relative. Some, on the other hand, had terms for "father" that included all of the brothers of both parents. Often they had a single term that grouped the sisters with all female cousins and the brothers with all male cousins.

Having discovered these patterns, Morgan's problem was what to make of them. At least three prevalent ideas in the climate of thought at the time helped to channel his conclusions. One was the belief in progress, which implied that societies had developed and improved over time. The second, which most of his Angloamerican contemporaries shared, was that Euroamerican society represented the pinnacle of development. This, of course, led to the third, which was a corollary to the first two: that non-European societies represented examples of earlier phases of human social development. This was the basis for a research strategy known as the **comparative method.**

The assumption of Euroamerican superiority ruled out the idea that other populations might be equally advanced in their own ways, let alone *more* advanced. The only logical conclusion, given this assumption, was that they were less advanced.

The comparative method indicated that these diverse cases of kinship categorization might represent examples of the sequence through which modern family structure had developed. They might represent living social fossils. In some respects, the comparative method addressed the old question of why human societies differ from one another. Notions of progress and evolution produced an answer; some had not progressed as far as others. The idea that they might represent equally valid alternative ways of life would have seemed absurd to many thinkers of the time.

An important ingredient of this assumption lay in the idea that logical thought, or rationality, is an absolute phenomenon. There was little recognition of the possibility that different but equivalent kinds of logic and rationality might exist. If other populations thought in ways that were different from the European style of rationality, it was because they had not yet developed the ability to reason like Europeans and Americans.

A corollary to this assumption was that if and when they *did* progress, it would be on a path that Europeans had already trod. This view has sometimes been referred to as **unilinear evolution.** It is based, among other things, on the assumption of what has sometimes been referred to as the **"psychic unity"** of humankind. The idea was not that humans all think alike, but that presumably, they *could*. And if they ever hoped to progress, they had better do so.

Turning this around, it was logical that examining the ways of life of "primitive" peoples might offer a look at Europeans' own past. The term "primitive," which continued to appear with embarrassing frequency in anthropological writing through the 1960s, has sometimes been excused as a term referring only to technology. In the late nineteenth and early twentieth centuries, though, the concept of the "primitive" generally referred to non-European societies in their totality (even some which, by most objective measures, were in fact extremely complex).

In sorting out the confusing array of kinship systems he had discovered, Morgan no doubt had many of these ideas in mind. Ultimately, he decided that the most primitive system was the form that bestowed the same kinship terms on siblings and cousins and linked parents with their siblings of the same sex, a system he called "Malayan." Modern anthropologists refer to this type of kinship terminology as the **Hawaiian** form.

The Malayan type was the simplest in the sense that it used the fewest criteria—only generation and sex—for differentiating kin. It also, Morgan reasoned, was compatible with the form of kinship system that probably characterized the earliest family form. The earliest humans, he assumed, must have been far less concerned with rules and no doubt had less control of their sexual urges than the nineteenth-century ideal family with its patriarchal decorum.

The rules of proper behavior, including the concept of incest, had surely been invented at some time in human history. There was no evidence that any non-human species had any such compunctions about their sexual activities. In the earliest human stages, therefore, sex must have been pretty much a free-for-all (although Morgan certainly would not have used such an expression). To apply the term for "father" to all males in the parents' generation probably reflected uncertainty as to whom one's actual father might be.

Morgan arranged the other kinship systems, which we now refer to as Iroquois and Eskimo types, in conjunction with what he considered to have been the gradual development of social rules pertaining to the family. With the prohibition of incest, collective marriage of brothers to a group of sisters developed. This gave way to *monogamy*, with terminology differentiating the nuclear family from aunts, uncles, and cousins (Morgan 1963).

This scheme had its problems, as we might expect of such a pioneering work. Although Morgan pointed out that the **"primitive promiscuity"** that gave rise to the Malayan (Hawaiian) terminology no longer existed in any known society, he did assume that living peoples who retained such a kinship terminology must be among the most primitive. (Remember, the comparative method saw living peoples as examples of earlier stages.)

As it turns out, though, the Malayan kinship terminology occurred among some peoples whose societies were highly complex. Not the least of these were the people of the Hawaiian Islands, who had elaborate systems of social ranking. On the other hand, Morgan's "Aryan-Semitic-Uralian," now referred to as **"Eskimo,"** terminology, which emphasizes the nuclear family, occurs not only among Europeans and Americans but also among hunting and gathering peoples with relatively simple technologies in the Arctic and elsewhere. Morgan's linkage of kinship forms with evolutionary stages, therefore, had serious flaws.

Still, an emphasis on the ways in which people organize themselves has remained a central aspect of anthropological inquiry. Morgan's painstaking attempts to gather detailed information on this fundamental aspect of human life opened a wealth of discovery, debate, and inquiry over the next century and a half.

For nineteenth-century evolutionists, though, the point of the exercise was quite different from the issues that motivated the pursuits of later scholars. In the twentieth and twenty-first centuries, most researchers have attempted to understand other societies in their own right. For them, these societies offer rich and diverse examples of the human experience. As cases, they offer some insight not only into what factors have given rise to cultural diversity, but ultimately, they help address the more profound question of what it means to be human. For the evolutionists, however, these societies were interesting mostly as purported examples of the Euroamerican past. The object of inquiry was not to understand "primitive" societies as phenomena of interest in themselves, but to glean what they could tell Europeans about their own prehistory. In a sense, the evolutionists felt that they were studying their own ancestors.

The driving engine of change remained a question, however. The Enlightenment idea of increasing rationality persisted. For Morgan this rationality was manifest in technological innovation. New discoveries and inventions such as pottery, the bow and arrow, or agriculture led to new ways of living, including the development of new family structures.

One advantage of treating technology as an evolutionary factor, of course, is that for the most part it is inherently cumulative and sequential. Certain inventions must precede others. This is less obvious for such issues as family and social organization, which were to remain subjects of lively debate for many generations.

A threshold development, as Morgan saw it, was private property. This aspect of society bridged the technological, economic, and social. Knowing that many smaller non-Western societies maintain communal or corporate access to important resources, Morgan surmised that such patterns must have been characteristic of the earliest human societies. In Morgan's view, the departure from such primitive sharing was a major advance that gave rise to all sorts of developments, including an increase in brain size (Harris 1968:138).

As we noted, a clear separation of biology from culture was generations away. Morgan and others seemed to envision a feedback between levels of social and physical evolution. In many ways this view may also represent Lamarkian ideas positing the inheritance of acquired characteristics. This was not entirely inconsistent with the nineteenth-century concept of psychic unity, which assumed that sooner or later all peoples would develop the same kinds of solutions to similar problems. It merely emphasized the presumption that many peoples had a long way to go.

The hallowed place of private property in mid nineteenth-century thinking was hardly questioned, especially among those who had a great deal of it. Even Marx and Engels saw private property as an essential feature of the capitalist stage of development that must precede a more advanced socialistic society. Unequal access to the fruits of one's labor, in their view, was a contradiction that would contribute to the eventual breakdown and restructuring of the capitalist mode of production.

Other, more conservative thinkers held that private property added to social stability. Property was an aspect of the good society with a responsible citizenry and greater general prosperity. As to the obvious fact that not all citizens had equal access to this advantage—well, the aspects of competition and fitness came into play, did they not?

THE EVOLUTION OF RATIONALITY

The old emphasis on rational thinking as the driving impetus for evolutionary change remained important. British anthropologist **Edward Burnett Tylor** saw human advancement as a matter of people progressing beyond irrational ideas and folk beliefs. Calling anthropology "a reformer's science," he argued that its major contribution was to dispell archaic, leftover ideas from the past (what he called "cultural survivals") (Tylor 1958:16).

Tylor was less interested than Morgan in defining stages, although he did use this model in his discussion of the development of religious ideas. In keeping with the general evolutionist assumption that European society represented the epitome of human achievement so far, Tylor assumed that as far as religion was concerned, monotheism was the most highly developed form. The question, though, was how had this form developed from earlier types? And for that matter, how did it all begin?

In Tylor's time, many thinkers held that one obvious answer to the question of how religion originated was that God had revealed Himself (not

Edward Burnett Tylor (1832–1917)

Herself or Themselves, in the European case) to humans in the past. But Tylor, perhaps noting that monotheism was not particularly common among the world's peoples, saw the need for an alternative explanation. It is interesting that like most of his contemporaries, Tylor had his own personal religious beliefs. But he elected to take what, for the period, was a dispassionate approach, examining religion as one of many cultural patterns that had developed through time.

Using the comparative method, Tylor found ethnographic examples to identify what he felt were the most primitive features of religion, and he speculated on what experiences might have led early humans to develop religious beliefs. He seized on the phenomenon of dreams—a common enough human experience, to be sure. Early humans, he surmised, mistook the experience of dreams as evidence that the soul actually left the body at times, and no longer subject to the normal constraints of bodily existence, operated on a different plane of being.

From that idea it was a short step to imagining souls or spiritual beings with no connection to physical bodies. And from that point, one could easily attribute spirits or souls to other natural bodies or phenomena, such as rocks or springs of water—things that most Europeans would consider inanimate. From this he developed the idea of *animism*, the attribution of life to natural objects. The earliest form of religion, Tylor suggested, involved animism, the attribution of life and even awareness to objects of nature, or *"nature worship"* (Tylor 1871).

This progression from animism at the lower end of the evolutionary process to monotheism at the highest seems a bit out of keeping with the general evolutionary assumption that progress involved a movement from the simple to the complex. Certainly one could argue that a world full of various spirits seems more complex than one over which a single deity rules. But the view that monotheism was more advanced was consistent with the idea of progression from what seemed less rational to Victorians—a view that rocks are alive—to what seemed to them more rational—that an invisible patriarchal deity had created the world and continued to watch over it.

Tylor's version of evolution did represent a significant difference from those of others, however. He offered a view of culture as a phenomenon that was not dependent on biological factors but developed according to dynamics of its own. His definition of culture—"that complex whole which includes knowledge, belief, art, morals, law, custom, and any other capabilities and habits acquired by man as a member of society" (1958:1)—stands as one of the classic statements on the concept.

Tylor stated explicitly that race could not serve as an explanation for cultural differences (1871:7). This does not mean that Tylor did not share the view of most of his contemporaries that some races were inferior to others. But for him, the force for progress was rationality, not biology. On the other hand, it does not seem to have occurred to any of the major thinkers of the time that rationality could vary in its forms, or that one could question the assumption that European achievement represented the highest attainment so far.

> On the whole it appears that whenever there are found elaborate arts, abstruse knowledge, complex institutions, these are results of gradual development from an earlier, simpler, and ruder state of life. No stage of civilization comes into existence spontaneously, but grows or is developed out of the stage before it. This is the great principle which every scholar must lay firm hold of, if he intends to understand either the world he lives in or the history of the past. (1916:20 [orig. 1881])

This view of intellectual progress was also evident in the work of **Sir James Frazer,** whose studies of the development of religious concepts earned him a place among several scholars (including Tylor) who have been called "the father of anthropology." Among other things, Frazer addressed the issue of magic, which seemed to be a quintessential example of primitive thought. Magic, Frazer suggested, was actually a primitive form of science. It

James Frazer (1854–1941)

was *incorrect* science because it rested on erroneous premises of cause and effect (de Waal Malefijt 1974:156–157). But it did represent a primitive attempt to address and manipulate the world—an attempt at which nineteenth-century "true" science had been far more successful.

Frazer's suggestion that the development of science necessarily supplanted beliefs in magic and the supernatural in general is open to question. Despite vast technological advances since Frazer's time, research indicates that a significant number of Americans at the beginning of the twenty-first century believe in the existence of angels and/or Satan. Frazer did, however, offer a useful categorization of different types of magic. Much of the value of Frazer's, Tylor's, and Morgan's work rests on their assiduous perusal of the ethnographic examples available to them and in their attempts to categorize these beliefs in typologies. (See, for example, Frazer 1958.)

That being the case, these scholars still faced the problem of determining the quality of their data. Tylor argued that the range of consistent information from different, independent sources resolved that issue. As he stated in response to criticism of his method, "A story by a bushranger in Australia may, perhaps, be objected to as a mistake or an invention, but did a Methodist minister in Guinea conspire with him to cheat the public by telling the same story there?" (Tylor 1958:9–10).

This did not fully address the problem of **systematic bias.** Suppose that a European missionary, a sailor, and casual traveler all report a similar version of "savagery" on some Pacific island or other. To what extent did that version result from generally held European views of "savages" and what savages are supposed to be like, which all of the observers might have held before their travels?

These various models of evolutionary progress also implied similar sequences of development. Not all of these scholars were as explicit about stages as Morgan, but clearly, higher forms necessarily followed lower ones in their thinking. This is one basis for the term **unilinear evolution.** And not all societies seemed ready or able to jump stages and shortcut the road to progress.

EVOLUTION ACCORDING TO MARX

An alternative approach to the major principles of social change appeared in the second half of the nineteenth century in the work of Karl Marx and his colleague Friedrich Engels. Tylor had emphasized the growth of rational thought as the driving engine of cultural evolution. Morgan's emphasis on the impact of technological invention and discovery and the development of private property, with their implications for family structure, had placed the development of ideas in the forefront of human progress, even though he linked them to material aspects of life.

Marx, however, emphasized what he considered the most basic aspect of life: the fact that humans must draw subsistence from nature. The ways in which they do this produce certain kinds of social arrangements with a complex range of implications. In Marx's terms, a particular **mode of production** determines the form that **relations of production** take. Further,

> The mode of production of material life conditions the general process of social, political, and intellectual life. It is not the consciousness of men that determines their existence, but their social existence that determines their consciousness. (Quoted in Godelier 1977:17)

These basic facts affect the ways in which social systems change or evolve. Unlike Tylor, Marx did not emphasize the importance of rational innovation—the idea that humans could think their way through the evolutionary process. In Marx's view, the social situation acted as a constraint on human powers to transcend their situations. As he put it, people live in a history, but it is a history that is not of their own making.

This was particularly so because the true structure of relationships in a given mode of production lay invisible beneath the surface appearance of relations. In class-based societies, for example, the exploitative relationships between elites and the lower classes might be disguised by a paternalistic model in the guise of mutual benefits for all concerned.

Marx's materialism was far more complex than Morgan's, which tended to credit such technological innovations as the bow and arrow or pottery with having a direct relationship to the forms of social organization and, in effect, the evolutionary level. To the extent that Marx placed any importance on technological innovations, it was only insofar as they brought about changes in the relations of production. An example might be the role of machinery in altering the relationships between the factory owners and their laborers.

Marx and Engels had little good information on small, kinship-organized societies that lacked clear social class differentiation. In the late nineteenth century they discovered the works of Morgan and adopted many of his views on that subject, albeit with some reservations. Nonetheless, such societies offered a baseline model in which people were relatively free from exploitation and could directly enjoy the results of their own labor.

The question of how such a small, classless society would change to a more complex, class-based system was difficult to answer. One possibility was that among scattered, independent small communities of this sort, a common need for scarce resources might give rise to some sort of ruling class to regulate access to them. This could produce a situation in which the powerful elite could exploit the labor of the general populace while disguising the relationship as one of benevolent rule or religious legitimacy. The identification of the masses with a religious system in which the elite act as intermediaries on their behalf was one example of this relationship. Such a situation, which Marx referred to as an **Asiatic mode of production,** had developed in parts of Asia and Central and South America.

This model inspired considerable research in the twentieth century on the rise of despotic governments. **Karl Wittfogel** developed the idea of **"oriental despotism"** as a system arising from the need for a strong centralized government to regulate irrigation systems in desert areas. As we will discuss below, Julian Steward adopted the model in the 1950s as an aspect of his **multilinear evolution.**

In effect, Marx's view of evolution was also multilinear. Paying close attention to the variety of actual cases for which he had some documentation, Marx realized that evolutionary patterns do not necessarily follow the same path. The consistent element in all cases, however, was the power of the mode of production to determine other aspects of life, from social relations to ideology. In the European sphere Marx saw the **feudal mode of production** as a precursor to capitalism, which he predicted would in time give way to socialism.

Although the Asiatic mode of production showed remarkable stability, the feudal mode had given way to private property and subsequently to the ability of those who owned the **means of production** to exploit those who owned nothing but their own labor. The means of production might be plantations, shops, or factories. Whatever their form, the owners were in a position to derive profit from the labor of their employees and to withhold the full value of what they produced.

In Marx's discussion of the capitalist mode of production in the context of a market system and class-based society, a number of important concepts come into play. The **use value** of a product, for a worker, reflects its value to whoever might produce and enjoy it. A simple example might be the vegetables individuals produce in their gardens for their own tables. The **commodity value** of an item, on the other hand, is what it is worth on the market. A different aspect of value is expressed as **surplus value.** As Maurice Godelier puts it, "The surplus value is nothing more mysterious than the difference between the total value created by the use of manpower and the fraction of this value which is handed to the producer in the form of wages" (1977:23). The surplus value in a capitalist system is the *profit* the seller can realize beyond the cost of producing an item, including labor costs.

To express this in another way, as Marx did, let us suppose that a worker in a factory shows up for work at 8:00 in the morning and begins producing items. By 10:30, the worker has already produced enough of these items to pay for her day's wages. But she does not stop working at that point. She continues to produce items throughout the working day (which in Marx's time might have been from twelve to sixteen hours). The market values of items she produces after 10:30 in the morning represent profit for the owner who, in fact, has not produced anything himself. It is enough that he owns the factory. And rather than applying the profits to increase wages for the workers, the owner is likely to invest in the factory in order to increase production still more. The worker, on the other hand, who does not own a factory and has no other means of subsistence, has only her labor to sell. And in general, the price of that labor is determined largely by the employer.

This relationship is not usually obvious, or "visible." The worker may be happy to have a job, conscious of the many people in the surplus labor force who do not, who could be referred to as a "surplus army of labor." Their presence allows the employer to adopt a "take it or leave it" stance toward the employees.

Change in this situation, according to Marx, is likely only when the "contradictions" in the system that reveal the true nature of these exploitative relationships become apparent and intolerable. In this case, the powerful elite are not likely to relinquish their privileged position willingly. Revolutionary change, therefore, is likely to require a violent overthrow of the existing system, rather than gradual reform. The outcome of such revolution, if successful, would be a restructuring of the mode of production to permit the workers to realize the benefits of their own labor, free of the exploitation of capitalistic elites.

The existing system is perpetuated, however, by the principle that the true structure of relationships is not visible to those who participate—even, to some extent, to the elites. The privileged classes occupy a received status, for the most part, not one they have created themselves. And the oppressed classes may continue to see the elites as their benefactors. The belief system, or **ideology,** tends to reinforce and maintain this **mystification** until exploitative contradictions reach the breaking point.

There have been many critiques of Marx's evolutionary schemes—often pointing to historic events occurring long after Marx's death that seem to contradict his predictions. The end of the Cold War and the failures of purported socialist and communist governments loom large in these critiques.

Within anthropology, however, many scholars have found valuable insights in Marx's work. Given Marx's and Engels's focus on industrial societies, the applicability of their ideas to the small, kinship-based populations with whom anthropologists often deal may be debatable. Nevertheless, Maurice Godelier, Regis Terray, Marc Bloch, Eric Wolf, Peter Worsley, and other anthropologists have found much of value in them.

On a larger scale, a number of scholars have utilized Marxist ideas to explore the nature of power disparities in the relationship between so-called "First World" states and "Third" and "Fourth World" indigenous societies (see, for example, Wolf 1982; Frank 1972, 1975; Wallerstein 1974, 1984; Worsley 1984). (We discuss some of these issues in Chapter 4 on structure.) With regard to evolution, Marxist ideas greatly influenced the work of Leslie White and Julian Steward, as we shall discuss below.

THE DECLINE OF NINETEENTH-CENTURY EVOLUTION

It was clear even to the unilineal evolutionists that few if any human societies remained untouched by contact with other peoples. What about the mutual influences that usually occurred when that happened?

The evolutionists did not seem particularly troubled by that issue. Morgan expressed some frustration in applying his stages to Africa because of the mixture of ideas that had affected most societies there. Tylor confronted the spread of traits directly, and far from denying them, he attempted to trace some of them. He pointed out clear cases of such cultural **diffusion**, the most famous being his discussion of the appearance of almost identical board games in Mexico and India. For the most part, though, the fact that populations might influence one another or that cultural features might spread did not appear to pose a major challenge to the general sweep or direction of development.

Eventually, however, among some theorists the diffusion of cultural traits came to the forefront as the major explanation of culture forms. Some of them posed this phenomenon as a rebuttal to evolutionary models. A few diffusionists, in fact, challenged the very notion of progress, suggesting that culture actually lost complexity and degenerated as it spread from centers of "high culture" to peripheral regions (see, for example, Smith 1932; Perry 1923; Schmidt 1939, Graebner 1911).

Ultimately, though, the severest challenge to nineteenth-century evolutionary models did not come from diffusionism. The most compelling force for revision arose from the growing awareness that anthropology, if it was ever to achieve scientific integrity, needed a sounder and more extensive base of information. Rather than relying on second-hand or third-hand accounts of uncertain quality, the serious study of human societies required solid, first-hand observational data.

The tradition of anthropological field research began rather haltingly. A few individuals in the early nineteenth century—such as Henry Rowe Schoolcraft, who spent many years living among the Chippewa—had made great efforts to collect ethnographic information (1851). Some missionaries, despite their primary aim of converting indigenous peoples from their beliefs and practices, had also collected detailed information (see, for example, Codrington 1891 in Melanesia). Additional data had come from naturalists and others whose activities had taken them to remote areas, although often their observations of the local peoples were secondary to other interests, such as ornithology or botany. The term **fieldwork,** in fact, seems to be a carryover from the work of these naturalists (Stocking 1992:27).

If we care to think in terms of the "evolution of anthropology," it is tempting to see the shift toward fieldwork as the beginning of a developmental stage. In the early years of the twentieth century, British anthropologists Alfred Cort Haddon, William H. R. Rivers, and Charles G. Seligman secured

The Torres Straits Expedition: (standing, left to right) William Rivers, Charles Seligman, Sidney Ray, and Anthony Wilkin, (seated) Alfred Haddon

funding to take a research trip to the Torres Straits off the northern coast of Australia. Armed with notebooks, cameras, and calipers, they stopped at various islands to collect a range of first-hand information from the people. Still earlier, in 1871, Nikolai Miklouho-Maclay took up residence on the northern coast of New Guinea; he took pains to learn the languages and recorded what he could about their way of life while living in their midst—often at some personal risk (see Stocking 1992:219–232; Webster 1984). Other adventurous scholars had made their way to parts of the world of which Europeans had little understanding.

Fieldwork became thoroughly institutionalized at last, though, through the work of three scholars in particular. In England, **Bronislaw Malinowski** and **Alfred Reginald Radcliffe-Brown** spent considerable time in their own field research and subsequently sent dozens of their graduate students out to do the same. In the United States, **Franz Boas** was to play a similar role. We shall have occasion to consider the impact of these figures on the development

Bronislaw Malinowski in the Field

of the ideas of culture, function, and structure in later chapters. With regard to the concept of cultural evolution that predominated at the time, the combination of Boas's demand for scientific rigor and his painstaking collection of data from the field helped to deal a staggering blow to many of the assumptions underlying nineteenth-century evolutionary theory.

The evolutionary paradigm had also become vulnerable through the excesses of some of its practitioners. In both Britain and the United States, evolutionary theory, social Darwinism, and racism had become intertwined (see, for example, Brinton 1896; Sumner and Keller 1927). While these aspects of the nineteenth-century evolutionary models certainly repelled Boas, his critique of them addressed their scientific, not their moral, validity. Among other things, Boas challenged the assumption that the human mind everywhere tends to reach the same results. This assumption of "psychic unity," as we recall, was an essential premise of such concepts as Morgan's stages.

Boas argued that social features such as clans can arise from a variety of circumstances. These features could include segmentation of a larger population into smaller units or the amalgamation of formerly separate populations. Masks, as another example, can have a range of different meanings and purposes, including disguise, transformation, threat, or entertainment. Only a thorough examination of each particular case can determine whatever causal factors might have led to observed cultural features. One could say that Boas substituted the study of specific histories for general evolutionary schemes.

In Britain, Malinowski remained receptive to the general idea of cultural evolution, but both he and Radcliffe-Brown disavowed the "speculative history" on which most evolutionary models rested. Like Boas, they emphasized the need for accurate, detailed, first-hand information from the field. Unlike Boas, they were not inclined to inquire into the past events and circumstances that might account for these observational data. In either case, however, the upshot was that among English-speaking anthropologists, unilinear evolution was decidedly out of date by the 1920s.

HUMAN BIOLOGICAL EVOLUTION

The concept of evolution is, of course, a central aspect of research into the biological history of the human species. As many researchers have pointed out, the relationship between human biological and cultural evolution is complex, and to some extent the two are inextricably linked. The capacity for culture, after all, is a product of biological evolution, particularly the development of the brain. It seems undeniable that aspects of behavior such as tool use, social patterns, year-round sexual receptivity, and prolonged childhood dependency all have involved biological and cultural interactions.

Nonetheless, we can still consider some of the major questions regarding evolutionary changes in the human species as separate from cultural phenomena. What were our ancestors like physically at various times in the past? What forms and directions did changes take? (For more information on these issue, see Boaz and Almquist 2002; Tattersall 1999; Wolpoff et al. 2002.)

We might take note at this point that some people continue to reject the very idea that humans are products of biological evolution over millions of years. It is safe to say, however, that this point of view has little or no influence in anthropological thinking except, perhaps, as an interesting example of cultural cosmology.

One might assume that unlike other perspectives that have linked evolutionary concepts with the human experience, the issue of biological evolution should be relatively free of speculation. The issue does, after all, rest mainly on concrete evidence, mostly in the form of fossils. Most people involved in this research, however, would probably agree that this field has been at least as contentious as any other, and possibly more so than most.

As we have noted, facts do not speak for themselves, and fossil skulls are no exception. Data require interpretation, and the field has been a lively battleground of competing views. These disputes began as early as the mid nineteenth century with the discovery of the first Neanderthal skull near Dusseldorf in Germany. Many viewed it as the remains of some unfortunate deformed individual. The subsequent discovery of many more such skulls over the years eventually compelled acceptance of the idea that other kinds of human (or human-like) creatures had once existed.

This fossil evidence caused problems in reconciling the physical evidence with the Biblical view of divine creation—a conflict that continues in some quarters today, as we have noted. Nonetheless, the discovery of stone tools in undeniably ancient soil strata added still more weight to the revisionist view, as did still other fossil remains, some of them far older and more ape-like than the Neanderthals.

The relationships among these prehistoric humans and their place, if any, in the human biological genealogy have stimulated long and heated debate. One might expect that new evidence would have helped to resolve many of these issues and build a consensus. As it happened, however, additional discoveries seem to have had the opposite effect. Discoveries of multiple hominid forms raised numerous questions and competing interpretations, fed to some extent by the eagerness of some researchers to claim a crucial role in human evolution for their particular finds.

The place of Neanderthals was among the most persistent issues. Had Neanderthals been direct ancestors of modern humans? Or did they represent an evolutionary offshoot, a dead end? If so, had they disappeared through interbreeding with modern types of humans, essentially being absorbed into the larger population? Or were they eliminated in some sort of prehistoric genocidal conflict with more "advanced" humans, the so-called Cro-Magnon people?

This debate, like many theoretical issues, tended to reflect the prevalent social philosophy of the times. The idea of an ancient conflict resonated well with nineteenth-century social Darwinism, with its popular mantra of "survival of the fittest" and progress through competition. As often in such debates, continued findings required some modification of views, albeit reluctantly in some cases.

An early reconstruction of Neanderthals as hulking, bent-kneed brutes turned out to be incorrect. Better information showed that although they had been stocky and well muscled with pronounced bony growth over their eyes, their brains had actually been larger, on the average, than those of modern humans. Excavations at an ancient Neanderthal living site at Shanidar Cave in Iraq, dated at around 60,000 years ago, showed that these Neanderthals had cared for a disabled individual and placed flowers in the graves of their dead. It is interesting to note that this revised view of a "kinder, gentler" and more complex Neanderthal coincided with more recent relativistic views in social and cultural anthropology in the twentieth century that had turned away from the hierarchical models of the nineteenth century.

It has also become clear that about 35,000 years ago, when the most extreme Neanderthal forms continued to live in Western Europe, other, more modern looking human populations had existed in other parts of the world for at least 60,000 years. DNA research, which had not been available before, showed that Neanderthals seem to have been an evolutionary offshoot that was not ancestral to modern humans. Not all researchers, however, have accepted this conclusion.

The issue of human origins has involved far more than Neanderthals. Since the discovery of the first Neanderthal skull, much older forms with smaller brains, collectively known as *Homo erectus*, ranged from Africa to East Asia. Still earlier creatures broadly categorized as Australopithecines ranged from Ethiopia to southern Africa several million years ago. Australopithecines showed a variety of forms. The most interesting, from the perspective of human evolution, were small creatures about four feet tall who stood erect and walked on two feet, as modern humans do. The brains of these creatures were only about the size of a chimpanzee's, but they lacked the large canine teeth that characterize apes.

Among those involved in the debates raging over these finds, some sought to draw conclusions about "human nature" from the fossil evidence. One argument, as we shall see in Chapter 3 on culture, was that these small australopithecines had been predators, consequently passing on a heritage of violence and even homicidal tendencies to us, their descendants. Other researchers have concluded that the light-bodied australopithecines were scavengers or even that they were seed-eaters.

In general, the major issues have been over the unity of the human line—debates between the so-called *lumpers*, who tend to consolidate the diverse forms into a series of evolutionary "grades," and the *splitters*, who tend to emphasize the diversity of forms and posit a variety of lines, only one of them leading to modern humans. Although much of the debate has gone on within a relatively narrow arena of empirical discourse—a matter of trying to "get it right"—some have also attempted to draw more contentious social conclusions from the fossil data. Certainly the most heated exchanges in this regard have been over the biological relationships among living human populations—the issue of "race."

As we can see, there is no significant disagreement about the general concept of evolution in this field of inquiry, but this by no means indicates that consensus reigns. Numerous questions persist. Has the evolutionary process been essentially continuous, or has it occurred in a "punctuated" fashion, with fits and starts, catastrophes, and resurgences? What have been the factors producing evolutionary change? Have tool use, social living, sexuality, competitiveness, or any of a range of other phenomena played predominant roles?

Since we are discussing here one of the most "scientific" aspects of anthropology—the biological nature of humanness—we might expect that rigorous testing of hypotheses against the data should be especially productive. As the record has shown, however, it has not been that simple. How would one go about testing a particular hypothetical model of human evolution?

As an example, let us consider the discovery of a particular fossil mandible. What to make of it? Does it represent a "missing link" in the chain of human evolution, or is it nothing more than the sad remains of an evolutionary sidetrack leading to extinction? Do the patterns of its tooth cusps show a relationship to later hominid forms, or is this a superficial similarity? Certainly the perspective of the researcher will have a great deal to do with whether the mandible will negate an existing hypothetical model of human evolution, affirm another, or essentially be considered an irrelevant anomaly. It should not be surprising, then, that competing models of human evolution have proliferated over the years as more data have become available.

Nevertheless, we can see some aspects of the gradual refinement of hypotheses that Karl Popper and his followers envisioned. Many older models have indeed undergone refinement as a result of new finds that have led to additional insights. We can also see examples of paradigm shifts that Thomas Kuhn describes, as, for example, the development of better dating techniques for fossil finds drastically extended our understanding of the age of hominid forms. We could also see the discovery of Australopithecines, with a relatively "modern" body form and small brain, reversing the older assumption that the human brain had first become larger and more complex while our ancestors retained an apelike body from the neck down. In these cases, compelling new data forced the abandonment of an older paradigm—generally with considerable emotional reaction on the part of its adherents.

EVOLUTION AND HUMAN VARIATION

Certainly racism in Europe and North America is a historical phenomenon that long predates any good scientific understanding of biological evolution. In the early nineteenth century, when the Biblical version of creation was the prevailing model of human origins, many writers struggled to reconcile divine creation with their negative views of other populations. Hence, we had such ideas as **polygenesis**—the argument that God had created various "races" separately.

This idea gained some currency when a traveler and raconteur named Isaiah Glidden observed that ancient Egyptian art depicted some people who were obviously dark-skinned Sub-Saharan Africans. Given the assumption that the Earth was only about 6,000 years old (based on Biblical genealogies since the Garden of Eden) and the knowledge that the Egyptian paintings were about 4,000 years old, Glidden argued that this was proof of separate creations. The alternative hypothesis—that all humans share the same origin—was implausible, since the intervening 2,000 years or so would not have been enough time for such differentiation to develop (see Stanton 1960:50).

Competing views held that, in fact, humans were extremely malleable and susceptible to environmental influences. William Stanhope Smith in the late eighteenth century, for example, attributed the alleged "savage" qualities of Native Americans to the "insalubrious" fumes and vapors that pervaded the swampy woodlands of their domain (1810). Another idea with rather wide acceptance was that the different major human populations were descended from the various sons of Noah—Shem, Ham, and Japheth—who dispersed after the Biblical flood.

As we can see, these ideas were not particularly in mutual accord, except to the extent that they assumed the inferiority of non-European populations. When the idea of biological evolution became established, it did little to change this perception. The predominant issue became how so-called "racial" populations became differentiated in biological, rather than Biblical, terms. In essence, the fundamental questions remained. How did variant human groupings arise? What was the relationship among them? Many of the earlier attempts to address these issues, not surprisingly, reflected predominant social views, and in many cases they blithely ignored obvious aspects of reality. The issue of "hybrids" was one case in point.

With regard to the question of the relationship among populations, some writers posited that Africans and Europeans constituted different "subspecies," or even different species altogether. One problem with this idea was that according to established biological thinking, the defining characteristic of a species is that its members can mate and produce viable, fertile offspring. There was no doubt that, in fact, such activity had been a commonplace occurrence among humans, even in situations in which social barriers attempted to prohibit it.

Nonetheless, some prominent figures in mid nineteenth-century America, including the well-known physician and self-proclaimed scientist Josiah Nott, asserted that the "hybrid" offspring of "interracial" unions were less vigorous and, in general, deficient compared to either parent. An alternative view, somewhat contradictory but held at the same time, was that such "hybridization" constituted a threat to society by decreasing the overall fitness of the population, presumably because such "hybrids" would reproduce in great numbers (see Stanton 1960:159).

Although the weakness of these arguments is evident, perhaps it is worth noting that the term hybrid, which comes from the realm of plant and animal breeding, refers to artificially induced reproduction between closely related species or subspecies (horse and mule, for example). Normally, hybridization does not occur spontaneously in nature. In any case, the empirical data gave no support to these arguments. The anthropologist Franz Boas, in fact, carried out a study in 1894 demonstrating that the offspring of French Canadian and Native American parents were actually taller than either parent and showed no signs of any deficiencies (Boas 1894b). Such data would have falsified the hypothesis of "hybrid deficiency," if they had not been ignored by the proponents of this view.

By the mid twentieth century, arguments for the extreme differentiation of human populations continued to prevail, though they were increasingly under challenge. The anthropologist Ashley Montagu published a book in the 1940s called Man's Most Dangerous Myth: The Fallacy of Race, in which he argued that the very idea of race has no biological basis (Montagu 1997 [orig. 1945]).

Notwithstanding this growing consensus among anthropologists and many other social scientists, however, the anthropologist Carleton Coon in the 1960s published a book asserting that the so-called "major races" had separated early in the course of human evolution (Coon 1962).

In this case, Coon used information in the fossil record at the time, albeit selectively. Europeans, according to Coon, had evolved from Neanderthals; Asians had sprung from *Homo erectus*, while most Africans descended from "Rhodesian Man," represented by a heavy-browed skull from central Africa.

By this time, however, Coon's arguments had become an anachronism and met widespread criticism. Already, advances in population genetics had begun to establish the deep genetic unity of all living humans. Richard Lewontin, for example, showed that most genetic variance among humans occurs *within* populations rather than *between* populations (1972; Lewontin et al. 1984). Individuals within a single group, in other words, are likely to differ more from one another genetically than the average gene frequencies differ between two populations.

The identification of gradual and overlapping gene distributions, known as **clines,** lent further insights. In effect, it underscored the assertion that the traditional idea of race makes no biological sense.

Perhaps the most striking recent finding in this regard has come through more refined genetic research based on DNA. The Human Genome Project, controversial as it has been, has established that the genetic differences among human populations are miniscule compared to the genetic material they overwhelmingly share.

In the late 1990s, Alan Templeton put the various alternative models of human differentiation to the test by comparing mitochondrial DNA among a global sample of geographic populations that included the spectrum of those traditionally grouped as "races" (1998). His findings clearly were inconsistent with the "deep separation" model of the sort Carlton Coon proposed. In effect, Templeton substantiated the hypothesis that human population separations are not only relatively recent, but that they have remained incomplete. That is, gene flow throughout the entire human species has never ceased long enough for differentiation to become significant.

One might speculate that the year-round sexual receptivity of humans—unlike many species that have distinct mating seasons—might have contributed to this result. In any case, however, it would appear that sexuality, which has been such a volatile aspect of human history, has at a basic level kept us a single "human race."

THE RETURN OF CULTURAL EVOLUTION

Although cultural evolution fell into disrepute within anthropology early in the twentieth century, it seems to have become firmly entrenched in popular thought. To some degree, the decline of evolutionary assumptions in anthropological thinking had to do with their association with issues that were not necessarily inherent in the concept of evolution itself. Evolution had been misused to give racist social philosophies the appearance of scientific validity, but it was difficult to deny that overall, some aspects of human life had changed in a cumulative fashion. This was especially obvious for technology. It would be absurd to assume that iron implements had appeared before stone tools, or that the invention of a simple wheel had not preceded the chariot.

One could safely go farther than that. Archaeological exploration of the human past had become a serious pursuit early in the nineteenth century. By the middle of the twentieth century, archaeology had provided a fairly detailed picture of changes in human life over tens of thousands of years. There was no reason to doubt that hunting and gathering had preceded the invention of agriculture, or that food production generally had coincided with changes in population size and density. Hunting camps had preceded villages. Villages had preceded cities. All of these ways of life, undoubtedly, entailed different forms of social organization and probably different systems of belief.

Leslie White incorporated these factors into a revised model of cultural evolution that avoided much of the unnecessary baggage of the nineteenth-century versions. White acknowledged an intellectual debt to Tylor, Morgan, and others, and in fact, he modestly claimed that he was simply following in their footsteps. He argued that prejudices arising from reactions to nineteenth-century cultural evolution had come to dominate American and British anthropology and had prevented a fair assessment of the concept of unilinear evolution (White 1945). Unlike the nineteenth-century evolutionists, though, White built a model of evolution without racist overtones and, he claimed, without the evaluative implications of earlier ideas of progress.

Although the term *progress* itself tended to remain laden with its earlier associations of betterment, White defined progress in more objective, measurable terms. Progress, in his view, involved a concept of increasing scale in social phenomena, as in Spencer's model. But White separated this trend from the idea of an improved quality of life. He suggested, in fact, that sociocultural evolution had also brought about increasing alienation and a decline in the quality of social relationships that often characterized small-scale societies (see, for example, White 1988:252–254).

White's concept of sociocultural evolution shook off many of the unnecessary assumptions and social agendas that had cluttered it. Social evolution did not need to imply racism or ethnocentrism. This streamlined model still entailed one-directional change, or "progress," as it had in the past; but if progress did not necessarily mean betterment, what criteria could define it?

White focused on a measure that was potentially free of value judgment: *energy*. Every society exists by drawing energy from the environment. The amount of energy a population draws can differ widely, depending on whether people live entirely on wild foods, grow crops, burn coal and oil, or

Leslie White

use nuclear power plants. Energy is measurable. The number of calories a population uses is an empirical question, not one of value judgment.

The amount of energy a population draws from the environment also dovetails with other aspects of life. A small group of hunters and foragers will not only draw less energy from the environment than an agricultural community does, but they will also have a technology appropriate to their needs and capabilities. It is likely to be simple (even if ingenious), portable, and so on. Agriculturalists with a more sedentary existence, on the other hand, will have tools and equipment appropriate to *their* way of life. They can have a variety of belongings, since they need not carry all of their gear around with them.

The ways in which populations organize themselves and structure interpersonal relationships will also differ. Arrangements that work well for scattered and mobile hunters might not be as feasible for farmers who live together in denser, face-to-face communities and have to deal with different kinds of social issues. Finally, the ways in which people in these societies construct their intellectual realities are also likely to differ. In short, this concept of evolution offered an empirical basis for distinguishing one level of cultural evolution from another and posited linkages between energy, material culture, social organization, and belief systems.

A century earlier, Morgan had also clustered various social and cultural features in his successive developmental stages. But there was at least one important difference between Morgan's model and twentieth-century views of evolution. Morgan did not pay a great deal of attention to the *independent variable*—the prime determinant—of the stages. In Morgan's scheme, the general package of traits for each stage tended to be linked or at least mutually appropriate, but the overriding factor was the idea of progress through intellectual and moral development, which implicitly was linked to discovery and invention.

White, by associating progress with the use of energy, freed the concept of differential evolutionary levels from intellectual and moral issues. As many people facing environmental degradation and social problems in the early twenty-first century have learned, the two are not necessarily linked in a positive way.

White's model of overall evolutionary progress seemed to make sense, but it was difficult to apply it to particular examples. It took little account of local ecological factors or other details of specific cases. Perhaps more seriously, it seemed to ignore entirely the cases in which populations had changed their ways of life in directions opposite to the general direction of evolutionary progress. The Native American Absaroke, or Crow, of the northwestern Plains had abandoned village agriculture in the nineteenth century and become buffalo hunters. Other groups, such as the Cheyenne and Lakota, had done the same. Did these cases contradict the trend of cultural evolution?

Such exceptions did not particularly trouble White. His model of evolution, he pointed out, applied to the general sweep of cultural evolution—"Culture with a big C," as he put it—rather than specific cultures. Considerable debate ensued as to whether specific exceptions disproved the general rule.

In any case, even if White's overall evolutionary model was valid, it was difficult to see how anyone could operationalize it for the study of specific cultural data. To some extent it would be comparable to analyzing midwestern tornadoes by employing a framework of long-term climatic change over the past 10,000 years since the end of the Pleistocene. The model was not irrelevant, exactly, but its macro scale seemed remote from the domain of specific researchable questions arising from particular cases.

White's model did offer major refinements in establishing the directional nature of sociocultural evolution, however. While it might be easy to conceive of a population increasing its energy use, the reverse would almost necessarily be a matter of catastrophe. Generally, a significant drop in the amount of energy that a population draws from the environment would either have to be a result of major population decrease or a cause of it.

Returning to the Absaroke question, in this context, it would be interesting to know whether their switch from farming to hunting buffalo actually increased the energy they extracted from the environment. One could also suggest that perhaps the quality of resource extraction—high protein meat and fat as opposed to low-protein, high-calorie carbohydrates of farm produce—could complicate the simple measure of overall energy use.

MULTILINEAR EVOLUTION

Other ways of studying evolution were available. Why *not* look closely at local ecological factors? Why *not* pay attention to specific local variations? One could consider hunting and foraging societies as a general category, for example, and still take into account the obvious fact that societies in that category differ among themselves in important ways.

The particular causes of major shifts in energy use were one question. Why, for example, would people who had been living successfully on wild foods decide to grow crops? At one time theorists assumed that as soon as people discovered how to garden, they would do so. The old idea had some resonance with the Enlightenment emphasis on progress through rational thought. But upon reflection and with better knowledge of such societies, this scenario made less sense. Could any competent forager be unaware of the nature of plant growth?

Better observations through fieldwork, as well as common sense, made it clear that many hunters and foragers knew perfectly well that seeds dropped into fertile soil would grow into plants. Their livelihood, after all, depended on a good understanding of the world around them. Yet they had not bothered to put this knowledge to use.

On the other hand, why should they? Gardening is hard work. Why strain your back breaking the soil, planting seeds, and chasing birds away when you can pick wild plants that already grow by themselves? Not only that, but we now know that hunters generally have a more varied diet, including access to animal protein, than do most farming peoples.

Using these insights, the geographer **Esther Boserup** in the 1960s provided an important analysis of the dynamics that promoted reliance on agriculture (1965). She argued that increased production, with its concurrent increase in demands on human effort, would not have arisen simply because of the knowledge of how to do it. Population pressure would have been necessary to compel such innovation.

Decades earlier, the anthropologist **Julian Steward** had turned the focus in evolutionary studies to local conditions and strategies. In contrast to Leslie White's revival of unilinear evolution, Steward had introduced the concept of **multilinear evolution.** Rather than the old model of stages, Steward preferred the term **"levels of sociocultural integration"** (Steward 1955).

Hunting and gathering peoples, for example, represented one such level. But hunting and gathering groups lived in areas with vastly different environmental features and potentials. Whether people in sparse areas relied mostly on large herd animals or on small scattered game such as jackrabbits would make a difference in how they organized themselves.

The ethnographic record shows that in most hunting and gathering groups, men have done most of the hunting. For that reason, the distribution of related men would be significant. If young boys who grew up hunting with their fathers, uncles, and brothers remained with their own group after marriage and brought their wives to live with them and their relatives, local groups of hunters would tend to be relatively isolated because the hunters would not have to leave their own localities. This would be feasible if the game were scattered but evenly distributed, as jackrabbits usually are. In that case there would be little need for people to hunt in different regions.

But what about situations in which large game such as caribou move about in herds and might not show up on any predictable schedule in a given area? Hunters would have to be able to respond collectively to unpredictable opportunities over a wide region. They would need to be able to move to where the animals were and coordinate their activities for such projects as game drives.

In that case, according to Steward, it would be advantageous for hunters to have social ties with hunters in other regions, effectively maintaining a precondition for cooperative hunts. For that situation it would be more useful to have men move *out* of their family groups and live with their wives' people. Not only would a man find new hunting partners and learn a new territory, but he would also retain ties with his brothers, uncles, and father in other places. When the time came for large numbers of hunters to come together for collective game drives, these latent ties would become active links for coordinated efforts.

This approach and the set of questions it addressed was a long way from the generalized evolutionary schemes of unilinear evolution. For one thing, the questions now focused on how populations developed particular strategies to meet immediate problems. Local adaptations took precedence over macro-level forces for change.

With regard to higher levels of sociocultural integration, such as intensive agricultural societies, Steward's approach was consistent. Using insights from the work of **Karl Wittfogel,** for example, Steward discussed the development of strong centralized governments in situations in which irrigation systems required overall coordination of access to water and ditch maintenance (Wittfogel 1953). In all cases, this evolutionary model rested on material/ecological considerations.

Steward did not assume that all aspects of culture relate in some clear way to the needs of making a living, whether it be hunting jackrabbits or farming rice paddies. Nonetheless, he pointed out that many aspects of social and cultural life, including social arrangements, *are* subject to such consider-ations. Steward chose to label those aspects of life arising from the food quest the **culture core,** distinguishing them from other cultural features that may be more variable or arbitrary.

This model of multilinear cultural evolution resembled White's model and even Morgan's in positing relationships among social, cultural, and ma-terial features at each level. It differed, though, in its attention to particular cases and the variations among them. It is probably safe to say that among all of the models we have discussed so far, Steward's multilinear model offers the most potential for generating researchable questions.

For a time in the 1950s and 1960s, the differences between unilinear and multilinear evolution and the validity of evolutionary models in general produced a fair amount of controversy. Some of White's former graduate stu-dents in the 1960s attempted to reconcile the models of unilinear and multi-linear evolution by suggesting that White's **general evolution** and Steward's **specific evolution** were perfectly compatible; they just focused on different levels of abstraction (Sahlins and Service 1960).

Some interesting concepts arose from this discussion. Service's **"law of evolutionary potential"** incorporated the factor of diffusion into evolution-ary dynamics (1960). Old industrialized states, for example, which had reached advanced stages of production sooner, were saddled with outdated factories as technology advanced. Newly industrializing states, on the other hand, could adopt the most modern technology of the day without having to pass through the same developmental phases—essentially taking an evolu-tionary shortcut. In another volume, Elman Service offered a discussion of the sociopolitical distinctions among **bands, tribes,** and **states,** which in some ways seemed to offer another version of evolutionary stages (1962).

Morton Fried worked with the issue of the origins of the state, incorpo-rating an evolutionary perspective (1967). He also critiqued the idea of "tribe" as an evolutionary stage, arguing that historic tribes are products of state expansion.

Despite the fervent defense of evolutionary models during the 1960s, it appears that whatever aspects of this concept came to seem useful eventually found their way into general anthropological thinking with little fanfare. By the end of the twentieth century, proponents of evolutionism no longer con-stituted a significant opposition party within the anthropological main-stream. Few anthropologists would question the idea that technology has advanced cumulatively, or that changes in material culture have had reper-cussions on other aspects of life. The old ideas that cultural evolutionary change had a particular direction, however, and the value judgments associ-ated with that assumption became more or less relegated to intellectual history in anthropology, if not in all of the social sciences.

Ironically, nineteenth-century evolutionary thought seems to have had far greater staying power in some of the other disciplines and in popular thought. In government agencies, the idea of "underdevelopment" continues to influence the economic policies of industrial nations toward the "Third World." Rather than attributing the poverty of former colonized countries to their systematic exploitation by more powerful interests, conservative economic models "blame the victims" for not having developed sufficiently modern economic structures. And in the news media—even in the respectable *New York Times*—we still read occasionally about "Stone Age tribes."

In anthropology, however, such views have given way to a more sophisticated understanding of the dynamics and diversity of the human experience. One of the most important conceptual tools in achieving this understanding has been the concept of culture, which we consider in the next chapter.

FOOD FOR THOUGHT

Does change in human life have any particular direction?

Can some aspects of life advance while others either remain stable or decline? Why/why not?

Is there any "prime mover" in human affairs?

Is evolution best conceived as a straight line or a branching bush?

Can the analogy of society as a living organism be applied to the idea of cancer and uncontrolled growth of individual cells? Could this be a model for unhindered growth in society?

Has progress in the history of human society always coincided with environmental degradation?

Chapter 3

THE IDEA OF CULTURE

We might find some irony in the fact that culture, the central concept of anthropology, is also one on which anthropologists have never reached consensus. As Robert Borofsky puts it, "Culture is what various people conceive it to be . . . different people perceive it in different ways for different ends" (2001:433). But before we begin to address the disagreements and points of contention, it will be useful to consider some fundamental points of agreement.

All anthropologists would agree that culture is *learned* rather than biologically inherited. And all would agree that culture is *shared* among individuals rather than being idiosyncratic, or unique to a particular individual. These concepts involve a third point of agreement: culture requires *language*.

These ideas are both old and new. As we noted earlier, writers as early as Herodotus described the customs of different peoples without attributing these varied ways of life to inherent physical differences. If anything, they tended to ascribe physical differences to the influences of custom rather than the opposite.

We have also discussed the rise of biological explanation among the social Darwinists of the nineteenth century. We have seen the continuation of biological explanations for human behavior up to the present that are marginal to, and often in opposition to, most anthropological thinking. We will discuss that point later in this chapter. To some extent, the development of the modern anthropological view of culture arose as a rebuttal to nineteenth-century racist views that attributed human behavioral differences to biology.

Although the term *culture* is common enough to have become commonplace, the idea is not altogether obvious. The use of the term *culture* itself implies a particular viewpoint about humanness and has important implications.

Culture shares the same roots with the term *cultivate:* "to grow," or in another sense, "to influence the growth or development of. . . ." It reflects a view of humans as products of particular social and environmental circumstances and influences, as opposed to being preformed or predetermined entities. In that sense, culture offers a counterpoint to the common idea of "human nature" that implies that humans have fixed, inborn characteristics that manifest themselves "no matter what."

Either of these views, if taken to extremes, becomes absurd. Few people who tend to account for the behavior of their friends, relatives, or colleagues in terms of "human nature" would deny that these people's life experiences have had some effect in causing them to become the way they are. And no anthropologist who places a heavy emphasis on culture to explain human behavior would deny the common biological nature of human beings. These concepts do, nonetheless, represent two ends of a spectrum with plenty of room for dispute between them.

Clifford Geertz represents the view of many anthropologists in arguing that culture is a necessary aspect of being human. As he has put it, a cultureless human being is an impossibility, since humans do not have sufficient inborn behavioral guides to make survival possible without learning from other humans (Geertz 1965). Humans *produce* culture, but we are also *products* of culture.

The crucial aspect of culture is that it is distinct from the physical being. It is **extrasomatic,** "outside the body." As some have expressed it, culture constitutes social rather than biological heredity. This idea has profound implications. To the extent that humans must learn to become who they are, they can learn many ways of being. It also means, in effect, that as far as culture is concerned, humans at birth are essentially interchangeable.

Like racial explanations, cultural explanations deal with human differences. Unlike racial explanations, cultural explanations can accommodate the *production of difference* without weakening in any way the assumption of an underlying common humanity.

THE DEVELOPMENT OF THE CONCEPT OF CULTURE

The idea that people in a given society share and pass on specific customs is far from new. It probably is safe to assume that in every functioning community in the world for tens of thousands of years, people have concerned themselves with passing on their customs and knowledge to subsequent generations. They have told moralistic stories to their children. They have put their young people through rites of initiation to instill a strong sense of who they are, or should be. They have alluded to the improper ways of neighboring groups as negative examples. They have often, with pride, referred to themselves as "the (genuine or proper) People," as opposed to others less fortunate or enlightened.

Historically, a significant aspect of European thinking with regard to these phenomena was the nineteenth century's unusual linkage of custom with physical characteristics, followed by disengagement of the two, gradually and contentiously, in the twentieth century.

It is useful here to draw some distinction between the linkage of physical nature and custom, on the one hand, and the linkage of physical nature with personal proclivities, on the other. For much of European history, as well as history beyond the European realm, people have had a tendency to assign *emotional* qualities to other groups. "The A are short-tempered; the B are a sneaky people; the C are lustful and immoral; the D are industrious but timid," and so on. Most anthropologists would probably argue that the acts of creating such *stereotypes* about others are the very stuff of culture. So, too, are the grains of truth they may contain. At both ends of the phenomenon—the actor's and the observer's—these stereotypes represent behavior that is learned rather than biologically inherited.

These attributions of personal qualities to others do, however, differ from the realm of describable custom and belief as anthropologists generally know it. In anthropological thinking, the issue has been that custom and belief slowly became freed from suppositions of "innate qualities" of particular populations, along with a developing recognition that such traits or qualities are manifestations of culture. To the extent that attributed characteristics have any validity at all, they are acquired through experience rather than being passed on "in the blood."

The term *culture* (or its German version "*Kultur*") actually appears quite early in scholarly writing. The philosopher Immanuel Kant used the term in the late eighteenth century. The "German concept of *kultur* places special stress on national differences and the particular identity of groups . . . " (Elias 1994:5). Robert Borofsky notes that "Anthropologists often draw on this tradition to emphasize a people's shared beliefs and behaviors that distinguish them from others and, at the same time, offer them a sense of shared meaning" (2001:433).

For much of the term's intellectual history outside anthropology, though, culture has tended to refer to what we might call "high culture"—art, music, literature, and so on. This meaning still tends to predominate among some historians and other social scientists.

As Edward Tylor's definition in the last chapter shows, however, anthropologists by the late nineteenth century had come to extend the concept of culture to far more prosaic aspects of life and to emphasize its collective nature. Music, dance, and theater were aspects of it, but so were nursery rhymes, good luck charms, common greetings, and ways of sneezing. The question of culture in this vein was not whether a gentleman wore an appropriate necktie for the occasion, but why Englishmen wore ties at all.

SYMBOLS, MEANING, AND THE TOTALITY OF CULTURE

If culture is learned, shared behavior, does this mean that *all* learned, shared behavior is culture? What do we conclude about a squirrel that learns how to steal seeds from a metal "squirrel-proof" bird feeder? Still more troublesome, what about other squirrels that observe that behavior and learn to do the same thing? Are these squirrels displaying culture?

Certainly metal bird feeders have played no role in squirrel evolution. So it seems improbable that squirrels could have developed an "instinct," whatever that means, for solving this particular problem. No, we are talking about squirrel learning here, on at least two levels. The first squirrel figured out how to solve the problem, and other squirrels learned from the first. A creature with a brain the size of a pea has once again outdone human strategic planning.

The annals of wildlife interactions with humans are rife with such animal triumphs. As far as the feeder issue is concerned, are we really confronting a squirrel version of culture? Has robbing bird feeders now become a squirrel custom? Is it a part of squirrel tradition?

With regard to the "custom" part of it, some might define the term in such a way that the squirrel behavior would qualify. As far as squirrel "tradition" is concerned, however, the answer is far easier. Squirrels have no tradition. Why not? Because tradition requires passing on information that does not rely on immediate experience.

A squirrel that learns to defeat a squirrel-proof bird feeder through trial and error will probably remember how to do it next time. A second squirrel that observes the first one's success may try the same thing, and if successful, may also remember how to do it next time. Theoretically, there is no end to the number of squirrels that might learn the same thing through observation. But no squirrel out of sight of the bird feeder can tell another squirrel the technique, let alone explain the method to an audience of squirrels in some sort of squirrel workshop. The first squirrel that fails to observe the technique first-hand is a squirrel that must either figure it out from scratch or give it up.

The reason has to do with a third essential aspect of culture: the **symbol.** What is a symbol? Essentially, a symbol is something—anything—that is arbitrarily used to stand for something else. As simple as that sounds, it opens a vast gulf between human culture and the learned, shared behavior of other animals.

Like many apparently simple ideas, the concept of symbols requires some discussion. Humans can decide and agree that an acorn stands for any number of things, including some abstract concept: it can symbolize an orga-nization; it can stand for the abstract concept of growth or even world peace, if this is what people decide it should mean. To a squirrel, though, an acorn can only represent what it is—a piece of food. If an acorn means anything else to a squirrel, it can only represent an example of other acorns.

A more important aspect of this concept, though, is that humans can agree that some arbitrary *sound* means acorn, even when no acorn is any-where in sight. Speakers of Italian, for that matter, can decide that the object that English speakers call an "acorn" is a *ghianda*. And if humans can express the abstract idea of acorns, why not philosophical principles, visions of spir-its, dreams of ghosts, or behavioral prescriptions through the use of a variety of symbols?

The ability of a symbol to *stand for* something opens the power to com-municate abstract information. Put simply, it means that humans can commu-nicate information about anything without having to demonstrate a concrete example of it. This phenomenon, and particularly its role in language, is the fundamental prerequisite for culture. It allows humans to pass abstract infor-mation over generations, and it allows that information to accumulate over time. To put it another way, it allows humans to *conceive of ideas* rather than merely to perceive what happens to be in their environment.

This brings us to another set of questions, however. Just what does cul-ture consist of? Is it information? Belief? Cognition? Is it the actual behavior of people in a particular group? Is it both? On the other hand, is it anything? Does culture really *exist*, or is it just an imaginary construct based on a sum-mary of lots of different incidents of behavior? And what about "society," which concerned people like Spencer and Morgan? Are culture and society different? Is society an aspect of culture, or vice versa? We will address all of these issues below. We begin with the refinement of the culture concept in the twentieth century.

As we noted in the last chapter, we can credit Tylor with one of the ear-liest formal definitions of the concept of culture. But little in his work indi-cates that he thought about culture in a sense that would permit us to talk about "cultures" or even "a culture." He did not go very far in developing the idea of culture as representing the total coherent and unique way of life of a particular community or population. We have, for example, his unfortu-nate comment that "one set of savages is like another" (quoted in Sahlins 2000:504). For Tylor, culture was a shorthand way of referring to the range of things that people think and do, but his main concerns tended to focus on the extent to which aspects of life such as customs and beliefs were *rational*, rather than focusing on the unique cultural repertoires of specific popula-tions.

The work of Franz Boas refined the notion of culture in two major ways. While he retained the general inclusiveness of Tylor's concept, Boas dis-missed Tylor's absolutist concept of rationality as an evaluative criterion.

The main task was no longer to assess whether the practices and beliefs of a given society were more or less rational in European terms, but to learn as accurately as possible just how the people in that society viewed the world. The issue was to *understand* other systems of rationality *in their own right*, rather than to evaluate them according to some absolute scale. Another way of putting this is to say, as Boas did, that the study of culture meant the search for *meaning* from the perspective of the community one was studying. It meant trying to fathom people's symbolic as well as their material realities (Boas 1896).

CULTURE AS A SYSTEM

Having established that culture is learned, shared, and that it depends on symbols, we can go a step further. It would be possible to conceive of culture as merely a bunch of learned, shared symbols and let it go at that. But do these symbols have any relationship with one another? If we extend the concept of culture to include not only symbols but also behavior and technology, do they simply amount to a random assortment of human phenomena, or are they components of an interactive system?

In the past some scholars might have held a relatively simple view of culture as a haphazard collection of customs and beliefs. But in the twentieth century a good deal of anthropological analysis involved exploring the extent to which these aspects interact with, affect, and reinforce one another. To at least some degree, they have a *systemic* relationship.

What does it mean to assert that something has the characteristics of a **system?** At a basic level it means that its component aspects share some sort of relationship rather than simply being a collection of independent elements. The implication is that potentially, at least, they can affect one another. A change in one is likely to have repercussions elsewhere in the system.

For this reason, some anthropologists have talked about culture as an **emergent phenomenon.** An emergent phenomenon is more than just the sum of its constituent parts. The relationship among its parts creates a new order of being. A significant drop in temperature, for example, causes liquid water to take on the emergent properties of ice. A chicken is more than just a beak, feathers, gizzard, and so on. One could assemble all of the materials necessary for a chicken and still not have a real chicken. By the same token, a work of art is something more than merely the daubs of paint and woven canvas of which it consists. Many would say that what a painting is really about is what it *conveys* to the viewer, and perhaps to the artist.

The idea that the various aspects of any culture stand in a systemic relationship to one another is an important insight. It amounts to the realization that the culture of even the smallest population with the simplest technology "makes sense" at some level, rather than simply consisting of the blundering habits of people who don't know any better. We explore this issue more fully in Chapter 5 on functionalism.

If the aspects of culture constitute a system of sorts, what are the boundaries of that system? What sorts of things do we include in, or exclude from, the field of culture? What, in other words, does culture consist of? Is it the constellation of symbols and the intellectual realm that impels human action and shapes belief? Or is it the behavior and the observable *expression* of knowledge and belief?

This problem involves a longstanding and unresolved discussion and takes us down several avenues. Is culture a mentalistic realm that we can only surmise indirectly from observation, or is it the material actions and expressions that any observer could perceive, or both? Some anthropologists argue that the "mentalistic" approach gets at the true essence of culture, which is the deeper reality that lies behind what we can see and hear. Others assert that this path leads to unscientific speculation and poses the danger of studying phenomena that exist only in the observer's imagination. In this view, only observable phenomena can lend themselves to valid scientific investigation.

The debate has roots in an ancient philosophical dispute involving what some have characterized as **dualism** and **monism**. Dualism is the position that perceptible reality is a reflection or manifestation of a deeper reality. The Greek philosopher Plato expressed this in terms of "ideal forms." When we look at an object of furniture and identify it as a table, on what basis do we reach this decision? Certainly not all tables are identical. Some are round, some rectangular; some have only one leg, some have four or even more; some are wooden, some metal, and so on. So how do we decide, without thinking much about it, that a dining room table and a pool table are both tables? The answer, Plato asserted, is that somehow we have in our minds the concept of an "ideal" table that we use to identify actual tables, even though the actual tables may be imperfect examples of the ideal model.

A monist would dismiss the argument that some "ideal" table exists. From the monist perspective, what you see is what there is. There is no underlying reality beyond perceptible reality.

Some anthropologists have argued that the sense of culture as an entity of sorts—a "thing in itself," as Raymond Williams expressed it—has inherent problems (Williams 1981:10; see also Williams 1958). Fredrik Barth, for example, argues that culture should play a secondary role in an attempt to understand human life, with the primary focus on the actions, thoughts, and vagaries associated with human life. Culture, he argues,

> is an abstraction from innumerable occurrences where people act in complex social and physical contexts. These actions are furthermore always associated with cognition, and with will and purpose. (2001:435)

PHENOMENOLOGY AND THE PROBLEM OF REIFICATION

In summarizing perceived patterns and seeking to construct general statements about human phenomena, some anthropologists have taken issue with the very idea that theory has glossed over and disguised the rich diversity of human life (see, for example, Jackson 1996). This view, often referred to as **phenomenology,** stresses attention to the specific, the unique nature of human events and individual perceptions. The premises of phenomenology derive in large part from the work of the philosopher Edmund Husserl (see Husserl 1931, 1970).

We can see varying degrees of this approach in the work of many anthropologists. Boas, notwithstanding his role in refining the concept of culture, did not view culture as a uniform, stable determinant of behavior. His focus remained on the meaning that custom and experience have for individuals within a given social context, with recognition of their diversity. To a great extent, this interpretation was consistent with his inductive approach that gave priority to observational data, even to what some would consider the minutiae of life, rather than any attempts to produce sweeping and, in his view, premature general statements.

We should note that Boas has been a target of criticism for being too "particularistic" by those who advocate a more "scientific" method capable of producing general laws or principles with broad application (see, for example, Harris 1968:251). We can also see some elements of this Boasian (or phenomenological?) approach in the work of Clifford Geertz and other anthropologists who favor an interpretive approach to culture, as we shall discuss below.

Some phenomenologists argue that the attempt to devise "ahistoric" theoretical models—that is, models of sociocultural patterns that transcend particular times, places, and instances—amounts to imposing the observer's perceptions over the "commonsense" knowledge of the people in the community studied. Michael Jackson, referring to the views of Max Horkheimer and Theodor Adorno (1972), writes that "Instrumental rationality [of the observer], with its preoccupation with pattern and order, is linked historically to a concern for controlled nature and dominating other human beings" (Jackson 1996:5).

While not all phenomenologists would attribute such dire motives to theorists (whether conscious or not), they would dispute as untenable the assumption that scientific knowledge is objective and somehow produces a cleaner, more objective engagement with a reality that is not apparent to the members of the community. The perceptions of the outside observer, they maintain, are simply another individual's perceptions, no more valid than the commonsense understanding that individuals within a given society have of their own circumstances and actions. As we shall see, elements of this point of view also play a large part in post-structural and postmodern ideas.

In general, it appears that phenomenology does not present a total opposition to explanatory theory that an outsider might construct, and which delineates aspects of life that may not be evident to people in a community. The objection is to privileging such a version of reality over the perceptions of the people involved.

This debate also takes us to what we sometimes refer to as the problem of **reification,** or the "problem of misplaced concreteness." The word *reification* comes from the Latin *re*, meaning "thing." Essentially, it amounts to the error of treating something that is *not* a thing—that is, an abstraction—as if it *were* a thing.

This error is one aspect of the debate over whether it is feasible to study culture in a scientific way. The issue of what is or is not "scientific" is a complex discussion in itself, but most would agree that, at a minimum, any subject of scientific study must be "real." The problem becomes a bit fuzzy when we enter some avowedly scientific areas of inquiry for which the evidence is rather tenuous, such as the dynamics of black holes or other phenomena of deep space. On the other hand, such theories, if they *are* scientific, stand ready for testing against whatever evidence eventually becomes available.

With regard to culture, many anthropologists argue that if sociocultural anthropology is to define itself as a scientific enterprise, it should focus on those aspects of human life that we can see and measure. Moreover, the goal of scientific inquiry should go beyond observation and recording the particular case and attempt to produce hypotheses and theories about general principles, causal laws, or correlations that apply to multiple cases and that are testable.

From that perspective, the issue of what people think and feel and how they categorize reality, though interesting, cannot be the stuff of scientific inquiry. This is particularly so because of the unique configuration of each culture's intellectual realm. How could one compare the Hopi concept of harmonious balance in the universe with the Aztec view of a universe involved in a constant battle between forces of good and evil? Multiplying these diverse and rich world views on a global scale, what sort of scientific conclusions or general statements are possible?

Others would define science more broadly, referring to science's fundamental meaning "to know," which they take as the pursuit of accurate and deep understanding of particular cultural systems. Still others, however, would agree that human cultural phenomena in their totality are not appropriate subjects of study through the conventional methods of science. In this view, if we are to understand cultural phenomena, it must be through an interpretive approach more akin to the way we understand music, painting, or other forms of art. We might analyze a painting by measuring brush strokes or doing spectrographic analysis of the paint, but that would miss the point. This is not what a painting is all about. The most significant aspects of culture, according to these anthropologists, is the meaning and texture of ways of life. A hard-nosed materialist approach, in their view, leaves out some of the most interesting aspects of life.

LANGUAGE AND CULTURE

Questions regarding the systemic nature of culture and its reification have involved discussions of language. Language is particularly interesting in this context because, like culture in general, it is learned rather than inborn. On the other hand, the human propensity to learn language—many would say the *need* to learn some language or other—does seem to be genetically inherent.

But language is important in another way as well in our conception of culture. Language, after all, is not only a component of culture but a prerequisite for it. And as aspects of culture, languages do appear to constitute systems in their own right. That is, languages display internal regularities (with plenty of exceptions, of course—we all know about irregular verbs and so on). Languages also constitute systemic *entities* that we can study without taking particular notice of what real people actually say in real time.

Another way of putting it is that we can differentiate language as an abstract system of symbols with its own rules for their combinations from the actual utterances of a particular speaker on a given day. We can even study the ancient Sumerian language, despite the fact that no one speaks it anymore. The linguist **Ferdnand de Saussure** made this point earlier in the twentieth century, distinguishing *langue,* or language as a system, from *parole,* or speech (1959). Acts of speech are unique events that occur within real time; language as a system, however, exists independently of who says what to whom in the short run.

Speech needs to conform to the rules of language in order to be intelligible, but clearly, discrete acts of speech, on the one hand, and a language in the broader sense, on the other, not only represent different levels of abstraction but different levels of reality. Few would argue that only speech is real and that "language" as an abstract set of rules exists only in the imagination. This set of rules is real enough to cause a range of reactions, often negative, if someone's speech violates them. With language, then, we have an example of learned, shared behavior utilizing symbols according to a system that is abstract, but undoubtedly real.

EMIC AND ETIC APPROACHES

As we noted earlier, definitions of culture lead us into a maze of other avenues. Related to the question of whether anthropology is or should be a science or a branch of the humanities, some anthropologists have drawn a distinction between **emic** and **etic** forms of inquiry.

These terms arise from linguistics, and in particular from the analysis of sound systems in language. The study of the basic units of sound from a physical or mechanical perspective—how sounds are formed—is known as *phonetics*. The study of how these sounds operate in a particular language is *phonemics*. Phonemics is the perspective from *within* a language. Phonetics is the perspective from a broader, external viewpoint. Whether a sound is vocalized and bilabial (the English /b/, for example) is a matter of observation. Whether that sound is a significant part of a particular language is another matter.

Kenneth Pike (1954) suggested this principle as an important distinction in the study of culture, using the last parts of these terms: "etic" and "emic." An *etic* approach focuses on those aspects of human life that any objective observers with sufficient information can agree on. How many houses are there in the village, and what are their relative sizes? Are some gardens larger than others? How many yams do they produce, and who has control over their use? Who does most of the gardening work?

An *emic* approach focuses on the meaning of these things and others to the members of the community. Do people consider gardening to be men's work or women's work, and why? What sorts of ideas justify this division of labor? What is the significance of one crop over another? Why do some people choose to live near others? What kinds of things are important in having a good life? What are the qualities of a good person?

It is clear that an etic approach would tend to be compatible with a materialist perspective, which focuses on things that lend themselves to measurement in some form or other. This approach seems consistent with the scientific ideal of testability on the basis of data. An emic approach, on the other hand, is congenial to the interpretive model in anthropology, which tries to get at the meanings of cultural patterns and attempts to express them effectively to others who wish to share that understanding. This approach seems to have the essence of a humanistic discipline.

This dichotomy is probably too simple (see, for example, Lett 1987:53). Even humanistic interpretations are subject to reassessment by outside observers and refutation by people in the community. Although the parameters of refutation may be less definitive, they do exist. We have the possibility, therefore, of etic approaches to interpretive analyses and scientific challenges to humanistic interpretation.

THE BASIS OF CULTURE

Whether we favor emic or etic approaches to understanding culture or some combination of both, neither position directly addresses the question of *where culture comes from*. How do particular cultural practices or beliefs arise in the first place?

Perhaps a materialist approach comes a bit closer to addressing this problem because it can deal with culture in terms of its adaptive value. From this perspective, the fundamental question of "why people do what they do" generally leads to an answer involving what such a practice accomplishes for people's lives, which could imply that certain cultural practices arise because they work better. (We shall return to this question in Chapter 5 on function).

Such a view has its pitfalls. It would be easy to jump to the conclusion that people have arrived at certain ways of doing things because they work best compared to possible alternatives, but that assumption is difficult to test. How do we know that some *other* way of doing things might not have worked just as well, or even better? Certainly the many possible ways of doing things among human populations offer enough variety to demonstrate that many options may be feasible. We could point out that certain customs *must* be adaptive because the people who practice them have survived over many generations. But this does not get at the question of why they do things this way rather than another way that might have worked just as well.

The systemic aspects of culture add another dimension. A certain way of inheriting cattle might be highly adaptive, for example, but only if it is compatible with other aspects of culture in a particular group. In a different population with another cultural system, the same practice might lead to disruptive conflict or have other disastrous consequences.

A materialist approach does, however, allow for easier comparison on the basis of the frequency of cross-cultural correlations. Does a custom of bride service, in which a man works for his in-laws for a period of time, often occur among hunting peoples in sparse environments? If so, then perhaps we could use this as a basis for arguing that such a custom *does* work better in particular situations.

Anthropologists who are more interested in interpretive approaches might argue that framing the question in this way leaves out a great deal of the substance of culture. It is one thing to see on-the-ground social arrangements as adaptive responses to the nuts and bolts of physical survival. It is a farther stretch to find correlations between those arrangements and aspects of belief, for example. Does a belief in ancestral spirits offer advantages over a belief that a cosmic serpent rules over the universe?

In any case, neither of these alternatives offers a specifically causal model of culture. Most anthropologists would agree that people do not usually sit down and decide what their culture will be like. To the extent that they ever have done so, there is little evidence that they have often succeeded. American history alone is full of frustrated attempts to change the population's behavioral patterns. This gives rise to a major conundrum in the social sciences. Even though people do not consciously invent culture, culture certainly *is* the creation of human beings. At least three approaches have addressed this problem.

Some scholars, as we have just noted, see culture and society primarily as *adaptive* phenomena. People may not consciously plan their culture, but they do confront problems of living on a daily basis. In doing so they make adjustments—usually, but not necessarily, within acceptable parameters of their existing cultural system. The cumulative effects of these minor adjustments, especially if they appear to be successful, can produce new or altered cultural patterns.

Others have argued that culture and society are *emergent* entities—phenomena that exist at a different level of reality from the people who make up their constituent populations. As such, cultures operate according to their own rules with an impetus of their own, independent of individual will. One way of expressing this is to say that culture is self-generating.

Still others have noted that even though humans collectively do create culture and cause it to change, no one is born in a culture-free environment. Individuals already are immersed in, and imbued with, their own culture. Whatever innovations they may attempt will necessarily occur in the context of an existing cultural milieu with its distinct set of values, concepts of appropriateness, and feasibility. This view preserves a sense of human creativity, while at the same time recognizing the constraints and orientations that culture places on the individual.

These issues of the sources of culture touch on broader philosophical questions. One of them is the question of free will, a question far older than the discipline of anthropology. On this concept, like many others, anthropologists have held a spectrum of views. Some, like **Edward Sapir,** have cautioned their colleagues never to forget that when we talk about culture, we are talking about an abstract summary based on observations of individual and collective behavior (1917). While Sapir certainly emphasized the influence of culture, his focus on the level of the individual tended to highlight the latitude of individual choice, and hence the volatility of human behavior.

Others, such as **Alfred Louis Kroeber** and Leslie White, have argued that the individual is swept along by the "superorganic" force of culture (Kroeber 1915, 1917, 1923; White 1949, 1959). In this view, the apparent effect of geniuses and other great innovators who have affected the course of history is deceptive. People of exceptional ability occur randomly among human populations. Only when the culture is "ready" do some of them rise to visibility, but they are only responding to the broader cultural context, not creating it. If a particular historical figure had not been born, according to this perspective, another would have been available to fill the bill.

CULTURE, CONSCIOUS, AND UNCONSCIOUS

These questions regarding culture also bear on the extent to which culture is conscious or unconscious. In a sense, it seems clear that much of culture is so deeply learned that people do not think much about it as they go about their business. It becomes so habitual that it comes to seem the only "natural" way of doing things.

Some would take this focus on the unconscious aspects of culture a step farther. **Claude Levi-Strauss** has maintained that the observable and overt aspects of culture often serve to disguise underlying contradictions and other uncomfortable realities. These contradictions often find expression in terms of deeper mental structures that organize reality on the basis of binary oppositions with a mediating element. Often this involves substituting symbols that allow for the resolution of contradictions in place of aspects of reality that do not. This symbolic substitution pertains especially to the realm of myth and, to a lesser extent perhaps, ritual. It may also be manifest in such aspects of life as the ways in which people express relationships between social and cultural categories through residence patterns or even facial decoration.

One troublesome intellectual contradiction, for example, is that humans are a part of nature and yet, in their own minds at least, are distinct from it. Being part of nature involves such troublesome consequences as mortality. Cultural ways of addressing, and in effect, disguising these contradictions symbolically may involve emphasizing a residential boundary between village (culture) and forest (nature). Levi-Strauss analyzed the unusual asymmetric face painting of the Nambikwara of Brazil as the expression of a subconscious wish to distinguish their (unnatural or asymmetrical) humanness from (symmetrical) nature—a means of stating that "we are a different order of being" (see Levi-Strauss 1961, 1963).

We discuss these ideas further in Chapter 4 on structuralism. For the purposes of discussion here, though, it is worth pointing out that in the view of structuralists such as Levi-Strauss, the subconscious may offer a more fundamental avenue to understanding human reality than the superficial overlay of recognized cultural patterns. People not only create customs and ways of doing things to meet their daily, practical needs. They also develop intellectual constructs that allow them to cope with uncomfortable discordances that human life presents, often by submerging them through symbolic substitutions that permit the emotional satisfaction of abstract resolution.

This debate can also lead to the issue of whether culture is a matter of each population's unique intellectual reality, or whether these modes of life are, in fact, comparable *among* cultures at some level. Taken to an extreme degree, the view emphasizing cultural uniqueness can become a form of **essentialism**—the idea that each population is unique at a level deep enough to preclude common understanding. This, of course, would be a fatal position for the pursuit of cultural interpretation. The view that different ways of life are somehow mutually understandable, given enough study, would imply that cultures in one sense amount to various diverse approaches to what are, after all, common human issues. For materialists, these issues might involve such matters as subsistence, resource allocation, and so on. For interpretivists, they might include such matters as coping with the knowledge of mortality or definitions of the self.

CULTURE AND THE INDIVIDUAL

Culture ultimately is a product of the human mind, and culture, in turn, undoubtedly has significant effects on the minds of individuals. A number of anthropologists have explored the nature of this relationship. Although numerous anthropologists have examined the effects of culture on the individual, explorations of the effect of the individual on culture have been relatively few.

In the 1950s **Homer G. Barnett** analyzed the process by which cultural change occurs through innovation. He did not push his inquiry into the issue of whether and why particular innovations (inventions, discoveries, or diffusion) might either become a part of culture or disappear without a trace. His primary interest was in the psychological processes involved in innovation itself. Basically, Barnett concluded that all innovation amounts to recombinations of existing elements (Barnett 1953). Despite the common conception that inventions and discoveries appear as new phenomena, in his view their novelty consists only in the new configurations of elements, not in their component aspects.

The automobile, for example, utilized the ancient idea of the wheel, the knowledge that explosions push things apart (the pistons of the internal combustion engine), the knowledge that it is possible to transfer kinetic energy through gears, and so on. All of these ideas had been available for a long time. The total system, however, was new. It amounted to an emergent phenomenon, a systemic entity that was more than the mere collection of its parts. As we know, it also was an innovation that had a significant impact on culture, but as we noted, cultural reception or rejection of innovations was not Barnett's major focus.

Other scholars have focused more on the effects innovators have had on cultural systems. In many cases throughout history, particularly in colonial situations, religious or political movements have arisen around charismatic leaders or prophets. **Anthony F. C. Wallace** explored this interaction with attention to the feedback or interactive relationship between culture and the individual in times of crisis. In pursuing this, Wallace developed the concept of **cognitive mazeway** (Wallace 1956).

In some respects Wallace's mazeway resembles the idea of world view, though with more accommodation for individual variation. According to Wallace, every person, through life experiences and cultural influences, develops a conception of the way things are and how they work—a sense of reality, a "mental map" or "mazeway." One aspect of this sense of reality or mazeway involves certain sets of expectations, or a sense of predictability.

Wallace developed his general idea of the interplay between cognitive structures and institutional change to account for the development of radical social movements. A disaster, whether a natural catastrophe such as a hurricane or earthquake or a social trauma such as foreign invasion, can shake or challenge a person's cognitive orientation. People who have undergone such experiences often feel a sense of unreality, of being in a dream. In situations of that sort, people's sense of reality has not been adequate to account for what has happened to them.

In such crises, according to Wallace, an individual may develop a restructured mazeway to help account for the new reality and to make sense of the altered situation. Usually this involves constructing a new mazeway in terms of the old, as a revised version of it. Such a person at times may be able to pull things together intellectually or emotionally in a way that offers others some psychological satisfaction or comfort.

In a society in which people believed that their ancestors would look after their well-being, for example, they might logically account for a disaster by attributing it to their ancestors' displeasure. They might even identify outsiders with deceased relatives, as a means of dealing with the unfamiliar and threatening presence by incorporating this new aspect of reality into a perception compatible with their existing concepts. Such revised versions of reality might serve as a basis for resistance to, or provide an escape from, their predicament. The new cognitive structure might prescribe certain courses of action to put things right or even to promote the coming of a new and better age. If an individual restructures her or his view of reality in a fashion that appeals to others, the result might be a collective social or cultural movement.

As Wallace notes, most such movements die out after a short time, usually when the results they promise do not occur. Some, on the other hand, may begin as what Europeans would see as new religions and develop into more secular political and even revolutionary movements. A few might grow and become part of the cultural mainstream. Wallace suggests that all of the world's major religions may have begun in this way (Wallace 1956).

Aside from the ideas of Wallace and Barnett, most explorations of the interplay between culture and the individual have dealt with the effects of culture on the individual, rather than vice versa. Early in the twentieth century, when the concept of culture was gaining ground over racist explanations of human difference, some anthropologists tended to see culture as more than merely an influence on individual behavior, but a determinant. A crucial aspect of the individual that aroused particular interest was personality.

The concept of *personality* is difficult to define in any way that lends itself to scientific analysis. Psychiatrists and psychologists have spent many decades in the study of individual "personality disorders." On the other hand, to discuss personality as a collective set of qualities that one could consider "normal" (or typical) for an entire population poses a different set of problems and pitfalls (see, for example, Barnouw 1973).

For one thing, this concept of personality implies a high degree of uniformity among individuals who share a particular culture. Without a precise operational definition of personality and some means of measuring it, such uniformity can only remain an assumption, often one based on subjective or impressionistic information.

One important early attempt to demonstrate consistency between culture and personality appeared in the work of **Ruth Benedict** in the 1930s. Benedict was a proponent of the humanistic, interpretive approach to the study of culture. One of her main points was that each cultural system manifests unique but coherent aspects, which she referred to as its **configuration.** Benedict argued that it was essential to understand each culture as a unique human creation in its own right (Benedict 1932).

Benedict asserted that it was possible to group cultures collectively in terms of major, broad orientations. Borrowing terms from the German philosopher Friedrich Neitszche's analysis of Greek tragedy, she suggested that we could describe the predominant orientation of some cultures as **dionysian** or **apollonian.** A dionysian approach to life valued excess, excitement, breaking beyond the bounds of normal human existence, and often

Ruth Benedict (1887–1948)

showed a propensity for violence. An apollonian approach, on the other hand, valued restraint and self-control. These terms, she asserted, could apply at the level of culture and portray the collective personality traits of constituent members.

It is important to remember that in describing and interpreting cultural systems, Benedict was trying to make them more understandable to readers who had little or no knowledge of them. She conveyed them as entities with internal consistency, as ways of life that made sense in their own terms. This was an essential point in an era when racist explanations and the popular denigration of non-Western cultures was commonplace in American and European popular thought.

It is significant, in this vein, that Benedict wrote for a popular audience. Her book *Patterns of Culture*, which came out in paperback in the 1930s, sold extremely well (for an anthropology book!). Being a pioneering attempt, however, the book had major flaws—particularly in its equation of personality with culture.

Even though Benedict in *Patterns of Culture* focused on whole cultures and allegedly typical personality characteristics, she did little in that work to address factors that produced or cultivated these personality types. **Margaret Mead**, a student of Benedict and Franz Boas, focused more on the effects of culture in producing these personality characteristics.

In the 1920s Mead first examined the experiences of adolescent women in Samoa, challenging the prevailing American perspective that this period in the lives of young women inevitably was a time of turmoil. Concluding that this was not the case in Samoa, Mead argued that it was *culture*, not "human nature" that molded the experiences of growing up (Mead 1928).

Mead's work in Samoa provoked some controversy. Surprisingly, perhaps, the controversy grew more heated after her death, more than half a century after *Coming of Age in Samoa* first appeared. Some critiques might be expected when a pioneering work remains in print long enough to become a "classic" and its flaws become easy targets for later generations. On the other hand, this book did raise some serious questions.

Mead had claimed that young Samoan women in the 1920s enjoyed a great deal of sexual freedom, compared to their American counterparts. Decades later, when many of these young people had become respected elders, some of them denied that Mead's account had been accurate. The shortness of Mead's stay in Samoa also provoked questions about the depth of her understanding of the complexities of Samoan life. Equally troubling to some, earlier descriptions of Samoan society depicted a much more hierarchical, authoritarian social system with an emphasis on premarital chastity, at least among people of high rank.

The issue broke into the media in the 1980s when the New Zealand anthropologist Derek Freeman alleged that Mead had fabricated her account of Samoan life in order to push a particular point of view—a Boasian emphasis on culture as the predominant factor in shaping human life (Freeman 1983). Mead's work seemed to demonstrate that even such essentially biological phenomena as adolescence were profoundly different experiences in different social settings.

Freeman espoused a perspective emphasizing biological influences on human behavior. He argued that Mead had ignored or suppressed some of the more competitive, even oppressive, aspects of Samoan life. In fact, the two versions were barely recognizable as depictions of the same culture.

In a sense, perhaps, they were not. Mead and Freeman did fieldwork in different communities at different times. Nonetheless, the issue brought to the forefront a crucial and nagging problem that continues to beset anthropology: How accurate is anyone's ethnographic description of another community?

There is little doubt that Margaret Mead, as a student of Boas, was a major proponent of a school of thought that had taken up the battle against biological determinism. As we know, Boas had made great advances in combating the racial explanation that pervaded the "conventional wisdom" of American popular and even scientific thought at the time. He had been the foremost advocate of the view that culture is independent of biology, and in fact, this had been the major thrust of Mead's findings.

Freeman's criticism of Mead's work remains a subject of debate (see, for example, Shankman 1996, 2001; Cote 1998). Many observers, while not particularly sympathetic to Freeman's position, have questioned some aspects of Mead's Samoan work, including some Samoans. It is important to point out, however, that this controversy did not extend equally to her more "academic" descriptions and analyses of Samoan culture, which Samoans apparently have viewed much more favorably.

For our purposes, however, we can also view this as another skirmish in the longstanding debate over the relative significance of culture and biology in shaping the human experience. We shall have occasion to return to this issue numerous times in the pages that follow.

Mead drew similar conclusions about the power of culture from her work comparing the thought patterns of children and adults in the Great Admiralty Islands of New Guinea (Mead 1930). In comparing concepts of "masculine" and "feminine" behavior in three New Guinea societies, she found wide variations that seemed explainable only by cultural difference (1935). In each case, she emphasized the role of culture rather than biology in shaping behavioral patterns. (We discuss the work of Mead later in this chapter and in Chapter 6 on relativism.)

By the 1940s, psychology, the discipline whose central task had been the study of the individual mind, had made significant advances. Freudian psychoanalytic theory, though already controversial, had long since achieved central stage. Some anthropologists utilized insights from these areas of research, carrying on a tradition of interdisciplinary perspective that was already well-established in the discipline.

At Columbia University, where Franz Boas had chaired the Department of Anthropology and where Ruth Benedict eventually took the chair after Boas's death in 1942, culture and personality studies continued energetically. **Ralph Linton,** an anthropologist with training in psychology, and **Abram Kardiner,** a psychoanalyst with an interest and some training in anthropology, developed the concept of **"basic personality"** and ran a seminar exploring its dynamics (Kardiner and Linton et al. 1945; Kardiner 1945).

Basic personality continued the assumption that at least some consistency of personality existed among people in small, cohesive societies. How did this personality develop? Linton and Kardiner took insights from Freudian theory selectively, particularly the idea that early life experiences have a profound impact on personality formation. Building upon this assumption, they developed the concepts of **primary institutions,** by which they meant customs and practices bearing directly on child rearing, and **secondary** (or "adult") **institutions,** which covered what most anthropologists meant by culture.

Sigmund Freud (1856–1939)

The model seemed to make sense. Certainly the standard experience of infants varies from culture to culture. It stood to reason that it must make some difference whether a child is bound tightly in a cradle board for hours on end or has lots of skin contact with the mother inside her parka; if a child gets the breast every time she cries or has to wait for regular, scheduled feedings; if a child is almost always with the mother or receives collective care among elder siblings, aunts and uncles, grandparents, or friends of the family.

As promising as this research seemed, though, some of its assumptions were subject to question. The subjective fuzziness of such concepts as "basic personality" were increasingly troubling and had drawn some criticism from other social scientists (see, for example, Lindesmith and Strauss 1950).

Not all observers were convinced of the determinative strength of early childhood experiences in molding personality. Moreover, how similar were the experiences of different children, even in societies with fairly standardized child-rearing customs? Even different siblings in the same family might have experiences that differ in significant ways.

The close linkage of personality with culture was particularly troublesome. With regard to Benedict's study of the Zuni, for example, other observers who worked in that community pointed out that many aspects of Zuni life involved far more conflict than Benedict suggested (see, for example, Li An-che 1937). These observers raised questions about personality uniformity even within small, closely-knit communities. Such observations also raised questions about the boundary between observable aspects of behavior and culture itself. If people conform to the prevailing cultural expectations and stipulations of their society, does this necessarily reveal anything about the internal psychological dynamics of the individual? How can we tell whether they simply suppress their true impulses and follow the social rules?

The concept of **modal personality** played an important role in this discussion. **Cora DuBois,** working among the Alorese of Malaysia, used projective tests, which are designed to elicit responses that reveal aspects of personality and/or psychological characteristics, to define in some objective manner the statistical modes or central tendencies of personality configuration among the people of that society (DuBois 1944). This method had the advantage of accommodating diversity while still focusing on "typical" characteristics. Even so, the range of difference among the responses of DuBois's research participants raised questions about the extent to which any meaningful central tendencies, or "modal personality" configurations, existed at all.

Some of the same questions arose in Anthony Wallace's use of modal personality. Wallace, who had worked for years among the Tuscarora, a Native American community in western New York, was dissatisfied with the subjective aspects of the "basic personality" concept. He applied projective tests to define Tuscarora modal personality more objectively. Like DuBois,

Wallace anticipated that the test scores would show one or more statistical modes or clusters of high scores that would demonstrate more precisely the shared personality traits in that community.

Whatever value the tests themselves might have had—and this is subject to question in its own right—the results showed that individuals in that community agreed very little in their responses. What the tests seemed to show, if anything, was an unexpected diversity of personality traits (Wallace 1952). The older supposition equating culture with personality no longer made as much sense as it had seemed to in earlier studies.

Many of these earlier models had drawn upon ideas reminiscent of the concept of **world view** (a translation of the German *Weltanschauung*). World view refers to a totality of understandings that people in a given cultural system supposedly share. The concept encompasses issues that might fall into categories of religious belief, practical knowledge, philosophical axioms, and so on. We can see examples of this idea in the work of Edward Sapir (1921) and Benjamin Lee Whorf (1956), which examined the ways in which cultural and linguistic categories shape habits of thought.

By the middle of the twentieth century, the implied uniformity of thought associated with the notion of world view had become troublesome. Anthony Wallace's work, in particular, seriously challenged older assumptions by demonstrating the individual diversity that exists even in a small and apparently close-knit community. As a result, Wallace developed a concept that he referred to as "the organization of diversity" (Wallace 1970). Societies, according to this view, are able to hold together not because their members share some mental uniformity, but because diverse individuals are able to accommodate one another.

Wallace's model linked the level of individual psychology, which develops under the influence of unique personal experience, with shared cultural perceptions. People in a given society, in other words, are not identical, but they do share a range of cultural precepts. These shared aspects permit a degree of social cohesion because they provide some predictability of behavior. One member of a society can be reasonably sure what to expect of other members in a given situation and can communicate with them easily, even though their individual mental characteristics, or "mazeways," differ in important respects.

The fallacy of considering culture itself to be a monolithic entity also had become far more apparent. Margaret Mead, much earlier, had equated culture with language—metaphorically at least—in the sense that one can learn a language through one or two people who speak it fluently. It would not be necessary, practical, or even useful to attempt a general survey of all speakers of a language in order to learn a language.

But as Roger Keesing noted in the 1980s, culture is not spread equally among all members of a society (1987). People in any community have specialized knowledge—knowledge that in some cases may even be secret from other members. Generally speaking, women know different things from men; adults from children; old people from younger people; specialists from non-specialists; and so on. This realization, which in retrospect appears to be a rather obvious aspect of common sense, has nonetheless served to complicate the concept of culture as a coherent entity. This is particularly so when some scholars have tended to equate "a culture" with "a society."

MEANING AND ACCURACY

Given the importance of grasping how the world looks to the people one is trying to understand, how can we ever be sure we have gotten it right? In the days when Europeans felt confident that "primitive" cultures were relatively simple, it seemed to many that the task was mostly a matter of collecting information. One merely needed to ask the right questions, record the information accurately, and put the information together in a coherent, erudite summary. Typically, such descriptions should reflect categories that to most Europeans seemed logical, self-evident, and universal: religion, family organization, kinship terms, technology, subsistence, and so on.

Certainly we can find beliefs and activities in any society that can fall into these and other categories. But what about populations who perceive deceased ancestors as having continued involvement in the lives of their relatives? Does this fall under "religion," "kinship," "social organization," or what? And suppose these ancestors are involved in punishing the living for misdeeds? Should we include them under the category of "law"?

What about cases in which people consider what Europeans might call "garden magic" to be part of normal agricultural practice? And how does "family organization" fit situations in which people believe that a child carries an animal spirit that entered the mother's body at conception? What do we make of it when people believe that as a result, this child shares an essence with other people who share this animal spirit, even though in European terms, they are unrelated?

With an increased understanding of non-European cultures through prolonged work in the field, it became apparent that these cultures were immensely more complex than most outsiders had assumed. It also became evident that the categories into which Europeans organized their own reality did not necessarily apply elsewhere.

Language played an important role here in several respects. It became clear that to begin to fathom the complexities of thought in any society, it was crucial to be able to discuss these issues in the language of the people themselves.

Languages, in that vein, involved deep windows into conventional thought, or world view—that is, peoples' assumptions and postulates about reality. Fieldwork was not merely a matter of being able to collect more detailed information. It was a matter of trying to grasp, through mastering a new language, a means of seeing the world in a different way. The Navajo language, for example, does not have a basic verb meaning "to be," as most European languages do. The equivalent Navajo verb translates into English as "to move," or "to go." Rather than reflecting a view of reality as a field of stable objects, the Navajo language carries a sense of reality as motion, change, and becoming (see Witherspoon 1977). We might note that if one tried to put cultural assumptions aside in order to determine which of these views offers a more accurate representation of *actual* reality, this would be difficult to establish by any objective means. In one respect or another, both appear to be true. Many objects exist in a state of relative stability in the short term, but not without some degree of change or motion, given enough time.

The problem for the concept of culture is whether such profound differences pose insurmountable obstacles to understanding other cultures. Can an outsider ever quite get it right? Moreover, if we can assume that the attempt to understand "meaning" in terms of another culture is more than just an individual adventure, is it possible for an outsider to *translate* these concepts accurately into another language?

We shall return to this issue in Chapter 6 on relativism. At this point, let us merely observe that anthropologists from Boas onward have recognized the pitfalls of interpreting other peoples' realities. For the most part they have attempted to be as accurate as possible without claiming to have reached "the truth" in any comprehensive sense.

We could also pose the question of why it should be an *outsider* who takes on the task of interpreting another culture. Would it not be better for someone within the society, a person who has grown up there and certainly knows more about it than anyone from outside could ever learn, to interpret it? A number of issues come into play here, however. There is no doubt that information from inside any cultural system is uniquely valuable. But in most cases, members of the communities that anthropologists have studied have not taken it upon themselves to describe their own culture to others. The most evident exceptions have been the numerous non-Western scholars who have become anthropologists. A major problem in limiting ourselves to "authentic" indigenous voices is that most of us have no access to them.

Another reason for the rarity of fully indigenous accounts that would be accessible to a general audience, aside from problems of language and literacy, has been the fact that one's own culture generally seems obvious, self-explanatory, and the most natural way of doing and seeing things. The impetus for undertaking the task of describing one's culture to outsiders requires a sense of, and an interest in, comparative cultural analysis and the ability to view one's own situation as a subject of study. Even if more indigenous accounts were available, there is a difference between attempting to describe cultural systems in a relatively dispassionate way and taking the role of advocate or spokesperson for that way of life. Certainly indigenous thinkers are capable of objective description to the extent that anyone is; but describing a culture in which one is fully immersed, and of which one is very much a product, presents its own problems.

In many respects cultural description, or **ethnography,** involves an interpretive brokering or mediation between two cultural systems and requires a familiarity with both. This does not mean that the ethnographer is unaffected by her or his own cultural system. Far from it. It does mean, though, that successful ethnography requires not only a good acquaintance with the culture being described, but also the ability to interpret that cultural reality to an audience utterly foreign to it and generally ignorant of it.

All of these issues add up to the fact that a total reliance on indigenous accounts is not adequate to meet the goals of anthropology. As we noted earlier, these goals not only involve understanding what people do, but why they do it. To these we could add another goal: to build a broad sense of the variety of cultures that have constituted the general human experience.

CULTURE AND SOCIETY

Among the various ways in which anthropologists have conceived of and approached the study of culture, the relationship between the concept of culture and the concept of society has not always been clear. Of the two, society is by far the older idea. People have long recognized that humans live in groupings with shared rules and expectations, differential rights, obligations, power relations, and usually some sense of social boundaries.

Long before anthropologists grappled with the concept of culture, Enlightenment thinkers had written about social contracts (see, for example, Rousseau 1938 [orig. 1762]). Spencer, as we recall, stressed the idea that society is *real*, not simply an abstraction. Like others before him, Spencer focused on society as a set of relationships.

As concepts, both culture and society refer to phenomena that are neither tangible nor visible. They are abstractions based on observable data that appear to configure patterned phenomena. Of the two, however, culture seems to be the most uniquely human. If we perceive of society as a set of patterned relationships, then the term *society* could apply to other species. We commonly speak of bees, ants, and termites as "social insects," and, in fact, they do have highly structured and regularized relationships among the members of their local populations. An ant colony clearly is more than just a large number of ants.

Few, though, would argue that ants or bees have culture. Their behavior seems to be almost entirely driven by biological factors, or at most, factors that arise from early physical experience. A female worker-bee larva can develop into a queen by ingesting "royal jelly," but this is hardly a matter of learned behavior.

With respect to human society, the issue is far less clear-cut. Although humans obviously form societies, many anthropologists would argue that almost anything and everything humans do and think is affected by learning—or by culture. So where does society end and culture begin?

During the time when American anthropologists were developing the idea of culture—some might say even taking it to extremes, at times—British and French sociologists placed far more emphasis on society, and particularly on the structure of social relationships. As we shall see in the next chapter, in France Emile Durkheim did refer to social facts and social forces in ways that might suggest a concept of cultural imperatives, but he did not use that term—and, in fact, these seem to have been expressions of the power of society itself over the individual.

Bronislaw Malinowski did pay a great deal of attention to such aspects of life as magic, religion, and value systems—phenomena that most American anthropologists would consider to be the very stuff of culture. But Malinowski did not seem to distinguish culture from society in any rigorous way, and apparently he considered them to be essentially components of the general totality of human life. Malinowski, in fact, saw both culture and society as human ways of meeting fundamental biological needs (Malinowski 1944).

Malinowski's colleague and rival A. R. Radcliffe-Brown focused far more on social structure. He recognized the concept of culture but accorded it little interest—possibly because in his view, social phenomena offered the possibility of revealing general social laws, while culture, being unique in each case, did not. To the extent that Radcliffe-Brown concerned himself with such aspects of life as religion, he considered it to be most importantly a social institution, an aspect of social structure (Radcliffe-Brown 1952b). Other features that American anthropologists considered aspects of culture, such as mythology, art, and most especially, personality, Radcliffe-Brown tended to relegate to the general category of ethnology, the study of which he left to his colleagues across the sea (Radcliffe-Brown 1949a, 1949b, 1952a).

In a general sense, we could say that while most British anthropologists before the 1940s considered culture to be an aspect of society, the Americans considered society to be an aspect of culture. This dichotomy, though somewhat oversimplified, does reflect the differences in emphasis between the two perspectives that prevailed during those decades.

From the middle of the twentieth century on, however, many British anthropologists incorporated cultural issues more intensively into their analyses. Even in the 1930s, E.E. Evans-Pritchard had focused on such issues as magic, witchcraft, and other aspects of belief. This, in fact, was a major emphasis in his work with the Azande of Central Africa (1937). Toward the end of his career, Evans-Pritchard stated forcefully that anthropology was not a science that could produce social laws, but a branch of the humanities comparable to history (1962).

Victor Turner, from his work among the Ndembu of Zambia, developed the idea of **communitas,** which involved social integration associated with the power of symbols. This approach focused on the ways in which public ritual drama, particularly in such events as initiation rituals, reinforced a sense of solidarity, and in some cases, provided a source of culture change (see Turner 1967, 1982).

We may tend to think of society in terms of stable institutions, formal and informal statuses, rules, and behavioral expectations. Yet it is also apparent that while these aspects of society itself may persist indefinitely, individual people do not. As we pass through childhood, adulthood, and old age, our place in society changes. We undergo transitions from one status to another, each with its own ranges of expectations. In a sense, the people who constitute the population of a society are continuously changing. Turner argued that such aspects of culture as ritual, as an acting-out of beliefs and symbolic meanings, plays a vital role in holding things together. A key aspect of this is the condition of **liminality.**

We could envision liminality as a condition of being in-between, neither here nor there, but in a state of transition. This, according to Turner, is perhaps most evident in rituals of initiation in which people leave one status or social identity, but have not yet entered another. Having left their former social selves behind, along with the various constraints associated with their former status, they come to be, in a sense, outside society, occupying a special realm of existence that leaves them more closely in touch with their basic humanness. The state of liminality often entails a certain power as well as vulnerability. Often those in such a state receive instruction and undergo physical challenges such as circumcision or other ceremonial body changes to mark their different identities. Typically, they receive knowledge inaccessible to them in their former status.

Many of Turner's ideas derive from the work of Arnold Van Gennep, who developed the idea of **rites of passage** (1960). Van Gennep pointed out that such ritualized changes in social status often involve three phases. The first signaled a *disengagement* from the former status. The second entailed a *transitional* process in which the participants, usually isolated from the community, underwent changes to prepare them for their new social identity. The third involved their *reintegration* into society in their new identity.

Turner's ideas went beyond Van Gennep's, however, in placing great importance on the liminal state corresponding to Van Gennep's stage of transition. The condition of being "outside society," and in a sense, outside of time, involved a socially anomalous position. It opened the way for innovation, even radical creativity. It was a realm in which individuals could escape the social constraints toward uniformity and express their basic humanness more freely.

Perhaps even more significant, the collective experience of individuals undergoing this state tended to produce a profound sense of commonality, or "communitas." With its volatile combination of creative license and mutual reinforcement among those sharing the experience, communitas offered not only a powerful mechanism for social solidarity but a potential source of social and cultural change.

Turner later extended the idea of liminality beyond the sorts of initiation rituals marking the transition from childhood to adulthood which some, but by no means all, societies practice. He also saw the experience of liminality— and even the conscious pursuit of such a state—in a variety of social phenomena ranging from the counterculture movement in the United States during the 1960s to punk rock.

As Turner stated, the creative tension between rebelliousness and social order could resolve itself in various ways. The communitas born of liminality could become a radical force for change, but it could also become absorbed into the social system, eventually becoming part of the established order. Turner cites European monasteries as an example of this process in which the state of liminality becomes an institutionalized part of the social structure.

Many theoretical attempts to deal with the integration of culture with society, like Turner's, have centered on the ways in which individuals have operated within social constraints and, in some cases, have rebelled against them (see Kuper 1983 for an extended discussion of this). In this vein, Gregory Bateson has referred to individuals in society as "energy sources" capable of generating change (Bateson 1972:126). Edmund Leach, another prominent anthropologist associated with the British tradition, drew attention to the creativity of individuals who often act in ways motivated by their perceived self-interest, sometimes in opposition to social norms (see, for example, Leach 1954:4–5).

From another perspective, Mary Douglas made the case that society in some respects serves as a model for the individual's perception of the self. She focused especially on issues of social and personal boundaries, suggesting that in societies with relatively rigid boundaries, cultural concepts regarding substances crossing the boundaries of the body—whether ingested or expelled—tended to be associated with more powerful ideas of pollution than is the case in societies with more permeable boundaries (1966, 1970).

In all of these cases, theoretical models have attempted to take into account and reconcile aspects of the society, abstract cultural features— particularly symbols—and the mind of the individual. We discuss these ideas more in Chapter 4 on structure.

SCIENCE OR INTERPRETATION?

We discussed earlier the question of whether the best avenue to the study of culture is from the stance of scientific analysis or humanistic understanding. To some extent this question touches on the differential emphasis on society versus culture. Few theorists have gone so far as to see one or the other as an exclusive domain, and as we have seen above, many have attempted to reconcile and define the nature of articulation between them.

This difference in emphasis relates to some degree to the German concept of a distinction between *Geisteswissenschaften*, the "human sciences," and *Naturwissenschaften*, the "natural sciences." This idea "insisted upon the existence of logical and methodological differences between the natural and social sciences" (Giddens 1995:154). The philosopher Wilhelm Dilthey and others associated these differences with a distinction between *Erklären* ("explaining") and *Verstehen* ("understanding").

In general, those who have embraced the explanatory model for the study of human social and cultural phenomena have been more receptive to the idea that an approach modeled after the natural sciences is the most useful and appropriate. Examples of such approaches have been associated with a tradition extending from Auguste Comte, who attempted to establish a "natural science of society," to such materialist theorists as Marvin Harris, who argued that anthropology must strive to develop **nomothetic** statements, or scientific generalizations approaching "laws" that apply beyond the particular case.

The alternative view is that a natural science model is not useful in developing a deep understanding of cultural phenomena, particularly with regard to the subtle, detailed nuances of symbolic domains. The German philosopher Friedrich Neitzsche expressed this perspective, asserting that cultural systems (or "worlds") should be seen as works of art and therefore subject to a range of interpretations (1968:no. 481). We can see examples of this from Dilthey through Franz Boas, who rejected what he called the "physicalist model," through Ruth Benedict, who saw individual cultures as unique configurations, to Clifford Geertz, who introduced the idea of **"thick description"** for the understanding and discussion of cultural life. As Geertz stated, anthropology is not "an experimental science in search of law but an interpretive one in search of meaning" (1973:5).

The attempt to understand the meaning of customs, practices, and events for those who perform and experience them has been a longstanding aim of cultural and, to a lesser extent perhaps, social anthropology. Boas was explicit in his admonition to "get behind the mask" and try to understand the way life appeared to people in other cultures. In recent times, however, Geertz has become the most prominent advocate and representative of interpretive approaches. His concept of "thick description," in effect, involves delving below the surface of customs and events and detecting deeper levels of signification. His now-classic example of various possible interpretations of a wink is a case in point (1973).

We could accurately describe a wink as a brief contraction of the muscles of the eyelid that causes the eye to close for an instant and reopen immediately. While this is essentially a true description of what happens when a wink occurs, that description leaves out a range of other, culturally significant information. Does the wink indicate flirtation? Acknowledgement of a shared secret? Is it a prearranged signal? An impudent gesture of disrespect? From this perspective the deeper meaning of even so simple an act, which may touch upon an array of broader signification, is the quest of anthropological inquiry. The object of "thick description" is to account for those meanings as accurately as possible. This search for meaning tends to focus on the intellectual and emotional aspects of human life, and most particularly on shared symbols—the "web of signification" that humans construct and within which they live.

Several aspects of this view are important to note. One, as we have mentioned, is that it focuses largely on symbols—that is, the meanings attached to actions, things, and experiences. Another is that such symbols and their relationships to one another are constantly being renegotiated and reinterpreted by the people who live within their realm. Moreover, the meanings of symbols within a given cultural system are generally "inexplicit"; that is, their meaning is not overt or obvious. Geertz's widely read discussion of the Balinese cockfight, for example, posits a range of underlying meanings for the participants, including the cosmological significance of blood sacrifice, the bolstering of male egos, a quest for personal honor, expressions of village rivalries, and so on.

Another aspect regarding symbols is that despite the individualist or even eccentric ways in which people in a community may use or interpret symbols, cultural meanings, within certain parameters, are shared rather than being entirely private. Even a wink, whatever its meaning, makes no particular sense if no one sees it.

As a number of writers have pointed out, this approach does have its drawbacks. For one thing, the issue of hypothesis testing through the possibility of falsification arises. To disprove an interpretation that claims authority based on "inexplicit" meanings is likely to be difficult. Moreover, as Geertz points out, the outside observer can never achieve a full interpretation of any complex event. At best, even the thickest of descriptions amounts to an interpretation of the participants' own interpretations. The resulting ethnographic accounts may be plausible but always remain contestable.

The most successful and accurate description of this sort is bound to be unique, dealing as it does with a specific time, place, and cultural context. The ability to draw conclusions from such studies that might be applicable to other cultures at other times and places seems doubtful. For this reason, some have seen this approach as an entirely nonscientific exercise in cultural reportage. Geertz would counter this by asserting that since the network of symbolic meanings in any culture is shared or "public," they can, in fact, be compared with other such cases.

If one accepts the broad definition of science as meaning "to know," then certainly the deep and detailed understanding of particular phenomena, and the ability to compare them with other such phenomena, seem to meet the criterion. Indeed, proponents might argue that the richness of close-focused information that this approach produces carries the goal of "knowing" farther than more generalizing approaches can. Those who would embrace an approach modeled on the natural sciences, however, tend to find this less than satisfactory.

CULTURE VERSUS BIOLOGICAL DETERMINISM

If other species of animals have something most of us call "society," how does that form of society differ from *human* society? Some scholars have argued that, in fact, the difference is only a matter of degree. In that view, the relationship between human and non-human society represents a continuum rather than a sharp qualitative break. Human societies differ from baboon troops mainly in terms of complexity and detail.

In this vein, the distinction or lack of it between culture and society becomes still more important. If we see culture merely as an aspect of society, the idea of a human/non-human continuum may seem more plausible. If we see culture as a qualitatively different and unique human phenomenon, then the break between humans and non-humans appears more distinct.

Many factors have clouded this debate. Let us first look at the concept of the human/non-human continuum. On the one hand, some proponents of the continuum model have accused their adversaries of romanticizing the special qualities of humans and, in effect, attempting to place humans "above nature." Some have even drawn connections to the Biblical view of humans as a special creation of God to rule over the Earth.

While almost any accusation might be true of someone somewhere, in general this assertion has little validity. The vast majority of anthropologists nowadays have no problem in seeing humans as one of many biological species and, in effect, as a part of "nature." The basic question is whether culture is just a fancy gloss on regular old instinctual drives or a particularly human phenomenon or specialized adaptation, a result of the same general evolutionary process that produced the ability of bats to locate flying insects in the dark through high frequency sound waves, or of earthworms to digest topsoil. The gist of the matter, then, after all of the painstaking debate over the concept of culture, is just how important culture is in human behavior. Are we just another species with an inflated view of our own special characteristics?

As we have seen, the idea that human behavior has a strong biological component is at least as old as the mid nineteenth century. This issue has often been divided into two major tracks. On the one hand, how much does biology impose a general "human nature" to which we all must conform as a species? On the other hand, to what extent does biology influence, or even determine, *differences* among humans?

These two strains converge somewhat when we consider differences that occur within societies but across social boundaries. We might consider male/female differences, for example. Since all human societies contain both types of people, are there some biological sex-based behavioral features that characterize females everywhere and males everywhere? Putting sex aside, are some individuals more favored than others in important ways? Does biology create "born leaders" or "born losers" in every society?

It seems unreasonable to doubt that all human beings have significant biological propensities. As we read this, people all over the world are sleeping, eating, and having sex—though presumably not at the same time. Most people share an urge for self-preservation. There may even be some biological propensity to seek additional sources of satisfaction such as social approval. And there is little doubt that humans are "hard-wired" to learn language. There seems to be little basis for controversy in these matters. As to biological destinies based on sex, as Margaret Mead sought to demonstrate many decades ago, cultural factors exert a preponderant influence on such complex aspects of human behavior.

In most societies men seem to exert greater control over resources than women. Is this "nature's way," or is it a spinoff—an **epiphenomenon**—of social or cultural factors, and therefore not necessary or inevitable? Is it built in, or is it a result of other less-than-deterministic factors? And even if there are biological components to such phenomena, to what extent can cultural or experiential factors free humans from biological propensities?

To address these questions, we might look again at some of the basics—food and sex, for example. It is one thing to say that all humans need nutrition on a regular basis. But how interesting is that? What about the differences between a wedding champagne brunch, a Kiwanis Club chicken roast, a Melanesian pig feast, a child's birthday party, or a Catholic Holy Communion? To what extent can biological factors help us understand these supremely cultural phenomena?

More to the point, what about cases in which culture overrides biological imperatives? Would any animal but a human refuse food to protest some political policy or to express religious devotion? And what about anorexia and bulemia, apparently culture-specific diseases that have caused illness and death in North America, but which most East Africans in the 1990s found all but incomprehensible?

As to sex, we might see it as one of nature's gifts to the human species (or a curse, depending on one's situation). In any case, how much does it tell us to learn that humans, like other species, copulate? In no human society do people "just have sex." Humans, unlike the other species we know of, have multiple, complicated, and varied rules about the whole issue: who can have sex with whom, what kind of sex, and under what circumstances. The fact that individuals might violate these rules at times does not nullify the fact that the rules exist, whatever they may be.

How does biology help us explain why in one society, first cousins are expected to marry, while in another, unrelated people who happen to be members of the same large clan suffer extreme penalties for incest if they engage in sexual dalliance? What about cases in which special occasions allow extreme sexual freedoms that are prohibited most of the time? We might conjure a rich array of social, cultural, and psychological theories to account for these phenomena, but reference to simple biological drives does not take us very far.

We have noted that the biological nature of humans is not in doubt among anthropologists. But most have seen culture as a specialized *capacity* of humans *based on biology*, particularly the evolution of the brain. From this perspective, there is no necessary contradiction involved in the cultural and biological nature of humans. The capacity for culture, in the view of many, is *part of the biological nature* of human beings.

One of the special aspects of culture—the transmission of shared, learned abstract information through symbols—has major implications. It lends *adaptability* to a variety of circumstances, rather than *adaptedness* to a special environmental niche. In the same vein, a capacity for culture favors rapid changes in behavioral patterns over and above biologically fixed patterns. Sometimes, as we know from recent history, these changes can occur within a generation or two. Such rapidity would be impossible if a species needed to rely on biological adaptation, which can only change over many generations through natural selection.

These are not merely empirical issues. Like most matters having to do with the study of humans, they have political implications as well. To the extent that human behavior is biologically programmed, it is not likely to change any time soon. To the extent that it is learned, it can change quickly. Of course, the latter would depend on changing the prevailing social, political, cultural, and/or economic conditions—not necessarily easy to accomplish in the real world, but a potential, nonetheless, and far more feasible than altering the gene pool. These matters have underlain many of the challenges to culture from outside anthropology.

To a great extent, as Walter Goldschmidt (2001) has suggested, the recent resurgence of biological explanations for human behavior seems to have moved in to fill the vacuum created when psychological anthropology and culture and personality studies fell out of favor. Both addressed the immediate or microlevel question of why *people*—not societies, but *individuals*—are the way they are. The "individual and culture" approach, stressing culture, was directly opposed to biological determinist approaches.

To this point, most of the biological approaches have arisen from outside anthropology. Nonetheless, the media have seemed very receptive to the idea of biological explanations for human behavior.

BIOLOGICAL DETERMINISM

As the senior anthropologist Walter Goldschmidt has noted in a retrospective article, "modern students of anthropology do not seem to realize how strong a hold biological determinism and racial explanation had on the scholarly community in the interbellum [World War I—World War II] era" (2001:79). As we noted above, much of Margaret Mead's early work amounted to a rebuttal to biological explanation in favor of the influence of culture. Franz Boas marshaled important critiques of racial explanation, even employing physical data. In a remarkable study, Boas showed that even a feature as apparently biologically determined as head shape could change within a couple of generations when people immigrated from Europe to the United States (Boas 1912). The head shapes of the children of immigrants differed significantly from the head shapes of their parents.

Perhaps the most crucial blow to biologically deterministic viewpoints in European and American thinking, ironically, came in the rise of Nazism and Fascism, the Holocaust, and World War II. In horrifying fashion, these events demonstrated the logical conclusion of such perspectives. Not that racism disappeared after these times by any means, but it no longer enjoyed a respectable position in academics.

After a hiatus during the 1950s, a number of developments brought a return of biological explanation from a variety of sources. Fossil discoveries shedding light on human evolution, especially in Africa, provided inspiration for one of the first of these developments. In the 1960s the playwright Robert Ardrey, fascinated by discoveries of the small hominid *Austalopithecus africanus* that appeared at the time to have been a human ancestor and a carnivore, constructed an exegesis on human ancestry that posited our descent from this purported "killer ape." Most significantly, Ardrey argued that this "killer" heritage had determined human nature ever since (Ardrey 1970).

In many respects Ardrey's tale was an *origin myth*—a "just so" story explaining how things came to be as they are (or supposedly are). More important, perhaps, was the implicit view of contemporary reality as Ardrey saw it. Ardrey was no anthropologist, but by the 1960s anthropology had provided a tool kit from which anyone who wished to could pick and choose tidbits to illustrate a point.

One problem with Ardrey's work, over which he had no control, was the limited information available to him at the time he wrote. That information is still limited, of course, but we now have a far richer base of fossil data. Other issues, however, illustrate some deeper problems in his reasoning. For one thing, Ardrey made a major point of the evidence that *Australopithecus africanus* had been a carnivore. That conclusion is open to serious question. But even if it had been true, what difference would it make? Ardrey assumed that the practice of killing animals for food was tied somehow to homicidal tendencies. What are the flaws in this assumption?

From what we know of both human and non-human meat-eaters, a hunter does not stalk and kill an animal because he hates it or feels a sense of rage toward it. Hunting is about getting food. People in many of the hunting societies that we know about have great respect for animals, over and above an extensive knowledge of their habits. Some such peoples, indeed, believe that humans and animals once could speak to one another. In the North American Arctic and Subarctic, hunters commonly believe that if hunters treat animals with courtesy and respect, they will give themselves to the hunter in the future. Conversely, disrespect for animals will cause them to avoid humans and cause starvation.

What about homicidal proclivities? It probably is safe to say that humans anywhere have the potential to kill one another, for a variety of reasons. If we examine the frequency of such incidents, though, it seems beyond question that people in agricultural and industrialized societies are at least as homicidal in their behavior as hunters, and often far more so. The deeper assertion, though, rests on the assumption that such behavior, even if it existed among our ancestors, continued to pass on through generations over millions of years as a biologically innate compulsion.

Ardrey's work received a great deal of media play, certainly inflated by the outrage that many anthropologists expressed at his unwarranted conclusions. Eventually it faded from public attention, however. Perhaps the most perplexing and disturbing question it raised is why the American public during that period found the assertion of an innate human propensity for violence to be so appealing.

Ardrey's work heralded a series of popular studies on "human nature" that either ignored or misused the anthropological information available at the time. One example was a book by the renowned scientist Konrad Lorenz, whose studies of animal behavior, or **ethology,** won him a Nobel Prize. His work with birds in particular had led to important insights into the role of instinct. Lorenz became interested in human behavior in the 1960s and 1970s and concluded—with no direct evidence—that humans also were subject to instinctive drives (Lorenz 1970).

The alleged instinctive drive to which Lorenz, like Ardrey, gave the most emphasis was aggression. Lorenz's book *On Aggression* received some media attention, but like Ardrey's work, it could not stand up well to scientific scrutiny. Much of the argument for an instinctual continuum between humans and other species rested on arguments from "common sense." But as we know, one person's common sense may be another person's nonsense. The human *potential* for aggressive behavior was beyond question. The central issue, though, remained: Is the expression of aggressive behavior best explained by cultural factors or biological factors, or perhaps some combination of both?

Other such works continued to appear through the following decades. Desmond Morris wrote a popular book titled *The Naked Ape*, which equated human gestures and facial expressions with non-human, and particularly primate, reflexive communication patterns. A human smile, for example, was a counterpart to a primate "fear grimace" (Morris 1967).

The most serious and effective argument for the primacy of biology over culture came from the field of **sociobiology,** essentially an outgrowth of ethology. **Edward O. Wilson,** its best-known proponent, had achieved an international reputation for his work with social insects, particularly ants. Like Ardrey, Lorenz, and Morris, Wilson argued for a human continuum with other species (Wilson 1975).

Wilson elaborated a bit more on the mechanisms that he claimed maintained this continuum. He not only postulated a strong biological influence on human behavior but argued that the purpose of this biological influence had little to do with the qualities most humans would consider important: happiness, fame, wealth, or whatever. The motivating factor was the drive to perpetuate one's own genes. Success in life, glory, or renown are not ends in themselves, according to Wilson, but are fundamentally the means to afford greater opportunities for mating and producing offspring.

Richard Dawkins, author of *The Selfish Gene*, carried this argument to its extreme (Dawkins 1989). Organisms, human or non-human, are basically little more than carriers of genes. Ultimately it is the genes, not their human carriers, that call the shots. This assertion presented a few problems. How could one explain situations in which a person or other animal sacrifices itself in order to allow others to survive? The simplest example would be a bird that sees a cat and cries an alarm, warning the other birds but exposing itself to greater danger. The sociobiologists' answer was that even though the heroic bird might end up as a cat's dinner, most of that bird's genes would survive in the bird's close relatives, which the bird had helped to save and would therefore live to mate another day. Sociobiologists refer to this as **reciprocal altruism.**

Despite the fact that these arguments come from distinguished scientists, just how scientific are they? If we define science as a process requiring testability against data, we have a problem. Yes, the birds in a flock of starlings are likely to be relatives and therefore share lots of genes. But is that the reason for a bird squawking when it sees a cat? For that matter, could we not just as easily assume that the bird who sees the cat first and sounds the alarm is likely to be the first to escape, squawking all the way?

All that aside, does it really make sense to equate the cries of a frightened bird with acts that we could call "altruistic" in a human context, or is this little more than a metaphor? It is one thing to state that animal reflexes resemble human behavior. In many respects, a college dining hall might remind one of a shark feeding frenzy, but at what level of analysis do these events fall short of being equivalent phenomena? Is reciprocal altruism really comparable, for example, to instances of self-sacrifice during wartime, or to a fireman rescuing a child he's never seen before from a burning building? Sociobiologists would say yes. Others would disagree.

An underlying issue here has less to do with science than with the use of language. The term *selfish*, for example (as in "selfish gene"), refers to human characteristics. It makes some sense to refer to a person who refuses to share the last potato chips in the bag as "selfish." That involves a conscious form of behavior, even if the person is *so* habitually selfish that he or she "doesn't know any better." But can a strand of DNA be selfish? When Dawkins refers to *genes* as being "selfish," it seems evident that he is employing a metaphor rather than suggesting literally that genes have personality traits or conscious motivations.

The line also blurs when we talk about birds being "altruistic." Altruism means a *conscious* choice to sacrifice one's own interests for the good of others. In using this term to apply to a panicky bird, we have jumped the gap between humans and non-humans in the realm of description. But does description equate with empirical reality? Is it useful to claim that a squawking, frightened bird represents altruism in the same sense that a human blood donor or someone who gives up a seat on the bus to an elderly stranger represents altruism? One could argue that neither the bird nor the human blood donor may ever realize who the beneficiaries of these actions may be, but certainly on the human side we have an *intention* to benefit *somebody*, even though the beneficiary of the act may have no biological relationship to the altruist. Does that matter?

This equation of humans with other animals through descriptive imagery works both ways in sociobiology writings. Birds allegedly display altruism, thereby supposedly acting like humans. The other side of the equation is that human behavior is essentially the same as animal behavior, arising from the same causes.

The substitution of metaphor for testability in sociobiology went further. Wilson posited genes for various complex human characteristics. Going beyond the "aggression" of earlier writers, Wilson argued that genes produce various personality characteristics at both the group and individual levels and, at one point, even a propensity for speaking one or another language (Wilson 1975).

On the issue of human biological programming to produce a general "human nature," critics have pointed to the broad cross-cultural diversity in the human experience as evidence for the power of learned behavior, or culture, in shaping humanity. On the issue of biological *causes* for diversity, critics have referred to the many cases in which people's ways of life, their cultures, have changed rapidly in a generation or less (see Perry 1980). Could the grandson of an Inuit hunter of seals who becomes an insurance broker and plays in a rock band in his spare time have undergone profound genetic change? Or is his lifestyle an example of cultural (and economic) change that has little to do with biology?

The work of the geneticist **Richard Lewontin** and his colleagues has posed a serious challenge to the claims of biological bases for group differences. Working with blood antigens among tropical South American groups, Lewontin discovered that most of the genetic variance in his samples—around 80 percent—was among individuals within the same populations. Average differences *between* populations accounted for only about 20 percent of the variance (Lewontin et al. 1984). The reasonable conclusion is that genetics does not support the perception that radical biological differences exist among human populations.

Broader research bears out this general conclusion, demonstrating that human genes occur in **clinal** distributions. **Clines** are distributional patterns in which a particular gene might occur with high frequency in one locality but gradually becomes less frequent the farther one goes from that center. Perhaps even more significantly, when it comes to mapping other human genes, their distributions typically do *not* replicate the clinal distribution of the first gene. Each gene seems to have its own clinal distribution. The more genes mapped, the more chaotic the distributions become. In other words, gene distributions do not present a picture of genetically distinct populations with clear boundaries. No doubt this is a result of the fact that human populations have always mixed their genes, and it also accounts for the fact that all living humans remain members of a single species.

If we want to be biological about it, incidentally, we might note that unlike many other species, human beings have no mating season but are sexually active all year round. We all know what that means. Throughout human history, group encounters have generally meant sexual encounters, which has meant the repeated mixture of genes. The bottom line is that the concept of biological "race" has little or no genetic basis. This being the case, the idea that differing cultural patterns are "biologically programmed" has no apparent scientific validity.

The traits that Lewontin recorded—blood antigens—are genetically simple. Whether or not a particular antigen shows up in an individual depends on the presence or absence of a single gene. When we come to visible traits such as stature, hair color, eye color, hair form, skin color, and so on, we are talking about genetically *complex* characteristics. That is, they depend upon the interaction of several genes, not to mention the effects of non-genetic *environmental* factors such as nutrition. That being the case, how much more complex are the causes of such things as temperament or language ability?

Having noted some of the scientific problems with arguments for biological determinism, we might wonder why the controversy continues—and continue it certainly does. One subset of the debate has been the question of genetics versus environment as determinants of *intelligence* (usually defined as scores on standardized tests, or in some cases, financial success. This is an issue at the center of much debate in its own right).

In the early 1990s, **Charles Murray** and **Richard Herrnstein** wrote a book titled *The Bell Curve,* one of a long line of treatises presenting a case for inherent differences in ability among racial groups (1994). For the most part, this book reiterated old, tired, discredited, and unabashedly racist arguments and assertions. Arguments for genetic differentiation addressed other social issues as well. In the 1980s Herrnstein and James Q. Wilson published "findings" that statistically, children with close relatives who had spent time in prison were more likely to go to prison themselves than were children whose relatives had not gone to prison. They presented this as evidence for a genetic cause for criminality. In doing so, oddly enough, they paid little attention to such environmental factors as the obvious possibility that difficult social and economic conditions that lead to criminal prosecution in one generation might have the same effect on the next (Herrnstein and Wilson 1985; Wilson and Herrnstein 1985).

Although these studies received attention in such distinguished media as *The New York Times,* many less publicized works have made similar arguments as well. H. Philipe Rushton, for example, has asserted for years that an inverse relationship exists between intelligence and penis size (see, for example, Rushton 1980).

As comical as some of these assertions might seem, it is evident that much is at stake in these debates. They derive at least as much from politics and personal philosophy as from science. It is clear that over the years, the seemingly innocuous concept of culture—the idea that human behavior is learned rather than inherited, changeable rather than fixed—has been liberating, subversive, insightful, and threatening to various constituencies.

Despite the guise of "science," we can also see these views as forms of contemporary folktales. We have already noted the resemblance of Ardrey's *African Genesis* to a "just so" story or an origin myth. Lorenz's theories on aggression seem to have much in common with parables or Aesop's fables—human lessons drawn from examples in the animal kingdom. And with sociobiology we find the sort of "unifying theory" which, like a grand myth, purports to explain almost everything of importance to human life on the basis of biology. Wilson's most recent book, *Consilience,* argues the need for just such a comprehensive world view in which the physical, biological, and social sciences merge (Wilson 1998).

The issue of culture will remain with us throughout the following chapters. Within anthropology, the view of culture as learned, patterned, symbolic behavior is generally accepted, although some anthropologists have focused more on other aspects of human life. **Eric Wolf** and others, for example, have examined such factors as power relationships and have tended to see culture as a secondary phenomenon. Others who have been more interested in structure have in some cases also tended to leave the study of culture to others. Some structuralists, on the other hand, have applied the concept of structure to the study of culture itself. We shall continue the discussion of structure in the next chapter.

FOOD FOR THOUGHT

To what extent can individuals ever truly generate their own opinions or behaviors? Are we so conditioned by society that we can only view things according to what we have been taught?

Where do we draw the line between one's actions due to "culture" and actions due to "personality"? Is it possible to draw a distinct dichotomy between culture and personality?

Is it possible for one to "unlearn" his or her culture in order to objectively analyze it? Or does analysis have to be done by an outsider, someone to whom the culture is new?

Wallace studied the development of radical social movements and dramatic changes in society. Do all radical changes occur after crises, or could they occur during "normal" times?

Chapter 4

THE IDEA OF STRUCTURE

Structure is about relationships. When we consider the term *structure*, we could visualize the framework of a house, and we might assume that the structure amounts to the component parts of that framework—the wooden studs, joists, rafters, and so on. These parts in themselves, however, do not constitute the structure. The structure is a matter of how they fit together, the *relationships* among them. Most houses nowadays consist of standardized and interchangeable 2 × 4 lumber, plywood sheets, concrete blocks, and the like. Yet houses built of these materials vary tremendously in their structures.

Like evolution and culture, structure is an old idea. In the broader social sciences, it generally has to do with the question of how society (or societies) work. It has been associated with the attempt to define relationships among social components, or in some cases, as we shall see, among cultural concepts.

We can find some inklings of structure in the writings of Enlightenment scholars. Rousseau's idea of the "social contract," referring to the understandings between the government and its citizens pertaining to mutual responsibilities, suggests some of the aspects of a political structure (Rousseau 1938 [orig. 1762]). Thomas Hobbes's work *Leviathan* presents a metaphorical depiction of society as a ponderous beast, which implicitly, at least, also suggests a structure (1958 [orig. 1642]).

In the nineteenth century, as we recall, Lewis Morgan saw relationships between such aspects of life as technology and family organization at different evolutionary stages. Although Morgan did not describe these relationships as "structures" characteristic of each stage, a certain degree of interdependence among these features was clear. One essential aspect of this view is the non-randomness of the various features that characterize the entire package of a social system. Certain things occur together; others do not.

We can credit Herbert Spencer with one of the earliest explicit uses of the concept of social structure to explain how society works and how it changes. Spencer argued that society is a natural phenomenon subject to laws of nature. One of these laws was the progressive internal differentiation of structure—the idea that as societies develop, they become more internally complex, with various components taking on specialized tasks. In totality, this array of tasks constituted for Spencer the structure of relationships of the society.

The idea that society consists of relationships, then, has been around for some time. But the crucial issue is the idea that these relationships conform to rules of which the human participants might not be aware. The average person may be fully cognizant of society's *overt* rules—one should not steal, one should not marry a close relative, and so on. But structural rules can also take the form of more subtle, mutually supportive interactions.

A religious institution, for example, might promote the value of hard work and humility, which supports industrial production while keeping labor costs low, providing in turn for good profits for factory owners. Spencer and Marx might disagree on the desirability of this situation, but both would agree on the interrelationship of these social features. And both would agree that these relationships are at least partly unconscious. Marx argued, in fact, that those in power tend to disguise or *mystify* such relationships, promoting a false consciousness among those who are most exploited (1973 [orig. 1858]).

The idea that there is some rhyme and reason to society was once fairly radical. To many people in many times, it has been just as reasonable to see society as a mindless hodgepodge of customs, rules, and privileges that have accumulated over the years for fairly capricious historical reasons. The idea that some implicit order characterizes social systems was not self-evident in the nineteenth century, nor is it today to many thoughtful people. To some extent, structure remains an unproven assumption.

The idea of structure also involved a fairly precarious path between the secular view that understanding society is a matter of science and the idea that some divine "guiding hand" is at work in human affairs. As we shall see, even some "scientific" views of the workings of society have lent themselves to accusations of mysticism. The assumption of structure also poses the dilemma, yet to be resolved, of where this structure comes from. If structure is not a matter of divine guidance, it must be a product of human thought and action. But if structure is not a part of normal human consciousness, how could humans have produced it?

This issue also touches on the old monist/dualist issue that we noted earlier in Chapter 3 on culture. People do things. Often they do them in much the same ways that other people do them, and they tend to do them rather consistently over time. Does this imply structure? Or is structure merely an imaginary construct built upon the summation of numerous discrete acts and the propensity for humans to act pretty much the same way other people act? Is structure really *there*?

The concept of structure offers the advantage of giving order to otherwise chaotic human events. It allows the assertion that somehow human social life makes sense, from a secular perspective. This idea of social order was particularly appealing in Europe and the United States during the nineteenth century.

SOCIAL ORDER

During much of the nineteenth century, Europeans and Americans faced the recent memory, immediate threat, and sometimes the reality of social disruption. The French Revolution had destroyed the old order just before the turn of the century. Revolutions erupted in several European countries in the late 1840s. In the 1860s the United States struggled through the devastation of its own Civil War, the deadliest war in American history.

In the social sciences, Karl Marx depicted social disruption as an inevitable part of the process of change, but much of the writing of other social scientists in that era amounted to a rebuttal of Marx's conclusions. They strived to show how society held together rather than why it should break down. The concept of structure was a useful image in this regard, since it conveyed a sense of stability and mutually reinforcing components.

In a sense, the fact that societies do hold together may pose a more interesting question than why they undergo disruption. The divisive factors of human life—conflicts of interest, rivalries, property disputes, and such—are fairly common aspects of the human experience. What keeps these things from escalating into more serious social breakdown poses a challenging problem.

To some thinkers, overall social forces have seemed to be a crucial factor in this cohesion. Some kind of overall social phenomena seemed to be at work to maintain the sort of order and solidarity required to keep society in operation. To some, it seemed evident that these social forces must be extremely powerful to override the strong conflicting interests that were bound to arise among individuals and interest groups. The French sociologist **Emile Durkheim,** in fact, argued that social forces not only supercede but *compel* individual actions and sentiments.

Emile Durkheim (1858–1917)

SOCIETY AS AN ENTITY

Durkheim's concept of society involved a sense that social forces have a reality of their own, over and above the people who comprise a society. Society, Durkheim argued, is more than the sum of its parts. Like Spencer, Durkheim visualized society as a higher life form, a superorganic entity (Durkheim 1938 [orig. 1895]).

Expanding upon this view, Durkheim asserted that it was no use trying to explain society on the basis of individual motivations and choices. Individuals may have minds of their own, but that, according to Durkheim, is a subject for psychology, not sociology or anthropology. The individual mind belongs to a lower level of existence. Its consequences do not provide the explanatory principles necessary to explain the higher level of society.

From this perspective, one could see reality in terms of a hierarchy of levels. Certain principles apply at the basic level of physics, for example. The study of chemistry requires some understanding of physics, but the laws of physics do not account for everything we need to know about chemistry. Chemistry has its own additional principles. At the level of living forms, biology subsumes the laws of physics and chemistry, but once again, these in themselves are not adequate. Biology has its own principles, over and above those that operate at the levels below.

Psychology, the study of the mind, once again assumes and incorporates all of the levels below it. Human beings certainly are subject to the laws of physics and chemistry. They are biological organisms with needs for nutrition, reproduction, and other imperatives they share with other species. But when we address questions of psychology, these laws are not enough. Additional principles come into play. The superorganic view of society places social phenomena at a still higher level of reality. Society requires and assumes living, breathing human beings. But no society is just a random crowd of individuals. Knowing all we can know about how a person operates will not account for collective social phenomena.

This brings us back to the issue of order. If society acts as a force in its own right, it stands to reason that society will tend to preserve itself, to act in its own self-interest. Such an assumption may strike many of us as a bit mystical. Some might question the existence of a superhuman phenomenon acting as it if had a will and motivation. This, in fact, has been a criticism that some have leveled at Durkheim. On the other hand, there is no doubt that broad social forces do seem to act in ways that have little to do with individual choice.

The pioneering statistician Adolphe Quetelet, for example, demonstrated this early in the nineteenth century (Quetelet 1842). In a given year, he noted, one could predict that a certain number of letters dropped into the mailboxes of Paris would be misaddressed or would lack the proper postage. Once could not predict, however, just *which* letters these would be. Although statistics rendered broad social phenomena predictable, the actions of a single person tend to be far less so. This distinction was consistent with the notion that the two phenomena represent different levels of reality, each of them operating according to a different set of principles.

Although Durkheim did not employ the idea of structure explicitly, his concept of social forces involved a sense of order imposed over and above the will of individuals, producing social *solidarity*. Durkheim was also aware that the mechanisms necessary to produce this solidarity would have to differ according to the type of society. Large societies with different social classes, varied occupations, and other forms of heterogeneity would face different kinds of problems in maintaining solidarity than would small societies in which everyone of the same sex or generation did pretty much the same sorts of things. In these smaller societies, according to Durkheim, differentiation was minimal. In that sort of community, he surmised, cohesion was based on the fact of social *sameness*. He called this form **mechanical solidarity.**

In larger, complex societies, mechanical solidarity would not be feasible because of the degree of difference among segments of the population. In that case, social cohesiveness would have to arise from the fact that these various segments of the population *need* one another because they carry out complementary roles. Durkheim referred to this mutually supportive differentiation as **organic solidarity.** Like Spencer, Durkheim saw different components of complex societies operating in a fashion similar to the internal organs of a living animal.

These forms of social solidarity have some bearing on the division of labor in such societies. On this subject, though, Durkheim's analysis departed in important ways from the approaches of Marx and most other materialists. To account for the development of a division of labor, many scholars would assume that a differentiation of tasks had something to do with greater productive efficiency. A person who can spend all day making pots for sale need not, and probably cannot, spend much time farming to produce food. The trade-off is that the potter can produce more pots—and probably better ones—than a non-specialist who makes a pot once in a while when the need arises. And since the potter does not really need to use any more pots than anyone else, she or he can trade the extras for food and other goods that other people produce.

But this sort of explanation was not satisfactory to Durkheim. He favored an approach that rested more heavily on the theme of internal social solidarity rather than drawing on more material "nuts and bolts" considerations. He was quite explicit, in fact, in disavowing any materialism in his approach.

> The division of labor appears to us otherwise than it does to economists. For them, it essentially consists in greater production. For us, this greater productivity is only a necessary consequence, a repercussion of the phenomenon. If we specialize, it is not to produce more, but it is to enable us to live in new [social] conditions of existence that have been made for us. (Durkheim 1938 [orig. 1895]: 275)

On this matter Durkheim remained true to the concept of society operating according to its own principles. The causes of social phenomena lay in the social realm, not in material considerations. Dukheim saw this as a matter of moral order, operating for the maximum benefit of all. His consistency in limiting social explanation to social causes, though, led to a model that many others have considered to be less than adequate, if not a bit bizarre.

The root cause of the division of labor, he argued, was a phenomenon he called **social condensation.** As a society grows, its capacity for mechanical solidarity diminishes. At a certain critical point members of a population may find themselves in competition, which is potentially disruptive of solidarity. The solution—a way to restore harmony and solidarity, in effect—is to divide the tasks. Like undifferentiated water vapor that spontaneously condenses into droplets when it reaches critical conditions of temperature, society differentiates itself when it becomes internally necessary to restore solidarity.

Durkheim's views on these issues reveal some evolutionary implications. For one thing, it seems undeniable that any transition from one form of solidarity to another would almost have to be from the mechanical to the organic form, not the other way around. Much of the preceding discussion had to do with how this transition would take place.

It is also worth noting that unlike many anthropologists of the later twentieth century, Durkheim apparently had few doubts about the differential value of these alternative forms of solidarity. Mechanical solidarity, he asserted, tended to oppress the freedom of the individual under the power of the relatively undifferentiated social order:

> It is wrong to contrast a society which arises from a community of beliefs (mechanical solidarity) to one which has a cooperative basis (organic solidarity), according only to the first a moral character, and seeing in the latter simply an economic grouping. (1933:228)

Far from having a romantic view of smaller, undifferentiated societies, Durkheim even argued that severe punishment for offenses was more common in societies with mechanical solidarity. With the advance in social complexity and organic solidarity, he felt, the intensity of coercive sanctions came to be replaced by "individualized" and more humane punishment—through imprisonment.

Some might take issue with this point, especially considering the realities of imprisonment in various state-level societies. In any case, the availability of better information on social sanctions in smaller societies tends to refute Durkheim's conclusions (see, for example, Hoebel 1954; Nader 1965; Starr and Collier 1989). It is fair to say, however, that most of this ethnographic information was not available to Durkheim.

We can see many of Spencer's ideas in Durkheim's work. The ideas of Durkheim, in turn, entered the intellectual milieu available to other scholars as well. The idea that regularized relationships give structure to human life developed further in the work of some of Durkheim's students, particularly his nephew **Marcel Mauss.** Mauss struck upon a fundamental aspect of human life that turned out to have considerable explanatory power: the principle of **reciprocity.**

Everyone knows that a big part of human interaction involves give and take. In Mauss's view, the regularities, expectations, and repercussions of exchanges provide a fundamental mechanism for social organization. One of his most important insights was that the essential aspect of exchange is not the item that moves from giver to receiver, but more important, that the transfer itself creates a social relationship (Mauss 1954 [orig. 1924]).

If the transaction involves reciprocity—that is, the receiver eventually completes the exchange with an item of equivalent value—it implies a balanced relationship between giver and receiver. If the receiver does not reciprocate, however, the interaction results in a difference in status between the two parties involved. The giver rises, the receiver drops. This simple fact of social interaction, Mauss argued, applies to a range of phenomena from personal relationships to political power among groups. One example would be the institutionalized competitive feasts or "potlatches" of the North Pacific Coast of North America, in which the group that is able to give more rises in status, while the "beneficiaries" of their largesse may be shamed if they cannot return at least as much (see Boas 1897; Codere 1950, 1956, 1957, 1959; Goldman 1975; Piddocke 1965 for discussions of the potlatch).

Some later anthropologists, most notably Pierre Bordieu, have refined this idea to take account of the ways in which the players in this exchange can employ their "feel for the game," or *habitus*, to manipulate the principle of reciprocity for various purposes. A recipient might return a gift immediately, for example, perhaps humiliating the original giver by terminating the relationship quickly. Alternatively, the receiver might fail to reciprocate for an inordinately long period of time, thereby sending a different message about the relationship (1990:58–66). In this sense, the issue goes beyond the analysis of structure as a matter of consistent relationships among components to the ways in which individuals can and do manipulate aspects of structure for their own purposes. Mauss's underlying principle of reciprocity and its power in social relationships, nonetheless, remains a valuable explanatory principle.

This basic issue of structure as reciprocity, or more generally, as a matter of binary relationships, will come up again when we discuss the structuralism of Claude Levi-Strauss in French anthropology. In British social anthropology, however, a somewhat different version of structure developed that found its greatest expression in the work of Alfred Reginald Radcliffe-Brown and his students.

STRUCTURE, EVOLUTION, AND HISTORY

We might note that while evolutionary models must involve an assumption of change, the concept of structure in itself need not. Structure is about relationships among components, not necessarily about transitions from one form to another. There is no reason why one could *not* take the issue of structural change into account; but it is possible to think of structure, unlike evolution, in a timeless or **synchronic** fashion without paying much attention to either the history of a particular society or the development of societies in general (see Radcliffe-Brown 1947). In the same way, one can examine how the various parts of a car fit together without paying any attention to long-term changes in the mechanics of cars, or for that matter, even considering

A. R. Radcliffe-Brown

how many miles that particular car has traveled. The idea of synchronic evolution, on the other hand, would be an oxymoron.

In anthropology the development of a synchronic approach to structure derived some of its impetus from the misuse of evolutionary models and the general decline in satisfaction with them by the early part of the twentieth century. By that time it was clear that many of these evolutionary constructs rested on poor or unreliable data. The conclusions had been too sweeping in some respects and inaccurate with regard to particular cases. This situation gave rise to a general realization that anthropology's bank of accurate data needed serious improvement. As we noted in Chapter 2 on evolution, that perception coincided with the establishment of fieldwork as the main research method in anthropology.

Although Durkheim did not carry out fieldwork, he did make use of the painstaking field research of others—particularly Sir Baldwin Spencer and Frank Gillin on Australian groups (Spencer and Gillin 1968 [orig. 1899]), which he used as a basis for his final book *The Elementary Forms of the Religious Life* (1915 [orig. 1912]). In Britain, however, anthropologists early in the twentieth century came to accept the necessity of first-hand field observation. For Radcliffe-Brown, field data and the concept of structure were integral aspects of his research strategy (1958).

Radcliffe-Brown was adamant that anthropology deserved a place among the sciences. As he put it, "I regard social anthropology as a branch of natural science" (1952b:88–89). He referred to his discipline as "social anthropology" to distinguish it from American cultural anthropology or "ethnology," which he considered less than scientific. At one time he also referred to his work as "comparative sociology," which seems to have arisen in the period in which he taught in South Africa. The term may have been an attempt to separate himself from the racist views of South African anthropologists of the time (Robert Gordon, personal communication).

In any case, Radcliffe-Brown's insistence on a scientific basis for anthropology led to several developments. As we have noted, it led him to distance himself from the cultural anthropology of the Boasians in the United States. Even though Boas himself took great pains to maintain high standards of scientific objectivity, the Boasian quest for meaning, the detailed and comprehensive focus on the unique features of particular cultures, and the interest in historical reconstruction seemed too subjective for Radcliffe-Brown. Social structure, on the other hand, appeared to offer a more solid basis for scientific analysis. "You cannot have a science of culture. You can study culture only as a characteristic of a social system" (1948:106).

Like Spencer, Radcliffe-Brown argued that society is not an imaginary construct. With regard to economics, for example, he wrote:

> The economic machinery of a society appears in quite a new light if it is studied in relation to the social structure. The exchange of goods and services is dependent upon, is the result of, and at the same time is a means of maintaining a certain structure, a network of relations between persons and collections of persons. (1952b:197–198)

This social reality deserved careful scientific study *on the scene*, and its analysis, in scientific fashion, had to rest on observational data.

These considerations led Radcliffe-Brown to reject both historical and evolutionary approaches. For most societies of the world, which lacked written records, the past could only be a matter of speculation, and speculation had no place in anthropological research. It was with these stipulations that Radcliffe-Brown developed his concept of structure.

For Radcliffe-Brown, like Herbert Spencer, the essence of social structure was a matter of relationships among *institutions*. Although Radcliffe-Brown held that social structure ultimately is a matter or relationships among persons, these persons were essentially interchangeable. Like Durkheim, Radcliffe-Brown saw no value in attempting to explain social phenomena by reference to the peculiarities of particular persons. People come and go. Institutions, however—the kinship system, the religious system, or the economic system—persist over generations. In a social sense, these institutions were more *real*, and more relevant, than the people who acted within their parameters.

Radcliffe-Brown took the idea of the organic analogy from Spencer, while rejecting Spencer's evolutionist suppositions, and argued that society is like a living organism. Like the various organs of an animal, institutions operate together in a mutually supportive manner to allow the society to exist. In their totality, it was the relationships among these institutions that constituted the social structure.

STRUCTURE AND CONSERVATISM

We have noted that this view of social structure did not necessarily offer much insight to account for change, and this aspect of Radcliffe-Brown's concept of social structure eventually drew serious criticism. To some, Radcliffe-Brown's model of society eventually seemed to be an implicit argument for the status quo. If the existence of a society depends upon a delicate balance of component institutions in a social "equilibrium," one could well conclude that change would only disturb that balance and be disruptive, and therefore undesirable (see Radcliffe-Brown 1950). In the 1960s, long after Radcliffe-Brown's death, some critics within anthropology asserted that this model of social structure manifested a deep political conservatism (Hymes et al. 1969).

The fact that Radcliffe-Brown and his students from the 1920s to the 1950s worked mostly in British colonies added some weight to these accusations. Were they acting as tools of the colonial powers, aiding in the oppression of non-European peoples? In some cases British anthropologists even justified their work as being of use to colonial administrations for developing better policies (see Evans-Pritchard 1962:109–129; Goody 1995).

As far as colonialism is concerned, though, it is worth remembering that this policy had been an ongoing phenomenon long before Radcliffe-Brown ever studied anthropology. For that matter, let us consider the prevailing view of Europeans at that time regarding the "dark races" of their colonial domains. Although horrifying now, the terms "wog," "fuzzy-wuzzy," "cheeky kaffir," and worse were a part of the common parlance early in the twentieth century.

Part of the ideological justification for colonialism, ignoring resource extraction and the brutal exploitation of labor, was the idea that it introduced "simple savages" to what was then considered "modern civilization." A corollary to this view, of course, was that the existing societies of these colonized peoples were primitive, undeveloped, and uncivilized. We have already sampled a dose of this attitude in the chapter on evolution.

In this context, what was the point of Radcliffe-Brown's insistence on the field study of particular societies and his emphasis on structure? To a great extent, the fundamental message was that these societies were intricately complex and self-sufficient in their own right. They were ancient ways of life whose histories might not be accessible to scholars, but which clearly had developed successful social systems over many centuries. The idea of equilibrium, far from being an argument for domestic political conservatism, was more pointedly an assertion of the viability of indigenous societies.

In making this argument, Radcliffe-Brown and others faced the daunting task of convincing many who had already made up their minds to the contrary, and who had a vested interest in retaining those negative views. As Jack Goody points out regarding the history of that era, colonial administrators in many regions were loathe to have anthropologists around because of the critical stand they took regarding government policies (1995:7–25). The myth of European superiority was, after all, far more comforting to many than the realization that the assaults of colonialism, rather than bringing civilization to ignorant masses, threatened to destroy, or had already destroyed, irreplaceable and unique human achievements.

We have seen the ideas of Spencer and Durkheim in Radcliffe-Brown's work. He was explicit in acknowledging these influences. But he did not mention another likely influence whose ideas also were part of the intellectual milieu of the time, and which clearly seem to have played a part in his thinking. This was the Russian anarchist **Peter Kropotkin.**

We might digress for a moment here and consider the philosophical position of **anarchism,** which enjoyed some prominence around the beginning of the twentieth century in Europe and the United States. Fundamentally, anarchism involves the belief that government is detrimental to human well-being. Some anarchists adopted militant strategies, planning attacks on the organs of the state, planting bombs, and so on. Others, like Kropotkin, embraced a more pacifistic position.

Prince Kropotkin had been a page in the court of the Czar as a young man at the end of the nineteenth century. For expressing radical views, he found himself exiled to Siberia. Since Kropotkin was a noble and his offense had more to do with attitude than with serious criminal behavior, he apparently did not suffer harsh imprisonment. During his time of exile, he observed Siberian peasant life and read Darwin. He was particularly taken with the Darwinian idea of relative fitness.

Unlike Spencer and even Darwin himself, who saw in this concept a natural propensity for fierce competition, Kropotkin became more intrigued by the evolutionary advantage of cooperation. Kropotkin was an early proponent of the concept that group fitness prevailed over individual competition. Those groups that provided the greatest mutual support for their members were more likely to prevail over those that suffered internal divisions and conflict.

On this assumption, Kropotkin concluded that humans had evolved with a natural tendency to cooperate. Why, then, were conflicts so much a part of human experience? The blame lay in government. In Kropotkin's view, it was government, whatever form it might take, that generated conflict, sweeping up the hapless populations who ultimately paid the price. Kropotkin expanded upon these ideas in his book *Mutual Aid*, which first appeared in England in 1901 (Kropotkin 1919 [orig. 1901]).

In England, anarchism became a popular fad among many intellectuals early in the twentieth century. Kropotkin, who found a warmer welcome there than he had enjoyed in his homeland, became a prized guest in many English drawing rooms. He visited the Royal Geographical Society as an honored speaker and even participated in public debates with Herbert Spencer.

In 1901 Radcliffe-Brown, at that time sporting the simpler name Alfred Reginald Brown, was an undergraduate student at Oxford. Somewhat the student radical, he had a particular interest in anarchism. His friends, in fact, gave him the nickname "Anarchy Brown." Could young Anarchy Brown have been unaware of Kropotkin, the most celebrated anarchist in England at the time? Not likely. (See Perry 1978 for a fuller discussion.)

The insight that formal government was not a necessary means of imposing order on human life seems compatible with much of Radcliffe-Brown's work, which dealt with relatively small, stateless societies. As we noted, many of these societies, in fact, were under the authority of a colonial government. But Radcliffe-Brown's work focused more on the internal workings of indigenous social structures than on those factors of their colonial situations that he seemed to consider external, foreign interference. Radcliffe-Brown has, in fact, been criticized for apparently ignoring this aspect of indigenous people's realities.

Certainly colonial authorities did impinge significantly on people's lives, and Radcliffe-Brown clearly was aware of this. But once again, the thrust of his work was toward showing how these systems worked in their own right. And to a great extent, of course, especially during the era of British "indirect rule," many local communities did manage to continue their day-to-day lives in relative autonomy.

Radcliffe-Brown's disavowal of "speculative history" led him and his students to ignore written history in some cases, as well as oral tradition. **Meyer Fortes**'s study of the Tallensi produced an elegant model of the workings of an **"acephalous"** society (literally, "headless")—that is, a society without a hierarchical, formal governmental structure (1945, 1949). As it turned out, though, the Tallensi earlier had had a strong indigenous governmental structure, but colonial conquest had destroyed the earlier political system. This information was available to Fortes, although it is not clear whether he was aware of it at the time. In any case, he produced a model that failed to take historical changes fully into account. The impression was that this smoothly operating, stable social structure represented a longstanding indigenous model of Tallensi society.

It would be a mistake to conclude that Radcliffe-Brown, Fortes, and others were not aware of the changes affecting the societies in which they worked. Many of these scholars expressed concern about what changes might overwhelm these societies in the future. Ironically, this concern for demonstrating the viability of indigenous societies as an aspect of their research strategies gave a later generation of anthropologists a basis for accusing them of being sympathetic to colonial oppression.

In the context of the times, however, the more immediate task was to demonstrate that these societies *had* social structure at all. Absurd as this might sound today, in the British colonial claims of the eighteenth and nineteenth centuries in North America and Australia, the British Crown denied indigenous rights to land on the grounds that these populations had no "true" societies (Williams 1986). This question was far from dead in the 1930s. The issue of how these societies had changed was secondary to the issue of demonstrating that they were ordered, viable social systems in the first place.

FRENCH STRUCTURALISM

As we have seen, Radcliffe-Brown focused primarily on social institutions in dealing with structure. But could the concept of structure also apply to other aspects of the human experience? Mauss's idea of reciprocity involved a rather simple dynamic that had considerable explanatory power, extending to a wide range of interactions and, in turn, accounting for such aspects of life as status differentiation. The idea of reciprocity offered a fundamental engine for constructing social organization.

Why not extend this idea to other aspects of life, including aspects of culture that Radcliffe-Brown had tended to ignore? The French anthropologist **Claude Levi-Strauss** took inspiration from Mauss and Durkheim. Taking the concept of binary or two-way relationships implicit in Mauss's model of reciprocity, Levi-Strauss developed a structural principle that pervaded aspects of life ranging from marriage systems to mythology.

Durkheim and Radcliffe-Brown had essentially dismissed the issue of human mentality from their analyses. Both, as we recall, tended to see society as a superorganic phenomenon (although Radcliffe-Brown showed no fondness for that term), operating according to its own laws. But Levi-Strauss attempted to deal with the totality of human life. The principle of *mediated binary opposition*—two opposite poles with a mediating element between them—pervaded all levels. And according to Levi-Strauss, its origins were in the workings of the human mind.

Levi-Strauss's model involved a distillation of ideas from several sources. The work of Sigmund Freud and others had established the realization that the mind operates at a number of levels, including the subconscious. Thus, important aspects of mental reality may not be overt or evident even to the individual involved. Indeed, the conscious mind may even *disguise* underlying mental phenomena. Could this idea apply to cultural systems as well as to the individual?

We might also note that Levi-Strauss's approach constitutes a rebuttal to the earlier work of Lucien Levy-Bruhl, who argued that the thought processes of "primitive" people are childlike and qualitatively different from those of adult Westerners (Levy-Bruhl 1923, 1926). Levi-Strauss's approach assumed universal structures on the basis of which the human mind works in *all* societies, obscure and elusive as these structures may be.

The study of language had also advanced tremendously by the early part of the twentieth century. Fernand de Saussure had established the distinction between *parole*, or language as acts of speech, and *langue*, or language as a structured system. One of Saussure's important insights was that the symbols, or "signifiers," of language not only have arbitrary relationships to the "signified," or the concepts to which they referred; these signifiers, as components of a system, also have meaning only on the basis of their relationships to other signifiers. These relationships were based on contrasts (Saussure 1959).

Saussure's work did much to refine the idea of language as a system with a structure, which is another way of saying that relationships exist among its components. They operate in a field of mutual effect. We have already seen that this aspect of language was useful in developing the concept of culture as a system for scholars like Margaret Mead, but for Levi-Strauss language offered more profound insights.

One of the major aspects of any language is the production of sounds. The problem of coming to grips with the tremendous range of sounds that humans are able to produce, as well as those that actually appear in one language or another, is enormous. One of the major developments in the analysis of *phonetics*, or sounds in language, was the idea that it is possible to describe any sound objectively in terms of a number of **distinctive features.**

Does a sound involve the expulsion of breath (aspiration)? Does it involve a closure of the lips to interrupt the flow of air (bilabial)? Does it involve a forceful hissing of air (fricative)? Does it involve vocalization (the difference between the English /p/ and /b/)? It is possible to express each of these and many other distinctive features in terms of "yes" or "no." A sound either is bilabial, or it is not. It is either vocalized or not. One can express these features on a chart with + or − signs to describe any vocal sound humans could possibly produce.

One of the foremost linguists working on these problems was **Roman Jakobson** (Jakobson 1971). By coincidence, Levi-Strauss accepted an academic post at the New School for Social Research in New York in the 1940s at a time when Jakobson was a member of the faculty there. In this case, the flow of ideas benefited from personal acquaintance (Levi-Strauss 1963:35). The binary system of linguistic features, combined with the concept of reciprocity that Mauss had developed, inspired Levi-Strauss to explore ways of interpreting culture through the contrastive analysis of binary structures.

Still other ideas and insights contributed to this approach. Marx's writings had a strong influence on Levi-Strauss. The concept of a dialectic, which Marx attributed to the work of Georg W. F. Hegel, seemed compatible with a model of binary opposition. In the view of Hegel, one could perceive aspects of reality only in terms of their opposites (Hegel 1910, 1956). Contradictions resolved themselves through mutual negation and the development of new syntheses. For Marx and Engels, contradictions in the political system would become increasingly intolerable until a revolutionary eruption would result in a new social order.

Levi-Strauss's structural model did not emphasize this sort of revolutionary social change, but he did develop the idea of a third, mediating element that could serve to resolve contradictory postulates. Much of his work on mythology, in fact, involved the ways in which myths "resolve contradictions" that are irreconcilable in social life. They do so by substituting symbolic elements, which *do* allow resolution, in place of "real life" elements, which do not (1966).

Perhaps one of the most important aspects of Levi-Strauss's version of structure, though, was that structure as an underlying feature appears in multiple aspects of life, not merely in relationships among institutions. One of his most significant arguments, in fact, linked marriage, economic exchange, and language as different levels representing the same general dynamic of communication (1953).

We might say that while Radcliffe-Brown's concept of structure involved a construct encompassing the entire social system, Levi-Strauss's view of structure involved a sense of internal dynamics operating *within* cultural and social systems at all levels. As we noted, too, Levi-Strauss did not draw the strong distinction between cultural and social phenomena that we see in the work of Radcliffe-Brown and many of his students.

STRUCTURE AND MARRIAGE

In the realm of social structure—if we think of social structure as involving rules or expectations pertaining to relationships among people—what could be more fundamental or important than marriage? Marriage, depending upon how one defines it, is either a universal or extremely common human phenomenon. No known human group exists in which sexual relationships between people are entirely free from rules of some sort; and in all known societies, at least some of these relationships involve rights and obligations regarding such issues as property and offspring. The most common form of marriage involves an institutionalized linkage of a man or men to a woman or women. Most other variants of this linkage—same-sex marriage, and so on—tend to replicate this general pattern in terms of the social rights and obligations surrounding the relationship.

This pattern reflects at least two major concerns. One involves the rights of partners with regard to property, children, and so on. The other involves the rights, obligations, and responsibilities of the *kin* of the marriage partners, both to the married partners and to one another. Marriage, in other words, creates **affinal relatives,** or "in-laws." For this reason, in most societies marriage is more than a matter of romance and personal attraction. Since it often involves relationships among a sizeable number of people, it is also a matter of politics and economics.

But if marriage offers fundamental social linkages, might these principles also apply to other aspects of life, as Mauss had argued? Levi-Strauss went beyond Mauss to point out that just as language involves the exchange of information through symbols, and economics involves the exchange of goods and services, marriage involves the exchange of women among social groups.

At the most basic level, marriage arises from incest rules, which dictate that the minimal family cannot reproduce itself indefinitely. That constraint necessitates marital exchange between families, which generally offers advantages. Tylor had pointed out many years before that groups whose members married out to establish ties with other groups would have a competitive advantage over groups who were isolated (Tylor 1889:267).

Given the need to marry out and the advantages of the resulting alliances, what forms could these alliances take? Conceptually, a simple possibility would be to have a rule stipulating that one can marry anybody who is not a close relative. (This does not, of course, address other issues, such as parental approval of the spouse, and so on.) This simple marriage pattern, which oddly enough is sometimes referred to as a **complex marriage system,** characterizes most industrial societies as well as many hunting and gathering groups. It produces networks of individual kin ties and usually occurs in societies with **bilateral kinship.**

Many societies reckon kinship in terms of descent through either the mother's or the father's line. In such societies, the people related in this way constitute **unilineal descent groups** such as **clans** or **lineages.** A unilineal descent group is a group of people—both males and females—who consider themselves to belong to a special category because of postulated descent through one line from a common ancestor.

If that line of descent is through the mother, then women pass the membership on to their children while men do not. If the father's line is emphasized, on the other hand, it is men rather than women who pass on membership to their children.

This does not necessarily mean that people in such groups totally ignore relatives in the other line. Some West African peoples, such as the Ashanti, recognize the mother's line for some purposes and the father's line for others. In the case of the Navajo, who have clans passed on through women (**matrilineal clans**), people recognize their mother's clan as the clan they are "born to" and the father's clan as the clan they are "born for."

With regard to marriage, though, unilineal descent typically involves a stipulation that one should not marry a member of the same group, even if that person may not be a relative in any traceable biological sense. Unilineal descent groups, in other words, are usually **exogamous.** (There are a few exceptions, such as the **bint 'amm** *endogamous* marriages in some Arabian clans, that need not concern us here.) In most cases, people must marry outside their own clan. This marriage prohibition may also extend to other clans as well, such as the clan of one's other parent.

Unilineal descent involves more than marriage stipulations, of course. It also produces categories of people these marriage ties can unite into political alliances within a society. There are several ways in which marriage ties can link these unilineal descent groups. Let us use clans as an example of such groups.

These possibilities, while they produce relationships among clans, are manifest in marriage rules pertaining to individuals. If clan membership stipulates descent through women, then naturally, all of the children of the same woman will belong to the same clan, and so will the children of the mother's sisters, since the mother and her sisters all inherit their membership in the same clan from *their* mother. These children of the mother's sisters are **parallel cousins.**

The mother's brothers also share membership in the same clan. Unlike the mother and her sisters, though, these males cannot pass their clan membership on to their children. Those children, the **cross cousins,** will belong to whatever clan *their* mothers belong to, but it would have to be a different clan because the mother's brothers could not marry members of their own clan.

If the descent principle is through the *father's* line rather than the mother's, the same general pattern will still prevail. Cross cousins are people whose parents include siblings of the opposite sex. Parallel cousins are children whose parents include siblings of the same sex. These features, which Morgan discovered in the nineteenth century, characterize what anthropologists now refer to as **Iroquois cousin terminology.**

A major point is that cross cousins are never members of the same clan. Parallel cousins are likely to be. In most societies with clans or other types of unilineal descent groups, the kinship terms for parallel cousins are the same as the terms for brother and sister. And like siblings, with a few exceptions, parallel cousins in most unilineal societies are not potential marriage partners. In many such societies, cross cousins, who are members of different clans—or other members of different clans—are fair game for marriage. So marriage to a cross cousin is equivalent to marriage outside one's own clan.

What could be simpler? But, remember that everyone who *has* cross cousins (that is, anyone living in a society with unilineal descent groups and an Iroquois type of cousin terminology) has at least *two kinds* of cross cousin. One type is on the mother's side (the mother's brother's children) and the other type is on the father's side (the father's sister's children). What difference does that make? From the perspective of relationships among unilineal descent groups, it matters.

Suppose we have a society with a dozen or so clans. And suppose it is permissible to marry anyone who belongs to a different clan. This is the equivalent of being able to marry *either* cross cousin. Structurally, then, we would have potentially reciprocal marriage relationships among any two clans. People of each could marry people of the other, generation after generation. Conceivably, those two clans could go on marrying each other's members forever, without having to bother too much with the other ten or so clans that constitute the rest of the society.

They probably would have other kinds of interactions with members of other clans, economic and otherwise. But as Levi-Strauss and many others have pointed out, nothing creates bonds like marriage, because marriage creates relatives, with all the rights and obligations that usually entails. Marriage bonds certainly have much to do with facilitating other kinds of relationships.

But what if people have a rule that a man can marry only a cross cousin on the mother's side, the mother's brother's daughter—or to put it another way, that a woman can marry only her father's sister's son? In that case, Levi-Strauss pointed out, there would be no direct reciprocity between clans.

A woman of Red Rock clan, for example, could marry a man of Cold Springs clan, and so could her sister. But the Cold Springs man's sister could not marry a Red Rock man. She would have to marry a man of the Mud Flats clan, or whatever.

The reason is that marriage to the cross cousin on the mother's side (from a male point of view) or the father's side (from a female perspective) leads to a one-directional circulating system. We could visualize this circulation as clockwise or counterclockwise, depending on whether one adopts the female or male perspective. In either case, the key aspect is that the direction never reverses. It does not allow for direct reciprocity between pairs of clans. Sooner or later, presumably, everyone has a chance to get married, but only to the extent that the marriage system involves all descent groups. Women from clan A marry men from clan B. Women from clan B marry men from clan C, and so on.

From a structural perspective, Levi-Strauss argued, this type of system has major advantages over a system in which pairs of clans can marry one another endlessly. With marriage in which a man can marry only his mother's brother's daughter but not his father's sister's daughter—which is sometimes called an **asymmetric marriage system** because it does not involve balanced reciprocity between pairs of clans—all descent groups must take part in a system that requires society-wide linkages. For this reason, such a system is also referred to as "generalized exhange."

But suppose the rules shift to the other direction. Suppose a woman can marry her mother's brother's son but not the father's sister's son; and a man, by the same token, can marry only his father's sister's daughter but not the mother's brother's daughter? It would seem obvious that the system would work the same way, in the opposite direction.

Not exactly. As Levi-Strauss pointed out, with this marriage rule the movement of men or women from one group to another would indeed be one-directional for a generation. In the next generation, however, the direction of marriage from one group to the next would reverse. In the following generation it would reverse again. The bottom line is that even though this type of marriage resembles an asymmetric or generalized exchange system in one phase, in the long run it has about the same effect as systems that allow marriage with either cross cousin. Eventually, direct reciprocity occurs. Men of clan A marry women of clan B. Then women of clan A marry men from clan B. The only difference is that the reciprocity takes two generations to work out. Some anthropologists have referred to this as a **delayed exchange** system (1969a).

A major debate ensued among some anthropologists over Levi-Strauss's assertions regarding the relative merits and frequencies of these systems among human populations. (See Homans and Schneider 1955; Needham 1962, 1964. Harris 1968 offers a summary of the debate from his own perspective.) Of more relevance here, though, is the role these marriage systems played in developing the structuralism of Levi-Strauss.

Forms of marriage, however we define "marriage," involve a tremendous array of features ranging from sexuality to economic exchanges. Levi-Strauss's structural concept focused on one major aspect of these complex phenomena: their implications for varied relationships or alliances among kin groups. Clearly this is not all there is to know about marriage in any society. The American entertainment industry alone has produced a ponderous volume of material on other aspects of this complex relationship. Levi-Strauss's approach, however, identified a *core*—a basic set of structures regarding one of the important things that marriage is about in most societies.

This form of structuralism involves a quest for a certain **totality**—that is, principles that extend beyond specific or isolated phenomena and have the power to unite them with other apparently unrelated aspects of society based on features or dynamics they share. In this case it involved the simple but powerful idea of reciprocity, which one could express in numerous ways: the relationships between binary poles or communication on numerous levels. It was about *relationships*.

MODELS

This discussion about marriage has been rather abstract. That is, it took the form of summations of marriage rules that are formal and removed from *actual* marriages of specific people "on the ground." They amount to **models.** Since models of social phenomena have played such an important role in these discussions, it is worthwhile to consider just what the term *model* means. The term is familiar, but like many familiar terms, it has numerous meanings. Basically, a model is a configuration expressing the relationships that characterize some entity.

Many children have built or played with model airplanes, ships, rockets, or race cars. How do we recognize what these models represent? We do not require that a model car be the same size as a real car, or do the same things, or even that it consist of the same materials. Any of them may be true, but they are not necessary. With enough skill or talent, one could make a model car out of toothpicks or mud.

Usually, though, models "look like" what they represent. Why? Because their *proportions* approximate the real thing. The component aspects bear at least a minimal resemblance to the parts of the "real thing," but perhaps more important, they stand in roughly the same relationship to one another as equivalent aspects do in the subject of the model. A model airplane usually has wings. It is not shaped like a basketball or a stepladder.

We also use the term *model* with regard to the fashion industry. In this case, the sense of "model" includes a participatory aspect that does not involve constructing a model of the apparel itself. The actual apparel is on full display. The model is intended to convey a relationship between the clothing and the wearer—what the clothing would look like in use. Generally, a person models clothing not to imitate the way it has looked on some other person, but to suggest what it *would* look like if the potential buyer were to purchase it and wear it. As we know, that suggestion may not always be accurate. A model in this case (and we might more accurately refer to such a person as a "modeler") is still representing a *version* of reality, however unrealistic or unrealized that version may be.

The issue of models presents serious problems in the analysis of human phenomena. By its nature a model is distinct from the social reality it supposedly represents. And being distinct from that reality, it leaves out a great deal of complex detail. The decision as to what features are more or less significant, ultimately, is a matter of the model builder's judgment.

Levi-Strauss grappled with the problem of social models by distinguishing two types, which he referred to as **mechanical models** and **statistical models** (Levi-Strauss 1953). *Mechanical models* express the essential mechanisms, the structure, or the social forms—the rules that apply. The marriage systems we discussed above are mechanical models. *Statistical models* are expressions of actual behavior. Rather than focusing on the rules and stipulations people are supposed to observe in choosing marriage partners, a statistical model focuses on who actually married whom, on a collective scale. How many marriages of various forms actually take place?

Models of both types answer different kinds of questions. We might assume that mechanical models are a more accurate reflection of structure. On the other hand, structure should also show up in what people actually *do*, should it not?

This brings us to another problem. In many societies—perhaps most societies—the difference between the general rules for behavior and the actual behavior of real people may be fairly wide. Even if everyone agrees that a woman should marry her father's sister's son, how many women actually do? Even if everybody agrees on the rules, what does it mean if hardly anyone follows them? In the case of such disparity between ideal rules and real behavior, the mechanical and statistical models will disagree. Which of them should have more weight?

This controversy has never been totally resolved. People say certain things, but they do other things. The relationship between the two is a fascinating and important area of inquiry, but not one that we can easily resolve without examing particular cases.

This debate did, however, have major implications for the concept of structure. If we choose to embrace a "strong" view of structure, we will tend to emphasize the consensus regarding rules and patterns. This also, we might recall, has much in common with the *dualist* view of human life: that behind the observed reality, a deeper reality (or deeper structure) exists. From a *monist* perspective, though, the behavior of people should take priority. Their versions (or the anthropologist's) of what the ideal situation should be, what the rules say, or what the "custom" is drops to a secondary level of importance compared to what they actually do.

We can imagine many reasons why behavior does not conform to, or even approximate, ideal models. An obvious one might be that the society has changed and that customs or rules that people once observed no longer have much power.

Another reason, however—one that is compatible with Levi-Strauss's view of the subconscious aspect of structure—might be that overt rules or customs may serve to *disguise* actual structures, particularly those that involve uncomfortable contradictions or power disparities. This issue remains unresolved, but it encompasses some important questions.

Despite these sorts of uncertainties, marriage systems do have some anchor in observed phenomena. Much of Levi-Straussian structural inquiry during the past few decades, though, has focused more on symbolism, and particularly on the study of mythology (1969b, 1973). Generally this study has involved a sense of totality in which the symbolism of myth merges with or confronts the social order.

STRUCTURE AND POLLUTION

We noted in the last chapter that Mary Douglas attempted to show that certain aspects of social structure—particularly the rigid or permeable nature of boundaries—tend to be projected to symbolic connotations of the human body. This appeared in attitudes regarding matter that either went into or came out of the body. In general, one could say that attitudes in societies with strictly defined social boundaries tend to be relatively "up tight" regarding bodily exuviae (Douglas 1966).

Douglas developed this idea of pollution much farther with regard to the social and cultural categories that all societies develop to grapple with, clarify, and simplify aspects of reality. It is important to remember that nature, or "reality," does not autonomously fall into evident prearranged categories. Such classifications become obvious only when they become part of the received cultural wisdom.

A glance at the variety of categories that various populations utilize provides ample evidence of this. We could imagine a category of "things that fly," for example, which would include birds, but also bats, and some insects. We have the example of the Apache and Navajo category of "things that move by themselves," which includes animals such as horses and also, early in the twentieth century, came to include cars. In our own cultural tradition, we have the example of "things that swim" that once included whales. But our present category of "things with warm blood that produce milk for their young," which separates whales from fish, is another possible way of doing it.

The issue of *folk taxonomies*, the ways in which various populations have constructed such categories, stimulated a flurry of studies and publications in the 1960s and 1970s (see, for example, Conklin 1955; Berlin and Kay 1969; Frake 1961, 1962). The point here, however, is that variable as the criteria for these categories may be, it seems to be a universal human characteristic to classify phenomena into general categories in one way of another in order to deal with an otherwise chaotic reality (see also Durkheim and Mauss 1970 [orig. 1903]).

Douglas examined some of the structural implications of these categories. One aspect of such groupings is that they tend to be imperfect reflections of nature. Whatever the criteria for classification, anomalies abound. One need only think of the strange little duck-billed platypus. We classify it as a mammal, since it has fur and warm blood and produces milk for its young; but it lays eggs, and it does not excrete milk through distinct nipples. We also have the echidna—a mammal that has scales. Such anomalies, things that seem to fall outside normal classification, often have an aura surrounding them. They may be associated with revulsion and/or pollution. On the other hand, they may be considered especially sacred, with a power that derives from their position "outside the system." In many cases the attitudes surrounding them involve a combination of both.

These anomalies are reminiscent of the quality of Turner's "liminality," which we discussed in the last chapter. In some societies hermaphrodites, who possess some of the overt genital characteristics of both males and females, or transvestites may have this special quality. In Native American buffalo-hunting groups on the Plains during the nineteenth century, the *berdache*, a man who adopted the clothing and socioeconomic role of a woman, often received great respect. We also have the examples of transvestite shamans in some Siberian groups. Transsexual *hijras* of India have power to bless infants. They can also curse entire families who refuse to allow them to perform the infant blessing ceremonies (Nanda 1999).

We might see such anomalous statuses as "anti-structural" in the sense that they defy conventional categories. In this respect they play into larger aspects of pollution and sacredness that extend into practices beyond the level of classification itself. They also underscore the importance of the structural categories, in a sense, by endangering them.

DYNAMIC STRUCTURES

As we noted earlier, most of the approaches we have discussed to this point give little attention to change. Radcliffe-Brown was primarily interested in how social structures are able to maintain themselves, rather than how they change. For Radcliffe-Brown, whatever laws of change might exist were secondary to laws of continuity (see Kuper 1983:54). Claude Levi-Strauss's attention to underlying structures did not preclude cultural dynamics, but he tended to regard them as relatively superficial epiphenomena over deeper realities.

A number of anthropologists in the British tradition after Radcliffe-Brown, however, paid attention to the dynamic and even volatile nature of structure itself. For some of them, this involved attention to individual actions within and against structural constraints. Edmund Leach, for example, explored the ways in which the self-interest of individuals could cause them to manipulate or even rebel against structures, to the extent that they could bring about change (see, for example, Leach 1954).

Leach's major study, *Political Systems of Highland Burma*, depicted indigenous social structures alternating between the extremes of a hierarchical state-like system (the *Shan* political system) and a relatively egalitarian system of intermarrying but essentially independent lineages (the *gumlao*) (Leach 1954). In between these phases, he described an intermediate form, the *gumsa*, in which rank disparities and differential control and access to resources develop.

Leach saw all of these phases as inherently unstable, with a tendency for each to develop into another under certain conditions. With the egalitarian *gumlao* phase, for example, some individuals and kin groups might achieve higher standing than others through strategic manipulation and/or luck, producing a *gumsa* system. The *gumsa* phase itself was inherently unstable, however, especially since it involved status and wealth disparities, and hence, conflicts of interest and the possibility of revolt. For that reason, the *gumsa* might revert to a *gumlao* arrangement. On the other hand, if power brokers were able to consolidate their positions and strengthen them, the structure could transform into the *Shan* system, in which power disparities become overt and more firmly established.

Max Gluckman also incorporated the issue of conflicting interest into his idea of structure. Gluckman made the point, however, that structural opposition in some cases may represent juxtaposition rather than overt conflict. A possible aspect might be that such opposition could, in fact, help to maintain a dynamic equilibrium of structure. A system involving separate lineages, for example, might entail a low level of sporadic conflict and personal differences, but at the level of allegiance to the chiefly authority, the juxtaposed lineages could constitute a coherent system. The chronic divisiveness among such segmentary lineages could keep larger interest groups from forming to pose a threat to the overall power structure.

The French social anthropologist Pierre Bordieu also critiqued the concept of structure as an ahistoric distortion that emphasizes formal rules and expectations at the expense of the actual behavior and choices of individuals (1990). Although Bordieu does not deny the provisional utility of recognizing such rules, they constitute only a part of the picture, perhaps merely as a background at that. Individuals operate within these expectations for their own purposes, rather in the way athletes compete within the rules of a game. The strategies and the skills with which they carry them out, for Bordieu, are of primary interest. He also makes the point that such human events occur in real, historic time as discrete events with greater reality than the timeless, abstract structures that observers may project onto them.

In a different vein, Renato Rosaldo writes of the problem of outside observers attempting to describe accurately such aspects of life as funerals.

> Neither one's ability to participate appropriately in other people's reactions nor the fact that people express their grief in culturally specific ways should be conflated with the notion that the devastatingly bereaved are merely conforming to cultural expectation. (1993:114)

STRUCTURE AND AGENCY

The interplay between the social structure and the individuals who comprise the population of the society, as we have seen, has been a concern of many theorists. Radcliffe-Brown tended to downplay the importance of individual motives and idiosyncrasies, seeing them as either shaped by social forces or all but irrelevant to the overall structure. Although Radcliffe-Brown referred to social structure as consisting of relationships between persons, his use of the term "person" rather than "individual" is important. A "person," in that sense, represents a position in society, a social status, rather than a specific human being.

Bronislaw Malinowski, who placed less stock in the idea of social structure, emphasized instead the role of the individual acting in his or her own self-interest as the crucial dynamic in understanding the way a given society works. Edmund Leach and Max Gluckman took up this perspective, working with the concept of structure but trying to reconcile it with what they saw as the crucial factor of human choice and strategy. We have discussed the work of Turner, Bordieu, and others in this regard earlier.

Fundamentally, though, the relationship of the individual to society has remained one of the most difficult problems in the social sciences. People live in a social realm that they did not create, but it seems obvious that society is a creation of human beings. On the other hand, there are few cases, if any, in which a committee has sat down to devise a social system and then successfully implemented it. Did society, then, spring spontaneously from human aggregations without people having control over it? Once begun, does society, as Durkheim asserted, act according to laws of its own, beyond the power of human will to deflect it? To what extent is human will, in fact, molded by social forces?

Anthony Giddens addresses this issue by asserting:

> We are all the authors of our own actions, no matter whether there be influences which affect us which we do not fully understand, or whether there be consequences of our activities which we do not in any way anticipate. (1995:9–10)

Perhaps a crucial element in this, as Marx pointed out, is history. People are born into a pre-existing social context. They need to learn to survive on its terms, even if they eventually manage—inadvertently or purposefully—to effect changes in it, or in some cases, to prevent changes from occurring, vigorously defending or clinging to the status quo in the face of "changing times."

The dynamic relationship between society and its individual members is in little doubt, even if one disputes the very idea of social structure, as some phenomenologists would. The nature of that relationship and the causal factors acting in either direction will no doubt remain a live question for the foreseeable future.

STRUCTURE AND POWER

Most of the theorists dealing with the concept of structure, even those who have considered ways in which rebelliousness or creativity have threatened its stability, have tended to view society as a coherent whole. Some, however, have addressed aspects of structural relationships that differentiate segments of the population within a broader social system. Often this differentiation entails differences in power inherent in, and maintained by, structured relationships. Edmund Leach, for example, has held that "social structure . . . consists of a set of ideas about the distribution of power between persons and groups of persons" (1954:5).

When it comes to power disparities, what better place to start than with Karl Marx? As we discussed in the chapter on evolution, Marx and Engels saw the model of production as a determinant of social arrangements or relations of production that involved structured relationships of inequality. It is especially significant that Marx did not assume that these were the conscious designs of conspiratorial bullies to exploit the lower classes. Such bullies might exist, but the structure of exploitation would continue to work even without them. Moreover, the lack of the workers' full understanding of their situation permits the structure to remain in place. The relations of production exist as a structured relationship, albeit invisible, beyond human choice.

Many theorists have directed their attention to peasantry, another form of structural differentiation that exists, even now, in many parts of the world. It has been said that most of the people who have ever lived have been peasants. Whether or not this is true, there is no doubt that peasantry has been an important part of the human experience, one that anthropologists largely ignored until the 1950s.

Most of the societies of interest to anthropologists up to that time had been small, organized on the basis of kinship, and essentially autonomous (at least until the advent of colonialism). Peasant communities, on the other hand, are rural communities that form part of a larger social and economic sphere. Generally they exist within the **hegemony** of an urban center or state system.

Eric Wolf describes peasants as "rural cultivators whose surpluses are transferred to a dominant group of rulers" (Wolf 1966:3–4). Maurice Godelier sees peasant societies as components of "class societies within which the peasantry constitutes an exploited class, dominated economically, politically and culturally by a class which no longer participate directly in production" (1977:31).

For this reason, peasant communities have been characterized as *part societies*. Typically, they remain geographically distinct from urban centers. Their social and cultural domain tends to be highly localized, to the extent that Eric Wolf described some Latin American peasant communities as "closed corporate" communities (Wolf 1957). Most important, however, peasant communities stand in a differential power relationship to the administrative centers.

Usually, for example, they are subject to taxation and military conscription. They may have their own internal administrative structure, but generally it is subject to the overriding power of the urban center. Yet in pre-industrial states, at least—and in areas not yet subjected to cash-cropping for the global market—the urban centers are dependent upon peasant production. Peasants are partially self-sufficient, producing for their own consumption and selling the surplus, if any, in urban markets in order to buy commodities they cannot produce themselves.

Generally this peasant-urban relationship involves "culture brokers" of some sort, typically priests or schoolteachers from the urban areas or traders who travel back and forth. In general, however, the peasant community's best defense against the oppressive relationship with the more powerful urban center is isolation and the maintenance of various barriers to outsiders.

Urban dwellers in almost any part of the world tend to look down on peasants as unsophisticated bumpkins. This is often the case, even when the urban dwellers themselves are former peasants. Peasants, perhaps awed by many of the glamorous aspects of the city, may tend to accept their lower status and intimidating aspects of the power center. Their likely strategy involves a posture of humility and gratitude toward their urban benefactors—whatever their deeper feelings may be.

The situation is inherently volatile, however. Eric Wolf (1969) and Anton Blok (1989) produced studies of historic peasant rebellions, ranging from the Mexican Revolution to the Vietnam War. From the perspective of structure, however, peasant studies became an important arena for exploring the dynamics of power disposition within broader social systems. They also led to closer studies of the localized structures that develop within these communities, at least partially in adaptation to the wider context.

Many studies have focused on some of the purported internal aspects of peasant communities. Robert Redfield, in his *Folk Culture of Yucatan* and his earlier study of the Mexican community he called Tepoztlan, tended to romanticize the internal harmony of life in the small folk community (1941, 1930). Oscar Lewis, revisiting Tepoztlan some years later, drew very different conclusions. Lewis found far more tension and aggression than Redfield had described—another example, perhaps, of the problem of ethnographic perception and interpretation. George Foster developed the idea of the **"image of limited good,"** which attributed a competitive, "zero-sum game" ethic in peasant communities, a sense that one person's good luck was another person's misfortune, that was conducive to envy and accusations of witchcraft (1965).

Studies of peasant communities reached their greatest florescence from the 1960s to the 1970s. Many works dealt with **leveling mechanisms**—practices and patterns that operate to enforce economic egalitarianism and prevent the internal development of individual power disparities. They might include ridicule and gossip, bilateral kinship (which extends kin ties broadly and horizontally and inhibits the growth of divisive lineages that could accumulate disproportionate power), beliefs in witchcraft that act to discourage people from arousing envy, and the "cargo" system through which a series of different people were obliged to sponsor expensive community fiestas that depleted their own wealth and dispersed resources throughout the community.

Some writers have predicted that peasantry is on the verge of disappearing as a way of life, as transnational firms acquire rural areas to produce cash crops, and former peasants become wage laborers, either on their own former lands or in cities. As yet, however, this predicted transition has not occurred universally, although in some cases former peasants have turned to growing cash crops of their own for the international drug market. In many such cases, they have become victims of a still greater power disparity: the so-called "War on Drugs."

In several parts of the world, peasant communities now find themselves caught between paramilitary or guerilla revolutionary forces and government troops, both of which can be deadly. The process of globalization for such populations has sometimes been catastrophic. Oppressive national regimes often have received financial and military support from such governments as the United States, with the rationalization of the need to interrupt drug production, especially coca and opium poppies used in the production of heroin. At the same time, these "First World" countries comprise the primary market for such products.

These issues underscore the fact that to understand crucial aspects of the lives of people in most communities, however remote they may seem, it is essential to consider their relationship with the range of forces that impinge on them within the wider global arena. Eric Wolf made this point forcefully in his book *Europe and the People without History* (1982). In this work he took anthropologists to task for a number of reasons. One was the historic trend toward focusing on the small community or population as if it were an isolated entity, ignoring broader relationships and power structures. He examined the African slave trade, the fur trade in North America, and other cases to demonstrate that many so-called "traditional" societies were products of such global interactions.

Wolf also took issue with the trend in the social sciences away from a comprehensive "political economy" approach toward a compartmentalization of disciplines. Many fields—including economics, sociology, and anthropology—came to focus on the maintenance of orderly relationships, in the process underplaying conflicts, contradictions, and the cross-cutting influences among these various realms. The emphasis tended to be on economic distribution and exchange (or how everyone gets what he or she needs) rather than on production, which may be rife with inequality, or on social order rather than internal conflicts of interest. Wolf advocated a Marxist approach to global relationships between states and indigenous peoples, with attention to the development of power disparities, exploitative relationships, and their consequences.

Wolf built upon the ideas of other theorists outside anthropology. Beginning in the 1950s, for example, Andre Gunder Frank developed what has come to be known as "dependency theory" (1972). Frank's model poses a direct challenge to older ideas of underdevelopment and modernization, which attribute the poverty of "Third World" countries to their internal deficiencies.

While "underdevelopment" models tend to focus primarily on economic indicators, "modernization" implies more inclusive cultural and social aspects of communities—"a state of mind"—expectation of progress, propensity to growth, readiness to adapt oneself to change (Lerner 1964:iix). In this view, such indigenous patterns as extended family households, corporate landholdings, and resource distribution are archaic obstacles to progress. There is a tendency for theorists with this perspective to attribute economic deprivation to "traditional" customs (see also Perry 1996:33).

In many respects this perspective is reminiscent of the older models of unilinear evolution that posited differential stages of development. Generally, underdevelopment models favor the achievement of capitalism as the primary indicator of progress. Poverty, in this view, results from the insufficient development of capitalistic institutions.

Frank challenged the concept that "First World" nations' contributions to "Third World" countries help them to improve their situations (1972, 1975). He pointed out that in times when such investments have been interrupted, as during major wars, the economic situations of poorer countries actually improved. This contradicted the conventional view, accepted by many economists and other political scientists, that wealth had been flowing from richer nations to poorer ones. Frank argued that the opposite had been the case. Richer countries had been extracting wealth from poorer ones, *creating* underdevelopment in the process.

Frank referred to the richer nations as "metropolises"—centers of wealth and power where the ownership of mines, factories, and plantations resided. At the other end, he referred to the poorer areas where raw materials are extracted as "satellites."

As a hypothetical example, let us suppose that, at the outset, people in a Latin American peasant community grow crops on their own land for their own use and sell the surplus in local markets. Then, let us suppose that a mining company based in a metropolitan area acquires their land; this could be through purchase, outright appropriation, or a combination of both. In many parts of the world small landholders have lost their farms through various methods of coercion.

The mining company has the wealth to set up an operation in the region, and the local people who once grew crops become mine workers for wages. The mining company is in a position to secure their labor for a low cost, although it might seem adequate in the local region, particularly since the workers have lost their alternative means of subsistence. From the perspective of the mining company, however, the cost of labor is small compared to the value of the raw materials they acquire.

The raw materials end up in the metropolis, where they are converted into commodities that the local miners would have been unable to produce themselves. Although one could say that the local populations had once been in possession of the raw materials and, in a sense, "owned" them, they derive little value from their extraction, even though they themselves contribute the labor in the process. The wages they receive become necessary for them to buy the food they once produced for themselves. Ironically, they may end up on the position of having to buy the commodities made from their own raw materials—if they can afford them. They become dependent upon their wages, and the wealth from their region flows to the metropolis.

This model, in addition to being based on a variety of actual situations, derives many insights from Marx. The mine owners (they could just as well be owners of coffee or tea plantations, or clothing or furniture factories) own the means of production. The local people, having lost their lands, have nothing to sell but their labor. Frank notes that the structure of this exploitative relationship is not susceptible to reform, largely because of the great disparity in power—including the ability to use force—that the metropolitan interests and their local representatives enjoy. Like Marx, Frank asserts that change can occur only through revolution to break the existing structure.

A somewhat related perspective appears in the work of Immanuel Wallerstein, who developed the concept of **World Systems Theory** (1974, 1984). In Wallerstein's view, the beginning of European colonial expansion in the 1500s led eventually to a global "division of labor" between what he calls "core" and "periphery." Like Frank, Wallerstein focuses on the appropriation and flow of wealth from peripheral areas to centers of power (see also Perry 1996:35–37).

Both of these models and others that they have inspired mark a distinct alternative to the nineteenth-century unilineal evolutionist views that have found their way into modern economic theory and public policy. A crucial aspect is that Frank's and Wallerstein's views pin the causes of Third World poverty on the extractors and beneficiaries of wealth rather than on their victims. It is worth noting, perhaps, that these views seem to have had little impact on policy makers, who continue to place the onus of "underdevelopment" on local inadequacies.

Neither Frank nor Wallerstein are anthropologists, despite the influence they have had on anthropological thinking. One aspect of their approaches that many anthropologists find troublesome, however, is their emphasis on structural relationships at the expense of attention to culture, or even to the specifics of the lives of people who have experienced the impact of these exploitative phenomena. Their principles would seem to apply equally, whether in Latin America or Indonesia. For many anthropologists, the details and nuances of indigenous responses and strategies remain an important, and perhaps a differentiating, aspect of this process.

POST-STRUCTURALISM

Whether it is possible or valid to explain culture and society as coherent phenomena has long been subject to question. For many centuries, thinkers have worked under the assumption that this coherence exists, whether its basis has been divine purpose or natural law. Yet most scholarship has been a matter of *interpreting* evidence rather than simply describing clear and unambiguous information. Because of this need to interpret rather than merely to describe, some scholars question the possibility that evidence of any sort can ever lead to unequivocal conclusions.

There is little doubt that the models of Levi-Strauss and other structuralists have been astute, creative, and perhaps even ingenious in some cases. But are they accurate reflections of human realities? And for that matter, what do concepts of "accuracy" and "truth" mean when they arise from the perceptions of human beings with their own agendas, whether conscious or not?

We have noted that with regard to some of the earlier uses of structure, a major point was to show the orderliness of society. Not that scholars such as Durkheim or Radcliffe-Brown were unaware of social conflict, any more than a physiologist studying the normal workings of the human body is unaware that disease occurs. Their structural models were involved in analyzing how society works, albeit under ideal conditions. Many of Radcliffe-Brown's analyses, in fact, addressed ways in which social institutions could forestall or resolve conflict. (See, for example, his 1924 work on the problem of the rights of a son over his mother's brother in South Africa.)

It may seem ironic that some of the most energetic challenges to the views of structure that Levi-Strauss's work represents came from French intellectuals. French structuralists such as Levi-Strauss did not deal with the concept of social structure as an overall organic model to the same extent that Radcliffe-Brown and others did. Levi-Strauss did, however, expend a great deal of effort on the ways in which structure shapes relationships, and in his studies of mythology in particular, the ways in which structure resolves contradictions on a symbolic plane. Importantly, Levi-Strauss saw structure pervading far more aspects of human life than the British structuralists did.

The reaction to this perspective began on more than one front. As we have noted, some scholars in the 1960s took exception to Radcliffe-Brown's overly elegant models that suggested, and perhaps overemphasized, social equilibrium. Real life, as everyone knows, is messier than that.

The reaction to French structruralism in the 1970s was a bit more contentious, possibly because by that time Radcliffe-Brown's version of structuralism was already out of fashion. Levi-Straussian structuralism, however, remained extremely influential. Among the general implications of structuralism, as Levi-Strauss presented it, was the power of structure to generate and to account for multiple levels of social life. To structuralists, this insight enhanced our ability to understand the complexities of society and culture. To critics who became known as "post-structuralists," though, such far-reaching models were suspect. To them, this sense of total comprehension implied a model of comprehensive control, perhaps even totalitarianism.

To many American anthropologists, this critique—largely from French intellectuals in literary fields rather than the social sciences—was difficult to comprehend. Its roots, some have suggested, go back to the Cartesian schooling that most French scholars had received early in their careers and against which many of them were happy to rebel. One aspect of Decartes's thought (*cognito ergo sum*—"I think, therefore I am") emphasized a linkage between thought and reality—that awareness proves the existence of the thinker, and in fact, of reality itself (Descartes 1960). In the view of many post-structuralists, this linkage was problematic. Some, indeed, argued that perception is capricious, and reality itself is subject to question.

Some have marked the beginning of the American post-structuralist movement to the visit of literary critic Jaques Derrida to a symposium at the New School for Social Research in the 1970s. According to legend, Derrida upon his arrival announced that structure was dead; the discourse was now all about relationships.

If he said any such thing, of course, it would suggest a deep misunderstanding of structure as most scholars had used the concept for many years. As we noted at the beginning of this chapter, structure has always been about relationships rather than about components as such. In this case, however, even the reality of the components themselves fell under skeptical challenge.

But the new perspective went far beyond that. A general sense arose that the concept of structure, with the validity of explanation for reality that it seemed to claim, was not only misleading but pernicious. To some it carried the unsavory aroma of control, the extension of power through privileged explanation.

Post-structuralism in the 1970s involved more than moving beyond structuralism, which the prefix "post" might suggest. In rejecting the concept of structure, it also took on overtly political claims. Structuralism was not merely mistaken, according to these views. It was also an instrument of oppression because it imposed the observer's own reality on those being observed and described.

The alternative to this alleged imposition was the assertion, perhaps even the celebration, of arbitrariness and disorder. To those outside the movement, this post-structuralist view sometimes appeared to be an example of monism gone mad and turned upon itself. It was not merely a case of arguing that discernible events are phenomena in and of themselves, responding to no particular underlying principles. There was also skepticism about the discernibility of these events at all. Are things really as they seem? To what extent are they merely artifacts of the mind of the observer, distorted by his or her own preconceptions, biases, and illusions?

Some of the roots of this view are very deep. **Skepticism**—doubt about the validity of any assertions, propositions, or claims to explain reality—was the central principle of a particular school of thought among classical Greek philosophers. Carried to extremes, it could take the form of **solipsism,** the idea that all reality is a figment of the viewer's imagination. The post-structuralist movement also drew some insights from the work of Saussure, who had pointed out the arbitrary nature of the relationship between the symbol (signifier) and object to which it refers (the signified) (1959). We shall have occasion to discuss this more in Chapter 6 on relativism, exploring the ways in which the post-structuralist agenda developed into the broader stance of postmodernism.

Despite the political stance that some post-structuralists styled as "radical," the post-structuralist view did not lend itself to any easily-defined "school." Indeed, many post-structuralists tended to engage one another in ways that were almost as hostile as the challenges they issued to structuralists and **positivists.** As a result, once we go beyond the anti-structure of the post-structualists and the varying degrees to which they rejected the possibility of engaging reality, post-structuralism did not present a particularly coherent body of thought.

One of the major themes of post-structualism has been the skeptical reading or "deconstruction" of texts. As the French linguistic theorist Roland Barthes wrote of history and historians, history is "an inscription on the past pretending to be a likeness of it, a parade of signifiers masquerading as a collection of facts" (quoted in Evans 1999:81). One could also apply this critique to ethnography, as many have done.

Derrida's call for deconstruction of texts arose from the detachment of the statement, the text itself (at the level of Saussure's signifier), from its message or content (the level of the signified). The implications of this are powerful, especially if carried to the degree that Derrida and many of his followers would (see Derrida 1967, 1972).

The idea that one could challenge the truth or accuracy of a statement or description is probably as ancient as language itself. Deconstruction, however, does not allow such a challenge on the basis of the data, or information about society. The central point is that since language is separable from what it signifies, and meaning depends on context, the meaning of any statement is essentially free-floating. There is no fundamental, stable association between signified and signifier. That being the case, there is no way to establish an inherent meaning in a text. The problem is not whether a statement is "true," because no statement can be true in an absolute sense.

This ambiguity invites creative play with any text, seeking various meanings and connotations for the signifiers; but it precludes the possibility of ever arriving at the "right" one. Derrida recognizes that in examining and challenging the conventional assumptions and concepts of Western culture that are associated with, or embedded in, a text, one has no choice but to employ concepts of a similar sort that are every bit as subject to question.

This view fascinated some anthropologists and annoyed others. At one level, the idea that our cultural lenses affect all of our perceptions was old news. But at another level, the implications for ethnography were staggering. From this perspective, the accuracy of cultural description was no longer an available question, if its pursuit meant matching the text to the "facts" it purported to describe. The game was all within the level of the text itself and what one could make of it, while the communities studied tended to fade into the background.

Although this view arose from the insights of Saussure, it probably took Saussure's ideas far beyond his intentions. While Saussure had pointed out the arbitrary relationship of the sound of words and their meanings, Derrida and others essentially denied that signifiers and signified had any consistent relationship at all. Meaning is ephemeral; language is "an infinite play of signification" without any particular grounding in the real world (quoted from Evans 1999:82). In this view, any "text" is really a matter of unanchored "discourse"—free-floating verbiage that has little to do with reality. Any historical or ethnographic account, then, has nothing to do with facts except possibly to distort them. Any text is merely a story, and no story is especially privileged. One is as good, or as invalid, as any other.

Clearly this position had devastating implications for any hope to understand the human experience. It discredited the entire concept of fieldwork and cultural analysis. In the post-structuralist view, there was no reason to differentiate the careful work of a twentieth-century field anthropologist from the speculative generalizations of a nineteenth-century armchair scholar—or from a bad novel, for that matter.

The posture of exposing the allegedly oppressive nature of pre-poststructural analysis tended to remain relatively abstract. Unlike much that had gone before, post-structuralism offered little in the way of description or analysis of particular cases or examples of human realities.

Michel Foucault, trained as a historian and one of the major figures of the post-structuralist movement, wrote extensively about the oppressive role of the state in Europe (see, for example, Foucault 1972). He challenged the idea that history consists of continuities and cumulative trends. History, Foucault argued, is discontinuous. Like speech or Saussure's *parole*, human affairs exist in the moment—"like a face drawn in the sand at the edge of the sea" (1973:387). For that reason, he rejected the concept of a "history of ideas." Ideas, he asserted, arise in the present. History is viewed according to present perceptions.

As an example of this historical disjuncture, Foucault examined the concept of madness. In the Middle Ages, he asserted, "madmen" wandered about, immersed in the social milieu. They were viewed with amusement, apprehension, and in some cases even as sources of wisdom, insight, and truth—but still a part of society. In the seventeenth and eighteenth centuries, the value of "reason" made such "unreasoning" individuals unacceptable. They became invisible, expelled from society and imprisoned. By the nineteenth century, madness came to be viewed as a medical condition. Asylums rather than prisons became the approved method of dealing with insanity (1976).

Foucault's point was not that one phase led inexorably to the next. Quite the contrary, he emphasized the apparent lack of continuity among these phases. Each way of dealing with madness and defining it reflected other social and cultural conditions of the times. With the overthrow of the French monarchy in the French Revolution, for example, human rights came to the forefront as a major public concern, and asylums, with their therapeutic rationale, took the place that prisons formerly held.

Foucault's views had important implications for anthropology. His point that history is constantly rewritten according to the perspectives of the historian could just as well apply to ethnography. This insight was troubling for those who hoped that some objective reality lay beneath cultural description. It did, however, offer a useful reminder that the concerns of the historical moment certainly affect the observer's judgment of which data are most significant or relevant, which questions are most interesting, and which interpretations are most convincing (or perhaps, satisfying). We might look at the belated attention to gender issues and women's lives in anthropology after the civil rights and women's rights movements in the 1960s as one example. Perhaps the impact of post-structuralism itself on anthropology after the mid 1980s is another.

Some historians have been critical of Foucault's historical work. Richard Evans, for example, observes that if history has to do with specific human actions and events in certain times and places, Foucault's work has contained little history (Evans 1999:137, 189, 222). It seems likely that such a critique would not trouble Foucault who, if he followed his own model, redefined history according to his own perspectives.

The post-structuralist position had important consequences for anthropology, however. If any attempts to depict reality are not only suspect but perhaps even reprehensible, how can one add to the body of information available for study? If no underlying principles or structures exist, the attempt to analyze them in any scientific way is absurd. If information is not trustworthy, any attempt to draw conclusions from it is pointless. The post-structuralist position implied a derailing of the intellectual developments in the social sciences of the past couple of centuries. It seemed to preclude any significant addition to our understanding of the human experience, except to expose and condemn the errors and misdeeds of the scholars of the past.

But if and when those enemies are vanquished, what comes next? After cultural description, structural principles, and other past sins have been expiated, what to do? One can always continue by extending the "search and destroy" mission to other realms, as we shall see in Chapter 6 on relativism. One can also scrutinize and attack other post-structuralists—a practice that offered both entertainment and an academic growth industry for a couple of decades beginning in the 1970s.

In general these ideas were slow to make their way from literary criticism into anthropological thinking, despite the role of Levi-Strauss as a prime post-structuralist target. Indeed, some anthropologists found the iconoclasm of Foucault and other post-structuralists provocative and appealing. Despite the stature of Levi-Strauss in Europe and America, not all anthropologists considered themselves structuralists. The critique of structuralism, in a sense, was not their fight.

At another level, many anthropologists had long since had a propensity for critiquing their own culture and society. Exposure to other cultural systems and the development of respect for their complexities and other qualities had instilled a tradition of skepticism toward the tenets of the researcher's own society. Perhaps for some of these reasons, the exercise of critiquing existing power structures, whether real or not, was a congenial idea for some.

This changed a bit in the 1980s when post-structuralism spawned postmodernism and began to generate more aggressive attacks on cross-cultural studies as well as engaging in internal cultural critiques. In this case, the attacks targeted many aspects of anthropology, and in some cases anthropology as a whole. Although a few anthropologists joined the side of the post-structural critics, others reacted with growing indignation. We shall look into this in further detail in Chapter 6. (For more discussion, see Perry 2000).

FOOD FOR THOUGHT

Durkheim argued that social forces "compel individual actions and sentiments." Do you feel that our own society has some sort of structure that compels us to do things and want to do things that we otherwise would not choose to do?

Why do we feel compelled to give gifts at birthdays and holidays? Is it to establish relations? Why do we feel the need to send a card to people who send us one?

Why did post-structuralism take on a political aspect? Why would enhancing the ability to understand the complexities of society and culture be interpreted as a controlling enterprise, or even totalitarian?

What causes a group made up of individuals to act so differently as a whole than the individuals would by themselves? Is it valid analytically to separate social structure from the minds of individuals in the society?

Can an individual thought overlap into collective thought when multiple individuals share a common thought, even though it does not conform to the collective ideal?

Chapter 5

THE IDEA OF FUNCTION

The idea that customs and practices make some sort of sense, or that they are instrumental toward some positive result, has a fairly recent history, although like most of the other ideas we have discussed, rudiments of the concept of *function* have been around for centuries. In the twentieth century, however, the idea of function incorporated two aspects of particular importance: one was that function is unconscious in its origins; the other was that function as a positive factor applies to human societies in general, rather than being the particular characteristic of "advanced" civilizations.

On the first point, early travelers and writers such as Herodotus or Thucydides often observed that the customs or behavioral propensities of other groups were conscious strategies or responses to environmental conditions. They also were fond of positing relationships among aspects of customs and beliefs. Describing the Persians, Herodotus writes:

> The most disgraceful thing, in their view, is telling lies. The next most disgraceful thing is being in debt; but the main reason (among many others) for the proscription of debt is that, according to the Persians, someone who owes money is obliged to tell lies as well. (1998:63)

Ancient historians also frequently treated customs as adaptations to the circumstances in which people lived. Regarding the Egyptians, Herodotus writes:

> In keeping with the idiosyncratic climate that prevails there and the fact that their river behaves differently from any other river, almost all Egyptian customs and practices are the opposite of those of everywhere else. For instance, women go out to the town square and sell retail goods, while men stay at home and do the weaving . . . Or again, men carry loads on their heads, while women do so on their shoulders. (1998:109)

These early writers seem to have given little thought, however, to the possibility that social customs might develop as the result of social forces rather than as the result of planned policy, on the one hand, or as automatic responses to the environment, on the other.

By the early twentieth century, however, views of function depicted society itself as the generator of customs that were neither automatic biological responses to conditions nor the results of strategic planning. Somehow function was a result of social or cultural forces that humans neither guided nor, for the most part, of which they were even aware. Social forces had little to do with personal wishes or motivation except as an indirect result of such factors on a collective scale.

In anthropological thinking, there has been a tendency to link function with structure. From the perspective of Radcliffe-Brown, the intersection of various components of social structure depended upon mutually reinforcing dynamics that he defined as **functions.** In that view, the function of a custom or institution ultimately was to allow the overall social structure, the society, to exist (1935).

But does the idea of function have to be associated with structure? Not necessarily. Radcliffe-Brown's model became known as **structural functionalism,** but functionalism could take other forms as well.

FUNCTION VERSUS PURPOSE

We should be clear about the distinction between function and purpose. *Purpose* implies some intention, motivation, planning on the part of someone. As we have observed, most concepts of function among anthropologists of the twentieth century have not implied any conscious purpose.

In many cases in various societies, people *have* attempted to alter ways of doing things. They have tried to institute policies, to change political structures, and even to initiate new customs. They have succeeded occasionally, but most social institutions have not arisen in this way. As far as we know, most examples of clan organization, descent rules, marriage systems, or whatever, have developed without the directives of any committee, board of elders, or public referendum. They have developed collectively but apparently in spontaneous fashion, often as **epiphenomena** of other factors. Despite the attempts of many would-be reformers to alter the course of social processes, social institutions and customs have a habit of going their own way.

As we have noted, this remains one of the major conceptual problems in the social sciences. Although people generally do not create customs intentionally, certainly customs and institutions arise from what people do. One possibility, as we noted earlier, is that function is a consequence of social forces that somehow shape, and perhaps even compel, collective behavior. Durkheim's view of society incorporated that sort of view. Function was not a matter of what worked to the benefit of individuals in a direct sense, but what worked best for society.

People were drawn along or were compelled, usually, as we have seen, without being conscious of it. From this perspective, even though individuals might feel that they are acting according to their own choices, needs, or preferences, their very wishes and motivations are products of social forces acting on them. This was one aspect of society existing at a higher level than the individual mind. The implication, of course, was that ultimately individuals *did* benefit from being part of a healthy, smoothly running and orderly social system—but the benefits were indirect.

This left Durkheim's model open to the criticism of mysticism because it suggested some "higher mind" manipulating human affairs. Durkheim vigorously denied this and maintained that his approach was purely secular and scientific. But the image of society lurking overhead as an entity in its own right, working on its own behalf, and capable of unleashing vague but powerful social forces that were invisible except for their supposed effects, remained a bit too spooky for some.

Durkheim's insistence that these social forces are something other than mere tendencies toward economic efficiency did little to resolve these misgivings. To ascribe social forces to economic or other material factors at least would have the effect of anchoring these alleged phenomena in the "real" or material world. But Durkheim would have none of it.

Of course, one could analyze *some* aspects of any phenomenon without feeling compelled to account for *every* aspect of it. We could certainly look at customs and institutions in terms of their functions without worrying too much about what factors generated them historically. To establish that social patterns were functional *at all* was no small thing, especially in light of the view prevailing early in this century that "primitive" practices were essentially irrational and based on ignorance. To argue that they fulfilled important functions was to argue that they did make some kind of sense in objective terms.

In this view, function became a different kind of answer to the problem of origins. The old question of why people do what they do was no longer a matter of when they started doing it. Instead, one could construe origins in terms of their function. The origins of customs in this sense had to do with what these customs accomplished. They existed *because they worked*.

A possible criticism of this approach, of course, is that such a model tends to confuse cause with effect. But this was consistent with the turn away from evolution and "speculative history" that we find in the work of Durkheim, and to a more emphatic degree, in the work of Radcliffe-Brown. Evolutionary or historical beginnings were no longer meaningful or useful questions.

FUNCTION WITH AND WITHOUT STRUCTURE

The problem of a linkage between function and overall social structure remained troublesome for some. Social structure still required that we assume a highly abstract entity of some sort, however real its proponents might insist that it is. It might be one thing for Radcliffe-Brown to assert that social structure is as real as a brick wall. But we can see a brick wall or bruise a knee on it if we fail to see it, tear it down, and rebuild it. Why should the idea of function depend on postulating the reality of such an abstract entity? Perhaps it was more sensible to see function in more down-to-earth terms. This was essentially the position of **Bronislaw Malinowski.**

Malinowski was well acquainted with the evolutionary models of nineteenth-century theorists. He had been an admiring student of Sir James Frazer, one of the most eminent proponents of cultural evolution at the time. But Malinowski had an advantage that Frazer never had. Malinowski lived for extended periods of time among the sorts of people that Frazer could only read about, write about, and imagine. Once again, the establishment of fieldwork as a basic research tool played a significant role in anthropological thinking.

Malinowski's time living among the people of Mailu and the Trobriand Islands of the South Pacific compelled him to confront the realities of life in these societies. Here were people with complex customs and practices that initially appeared inexplicable, and perhaps even irrational, to the outsider. But these were also human beings faced with fundamental problems of living. Like everyone else, they needed food and shelter. They needed to find ways of living together, to resolve conflicts, to regulate access to resources, to reproduce, and to help their children survive. These problems of living were basic, and they were problems common to all human beings. The answer to why people do what they do, Malinowski reasoned, must lie in their need to meet these basic human needs (1944).

This view depicted a very different actor from the "socially indoctrinated" member of society that Durkheim had in mind. Radcliffe-Brown, strongly influenced by Durkheim's ideas, saw persons primarily as social actors, but they were anonymous and relatively interchangeable. Malinowski's individual was far more calculating, conscious of self-interests that might conflict with social norms, and given to strategic manipulation, albeit usually

Bronislaw Malinowski (1884–1942)

within the rules. Such an individual was not merely an automaton carrying out social imperatives.

From this perspective, it seemed erroneous to consider people in small non-Western societies irrational or ignorant. In Malinowski's field experience, it was clear to him that their survival required intricate knowledge and calculated effort. Nor did it seem necessary to postulate some overall social forces or social structures as work. The key factors were much closer to ground level. No successful population could survive on the basis of irrational customs and practices. Not only would such practices be ineffective, but customs require effort and energy for people to perpetuate them over generations. Unless they have some value to balance this cost, Malinowski reasoned, they would eventually disappear.

This view stands in significant contrast with Tylor's concept of "cultural survivals." As we remember, Tylor considered many customs to be irrational carryovers from earlier times. In Tylor's view, people often went through the motions in thoughtlessly repeating customs that had once had some value for their ancestors, but whose original use and meaning they had long since forgotten. For Malinowski this view made little sense. Present customs would not have *remained* as customs unless they served some function. It was the task of the observer to discover just what these functions might be.

Malinowski's way of addressing this question did not require imagining some overall structure, but rather focusing on the set of day-to-day needs that face all human beings. We could say that while Radcliffe-Brown saw customs and looked upward at an abstract social structure, Malinowski saw these same customs and looked downward at the individuals who perpetuated them.

RATIONAL OR IRRATIONAL MAGIC

One of the more provocative questions associated with the rationality or irrationality of customs was the use of magic. For evolutionists such as Frazer, magical practices arose from ignorance, from mistaken ideas of cause and effect. But Malinowski had the chance to observe Trobriand Islanders' use of magic first-hand and to discuss their ideas about it with them (see Malinowski; 1948).

It became clear that Trobrianders did not rely primarily on magic to achieve their needs. When it came to gardening, for example, the Trobriand Islanders were highly skilled and knowledgeable in ways that Europeans would recognize. They were concerned about soil quality. They selected their seeds and cuttings carefully. They knew the proper seasons for planting. In these important respects, they employed methods that were as scientific as their experience and technology allowed.

Once they had employed this knowledge and expended their efforts, though, they recognized that certain factors were beyond their control. Like European farmers, they could not control the amount of rainfall. Although they had learned to expect when conditions would be optimal, they had no way to prevent vagaries in the weather or other factors that could affect the outcome of their labors and planning. It was at this juncture, Malinowski argued, that magical practice came in (Malinowski 1935, 1948).

In the view of Malinowski and other Europeans, magic could not ensure good crops. But among the Trobrianders, it could fulfill a different, important function. It could help alleviate anxiety by fostering the illusion that humans could influence crucial aspects of life over which they had no physical power. It could make people feel better. It could help remove some of the stress from their lives, particularly in issues of great importance involving some element of chance.

Malinowski also used the example of fishing magic. Not surprisingly, fishing inside the coral reef, where success was fairly certain but the payoff was likely to be small, had little associated magic. Deep-water fishing in the open ocean beyond the reef was fraught with various dangers, but it also afforded greater possibilities. As a consequence, deep-water fishing had a far more elaborate body of magic surrounding it.

Malinowski extended these principles to general aspects of life far beyond the Trobriands. His view of function incorporated consideration of human psychological as well as physical needs. For this reason Malinowski's approach is sometimes referred to as **psychological functionalism.**

MIND AND MATTER

The most important distinguishing aspect of Malinowski's functionalism was its grounding in the day-to-day needs of human existence. As we have seen, function for him involved "nuts and bolts" issues like food-getting and reproduction, rather than the maintenance of an abstract social structure or the workings of social forces. Even when Malinowski dealt with issues such as conflict resolution and the rules governing human interaction, he tended to depict them as ways of regularizing and supporting the lives of real people, rather than dynamics supporting the society as such. In that sense one could say that Malinowski's work tended to be far more *monist* than Radcliffe-Brown's.

Although this kind of functionalism arose from basic facts of human life, however, Malinowski stopped short of attempting to explain everything in economic or material terms. He recognized value systems and psychological motivations, such as the quest for prestige, as driving forces in their own right. His classic analysis of the Kula ring (1922), a huge trade system in the South Pacific in which the Trobrianders participated, was largely in terms of its ritual and social significance, rather than its material payoff.

The central aspect of the Kula involved ceremonial exchanges of ritual items that were not intrinsically valuable, but which had enormous significance as heirlooms with their own histories. Later scholars pointed out that these periodic exchanges also facilitated more economically important forms of trade in items ranging from fish to wooden bowls. The islands involved in the trade had varied resources, and these exchanges were a useful and perhaps even essential means of distributing needed goods. It would be consistent with the concept of function to emphasize the utilitarian trade and to see the formal Kula exchanges as a secondary lubricant for the system.

That sort of analysis would become more frequent in later years, particularly when cultural ecology developed as a field of inquiry. For Malinowski, though, the social and psychological value of the Kula exchanges, and the ways in which participants developed strategies to enhance their own benefit, appeared to be their most significant aspect.

Despite Malinowski's differences with Radcliffe-Brown, the two scholars did share an aversion to "speculative history." Oddly enough, perhaps, Malinowski saw nothing in his view of function to discredit the general idea of cultural evolution, although he did not pursue the evolutionary question very far. In his view, the specific history of particular customs was not a useful direction of inquiry. His position went beyond the argument that we can learn little about the specific histories of groups who lack written records, and whose accounts of the past often are not chronological in the European sense but take the form of myth.

Certainly one could see many myths as aspects of the present culture, rather than mere records of the past. Often aspects of oral history—such as accounts of the places where clan ancestors arose from caves, or which clans appeared first—can function to justify the relegation of rights in the present and might have little to do in a literal sense with actual past events.

The main argument, however, rode on the implications of function, which stipulated that no custom or institution could have survived to the present unless it served some human need, however indirectly that might be. The significant question, therefore, was what a custom did—what its function was—rather than how, where, or why it originated.

This ahistoricism came to seem extreme and ultimately unacceptable to many anthropologists. On this issue, though, it is worth remembering the times in which Malinowski worked. Like all important scholars, Malinowski was not simply describing and analyzing his finds in a neutral arena. He was engaged in an implicit argument with his contemporaries, especially those who gave "primitive" cultures little credit for rationality, not with those who built upon his work half a century later. In making these arguments, Malinowski's crucial point was that customs require understanding in their own right as aspects of present life. They are not simply mindless repetitions of traditions handed down from the ancestors. These ways of living are *situationally rational*, given the circumstances and premises of the living people who practice them.

We associate the concept of function most closely with Malinowski and Radcliffe-Brown, despite the differences between them and their views of what the term entailed. The debates surrounding these two theorists, which involved not only them but their students, helped to clarify some of the distinctive ways of viewing the concept. Partly for this reason, and because Malinowski and Radcliffe-Brown became the leading anthropologists of their day in England, functionalism has long been equated with British social anthropology in the first half of the twentieth century. The notion of function, though, also played a part in American anthropology, although perhaps with less enthusiasm than in England.

FUNCTIONALISM IN AMERICAN ANTHROPOLOGY

The treatment of history was probably one of the most important differences between British and American perspectives in the first half of the twentieth century. Boas's approach to the study of cultures had always emphasized thorough and detailed gathering of information in the field, and on this point there was no significant difference between the British and Americans. Radcliffe-Brown and other structuralists did tend to ignore many aspects of culture that Americans considered important, such as art, music, and oral literature. But the Americans disagreed most strongly with both Malinowski and Radcliffe-Brown on the importance of history.

For Boas, the fundamental question of why people do what they do called for attention to their past experiences, their unique histories. For this reason, Boasian anthropology has been referred to as **historical particularism.** Among other aspects, it involved attention to the ways in which cultures in the past had influenced each other through the process of cultural **diffusion.**

As to the *function* of various customs and institutions, Boas tended to reserve judgment. Customs might well serve some basic human needs, but this remained to be demonstrated, not assumed beforehand. Cultures most likely *did make sense* in their own terms, but not necessarily maintaining some overall social structure for its own sake. As to the overall influence of "social forces," these tended to be a bit too imaginary and speculative for many Boasians.

The British, for their part, had little use for the explanatory power of diffusion. Part of this aversion probably arose from the excesses of the several "diffusionist schools" that had enjoyed some popularity early in the century. Although the diffusionist models varied, their essential theme was that ideas from "high cultures" of the past had spread throughout the rest of the world, becoming weakened and distorted in the process. In this view, so-called "primitive" societies were pale reflections of former, grander things (see, for example, Smith 1928, 1932; Perry 1923).

The Boasians had as little use for these schemes as the British did. The Americans' use of diffusion was far more modest, usually limited to demonstrable evidence of contacts among populations in restricted areas. Even Kroeber's ambitious project *Cultural and Natural Areas of Native North America* (1939) and his other works dealing with diffusion generally focused on contiguous regions and demonstrated similarities.

From Boas's work on the Pacific Coast of North America, there was little doubt that neighboring groups had influenced one another in such cultural aspects as ceremonial feasts and art forms. To view each local culture as an isolated entity in its own right would have been to ignore clear evidence and distort the realities of their heritage. For British functionalists of either the Radcliffe-Brownian or Malinowskian persuasion, though, particular histories were not especially relevant. The most important question was not how or when a society adopted a Winter Ceremonial or Sun Dance, but how such a ceremonial functioned within the present society.

THE "CONSERVATIVE" NATURE OF FUNCTIONALISM

Like the concept of structure, the idea of function developed political connotations, many of which its proponents probably never intended and, for that matter, which they probably would disavow if they were alive to hear the accusations. We noted in the last chapter that one implication was that if the customs and institutions of a society either meet a range of basic needs or work to maintain the social system, then everything in the existing society is pretty much as it should be. Either model depicts a state of stability. More important, it seems to suggest that change is bound to be detrimental.

In one sense the assertion that a given society worked well ran the danger of being exaggerated or misinterpretated as an assertion that this was the *only* way it could work. This position might seem to imply that any change would likely disrupt the lives of the people.

This, of course, was not merely an abstract question. Whether the context was colonialism in the early twentieth century or overseas "development" schemes in later decades, interference with people's lives, even with the most benign intentions, was a debatable issue. For functionalists, the assertion that indigenous societies made sense and were viable and self-sustaining could shift from an argument for non-interference and lend itself to the implication that they were not only stable, but incapable of progress on their own.

Clearly these two propositions are almost diametrically opposed. It is worth taking time to explore this example of the ways in which a rather simple assertion could have been "teased out" into several directions, rather like an intellectual taffy pull.

Talal Asad asserts that British social anthropology was so deeply involved with colonialism that the independence of former British colonies in the 1960s threatened the decline of the entire theoretical approach. He draws attention in particular to the ahistoric nature of this form of functionalism, which supposedly ignored the past colonial and precolonial circumstances of the net nations (Asad1973:13).

> We are today becoming increasingly aware of the fact that information and understanding produced by bourgeois disciplines like anthropology are acquired and used most readily by those with the greatest capacity for exploitation. (1973:16)

This certainly is a serious charge. We find many of the same issues in the collection titled *Reinventing Anthropology* in the late 1960s (Hymes 1969).

To some extent, though, it seems fair to take into account the climate of the times in which these earlier anthropologists worked, compared to that in which the later criticisms arose. (Perhaps this is a case of Foucault's claim that history is rewritten in the perspective of the present, as we discussed in the previous chapter.)

There is no doubt that there is considerable diversity of points of view among those who refer to themselves as anthropologists. We would not find it surprising that not all historians, political scientists, or economists see things the same way or hold the same political and social opinions. The idea of condemning history as a discipline on account of a few problematic historians would seem rather silly. Yet anthropology—even in the minds of some anthropologists—seems to share an odd degree of collective responsibility.

Most of the colonialism debate focused on Africa, no doubt because so many anthropologists worked in British colonies there. We could just as well look at other parts of the world, however. The Pacific probably offers better cases of colonial participation by anthropologists. One of the most prominent early ethnographers in that region, F. E. Williams, was in fact a colonial officer (see Williams 1923, 1930, 1936). Moreover, Australian colonial policy in Papua New Guinea required that patrol officers have some academic training in the ethnology of local cultures. And at the risk of getting too far off track in that direction, R. H. Codrington, who wrote an extensive early ethnographic work on Melanesia, was a missionary (1891). Since British social anthropologists in Africa have been the center of most of these debates, however, it seems appropriate to explore that area more fully.

Whatever the disagreements among functionalists may have been, they were radical in the context of their era in arguing in one way or another for the validity of indigenous systems. Taken to its logical conclusion, this position amounted to an argument for non-interference. Given the world's political realities in the 1920s through mid-century, however, non-interference was a fantasy. Colonial powers' interference with the lives of indigenous people was long established and had gone on without any particular deference to anthropologists. Indeed, as we noted in the last chapter, many colonial administrators viewed anthropologists as unnecessary annoyances, to the extent that they had to deal with them at all (see, for example, Goody 1995).

It was in this context that the anthropological concept of functionalism developed. Its main thrust, as we have said, was that these colonized peoples with complex, viable social, political, and economic systems had existed for a long time without imperial guidance or supervision. There is some irony that decades later in the post-colonial era, this argument for indigenous viability came to be construed as an assertion that these social systems were incapable of change. What had earlier been a championing of indigenous societies became, retrospectively and out of context, a denigration of them.

Just as serious, perhaps, was the criticism that these functionalists saw societies as self-contained isolates. Again, it is necessary to examine the context of inquiry. To take an example from biology, an analyst might consider in detail the physiology of a horse. Does this mean that the researcher is unaware that a horse runs, interacts with other horses, or grows old and dies? This information, or any other that a researcher might consider (Was the horse a racer? Did it pull a popcorn wagon or dive off a circus platform into a tank of water?), has varying degrees of relevance to the questions under investigation.

British functionalists were far from unaware of the interaction of indigenous societies with other groups. The impingement of outside colonial forces was a part of the daily context in which they worked. One rationale for their work, in fact, was to mollify the effects of this assault by enhancing understanding.

This effort did involve compromise, to be sure. Overturning the long-standing British national policy of colonialism was out of the question, at least in the short term. Anthropologists were not cabinet ministers or members of Parliament. They were merely academics who, at best, were viewed as respected scholars, but in some cases as innocuous eccentrics. It was in this setting that some made the argument that their findings might help in the effort to develop more enlightened administrative policies. This does not in any way, of course, change the injustices, exploitation, and atrocities associated with colonialism. Nor does it alter the fact that these anthropologists lived in a society that perpetuated such injustices.

In the same vein, Americans at the beginning of the twenty-first century were part of a society that had enslaved hundreds of thousands, colonized a significant part of the world, not the least of which included its own indigenous peoples, and benefited from the economic exploitation of much of the rest. One might argue that for the purpose of evaluating theorists, a pertinent issue is the context in which people live and the choices they make within that context.

It seems fair to point out that the British functionalist anthropologists devoted their work toward demonstrating the complexity and rationality of peoples whom most others in their society were prepared to dismiss as backward and primitive. It also seems safe to say that Radcliffe-Brown, for one, if transplanted to the contemporary American political climate, would find himself considered well to the left.

Jack Goody, in his retrospective of British social anthropology in the first half of the twentieth century, offers useful insights into this matter (1995). As Goody points out, there were one or two cases in which a colonial officer with ethnographic interests produced valuable accounts of indigenous societies in the colonies. The best known of these probably is R. S. Rattray's work on Ashanti in the 1920s in what later became Ghana (1923, 1929). Malinowski, moreover, during the 1930s and 1940s, urged his students to become involved in studies of "change" that might lead to better and more enlightened administration of colonized peoples. To some extent, no doubt, Malinowski hoped to promote the image of anthropology as a useful endeavor worthy of government funding. As Goody notes, such funding never materialized to any significant degree (1995:54–55).

Many of Malinowski's students resisted his urging to involve themselves in "practical" research. Goody reports an alleged remark that Malinowski once made—sardonically, we must assume—that anthropology could allow the appropriation of South Africans' lands "according to their own customs" (1995:74). While this story may be inaccurate, it expresses the misgivings that many anthropologists had about the entire colonial enterprise. Malinowski, in his later work, argued that European colonialism had taken far more away from Africans than it had ever given them. Evans-Pritchard, while he did his work among the Nuer at the request of the colonial government, grumbled in writing about the tendency of some colleagues to linger around "the colonial office couch" (quoted in Goody 1995:73).

Asad states that "At any rate, the general drift of anthropological understanding did not contribute a basic challenge to the unequal world represented by the colonial system" (1973:18). In practice, however, anthropologists and colonial administrators generally did not hit it off. In the grumpy words of one administrator, anthropologists "... busied themselves with enthusiasm about all the minutiae of obscure tribal and personal practices," producing reports that are "of such length that no one had time to read them and often in any case, irrelevant, by the time they became available, to the day to day business of government" (quoted in Kuper 1983:107).

Evans-Pritchard wrote that "During the fifteen years in which I worked on sociological problems in . . . [the Nuba Hills of Sudan] . . . , I was never once asked my advice on any question at all" (Kuper 1983:103–104). The American anthropologist H. G. Barnett, who studied in England for a time, wrote that "the truth is that anthropology and administrators do not, on the whole, get along well together" (Kuper 1983:113).

To a great extent, no doubt, this disagreement involved many administrators' sense of anthropologists as annoying "do-gooders" critical of administrative policies. Kuper points out another significant factor, however. Much of the later criticism of British anthropologists' role in British colonies rests on the functionalist perspective that dominated at the time. If colonial administrators had had any anthropological training before taking their posts, it had been from the perspective of unilinear evolution—and generally of the most ethnocentric kind. That, of course, had been the "dominant paradigm" early in the twentieth century, when these officers had undergone their schooling. From that perspective, the officers' perceptions of their role was that of bringing civilization, a more advanced way of life, to "primitive" people at a lower stage of evolutionary development.

The functionalist approach, as we know, was the new wave in the 1930s. This approach, which began with the premise that indigenous societies were viable, complex ways of life worthy of respect, could not have gone down well in many quarters. Indeed, the view that "native" societies had value in their own right brought into question much of the rationale for the entire colonial enterprise.

The upshot of this was that very often, even when anthropologists received an assignment to carry out a project in a particular area, they ended up exploring questions and issues that seemed most important or interesting in the field, rather than following the original line of inquiry. This could hardly have been otherwise, since a new acquaintance with a way of life that outsiders knew little about would inevitably raise areas of research interest that would have been difficult to anticipate.

By the late 1950s, as the British colonial system was beginning to break down, many anthropologists worked in support of independence movements. Even in 1940, Radcliffe-Brown submitted a proposal for research into changing political systems that could be applied to "current problems of administration leading to self-government" (Goody 1995:195). Evans-Pritchard's papers, long after his death, indicate that he deliberately understated the authority of the Nuer leopardskin chiefs in order to protect them from British colonial harassment. Goody states that "to help the independence movement was more important for [Lloyd A.] Fallers in East Africa, R. T. Smith in British Guiana, and many in West Africa, than to assist the colonial regime" (1995:195).

Jomo Kenyatta, who became the first president of Kenya, studied anthropology with Malinowski and wrote *Facing Mount Kenya*, an ethnographic history of his own people (1953). Kwame Nhrumah, first president of Ghana, Kofi A. Busia, later prime minister, and many other African figures in independence movements and new states studied anthropology at Oxford and other British universities.

During the era up to the 1960s, anthropologists were among the few scholars who were interested in carrying out work in Africa among indigenous peoples. After that period, representatives of many other disciplines, such as political science and economics, found Africa to be of great interest and traveled there in great numbers—with significant funding, in most cases. Unfortunately, many of these researchers either ignored much of the anthropological work that had been done or attempted to discredit it. But this, of course, says more about academics than about Africa.

FUNCTIONALISM AND ITS PROBLEMS

As anthropology approached the middle of the twentieth century, the relatively extreme forms of functionalism that Radcliffe-Brown and Malinowski had developed fell out of fashion in the face of accumulating criticism. At this point we can take a closer look at the far-reaching implications of the idea of functionalism in its various forms and examine some of the problems that became associated with them.

Some of the critricisms arose from within the functionalist camp itself. E. E. Evans-Pritchard had been a student of Malinowski and subsequently, after a personal falling-out, became a student of Radcliffe-Brown. Evans-Pritchard's training was thus steeped in functionalism of both major types. But his perceptions also arose from extensive and lengthy field research among the Zande of Central Africa, the Nuer of the Southern Sudan, and the Sanussi Arabs of Cyrenaica (1937, 1940, 1949). Evans-Pritchard was truly a field anthropologist. In correspondence he confessed that the field was where he felt most at home (Goody 1995:63). His theoretical approach, then, arose not only from the ideas of his mentors, but like Malinowski's, from his experience in living with a variety of peoples and the intensely personal observations he was able to make in those settings.

Among the aspects of functionalism that troubled Evans-Pritchard was the stern disavowal of history. He was acutely conscious of the extent to which long-term experience contributes to people's present lives and the power of historical trajectories in shaping them. In the same vein, he also saw no reason to ignore the intellectual and emotional aspects of human life— ideas of magic, religious concepts, explanatory principles, and so on. The study of culture and society, in Evans-Pritchard's view, should encompass the full reality of all of these issues before it could approach anything like an adequate understanding of people's lives.

Evans-Pritchard also took issue with the idea that societies are subject to social laws comparable to the laws of science. On the subject of social laws, Evans-Pritchard took the position that what functionalists and structuralists claimed to be laws were essentially banal platitudes or meaningless general-izations that did little or nothing to advance knowledge. Declining any attempt to "prove" that no laws exist, Evans-Pritchard took the position that the burden of proof lay with those who claimed that they did. It was up to those who argued for such laws, he asserted, to tell us what they are (1962).

Evans-Pritchard asserted that the thrust of the assumption that social laws govern human life tended to relegate humans to the role of automatons (1950). It ignored the important aspects of individual choice, judgment, his-tory, and experience. Anthony Giddens makes a similar criticism with regard to the tradition associated with Durkheim and which also appears in the ap-proaches of Radcliffe-Brown. Giddens charges that this position leaves "no place for a conception of the actor as a reasoning agent, capable of using knowledge in a calculated fashion so as to achieve intended outcomes" (1995:195).

Anthropology, in Evans-Pritchard's view, was not a science but a branch of history. As such, anthropology should focus on the unique aspects of cultures, including their realms of meaning as well as social relationships. To the extent that anthropology attempted to imitate the physical or natural sci-ences, it distorted human reality and stripped it down to its most simplistic elements.

We have already noted one of the positive aspects of functionalism, which was to demonstrate that human societies are more than hordes of peo-ple practicing a hodgepodege of irrational customs. In that sense, functional-ism, implicitly at least, was egalitarian in its assumptions, asserting that whatever general principles operated in some social systems operated in every social system. The details of customs might differ dramatically, but all existed because in one way or another they served a function. In that regard, no viable ongoing society was any more or less rational than any other.

A corollary to this view was the rejection of racial difference as an explanatory factor. There was no denying that profound differences exist in the lives of peoples, but the explanations for these differences lay in factors other than biology.

Beyond that, the term *function* came to subsume a number of different meanings. As we recall, Malinowski looked for functions in the ways in which customs and institutions address biological human needs. Radcliffe-Brown saw function in the extent to which these customs and institutions meet the needs of the social structure. A third meaning, which Malinowski and Radcliffe-Brown shared to some extent, was the idea of function in a mathematical sense—that is, functions interacting with and affecting other functions.

This view involved the concept of culture and society as systemic phenomena; that is, internal functions acted in conjunction, not as isolated features. Even if one stopped short of Radcliffe-Brown's view of function as an aspect of structure, there was still the idea of functions working in concert, if not total harmony, with other functions.

This involved some problems. How, for example, could one *explain* function? We could say that a ritual exchange in a particular society exists because it serves some function. But is this a useful statement about the *reason* *why* that particular ritual exists, or simply an assertion about the *result* of its existence? Is this, as we suggested earlier, a matter of confusing cause with effect? As Marshall Sahlins asserted, "Proof that a certain trait or cultural arrangement has positive economic value is not an adequate explanation of its existence or even of its presence" (1969:30). Some scholars saw this as a form of description rather than explanation, and perhaps a questionable description at that.

FUNCTION AND EXPLANATION

We should take some time at this point to consider what we mean by explanation. The term can subsume a number of positions. One way of evaluating explanatory models is to decide which is the most useful or productive. A full, accurate description of some phenomenon can sometimes pass muster as an explanation. More commonly, we think of explanation as a statement of *how* or *why* a given phenomenon came to exist. We might see an explanation as a statement that a particular situation has occurred because of particular conditions that produced it or at least stimulated its development.

More formally, we could state that a particular situation (S) resulted from a specific condition (C). To make this more satisfactory, we should be able to determine whether condition (C) *always* and *inevitably* produces situation (S). Can condition (C) in some cases give rise to some *other* situations (S1, S2, etc.)? If so, why? For that matter, can *other* conditions (C1, C2, etc.) also sometimes give rise to situation (S)? If any of these are true, then additional factors must be at work. To construct a better explanation, we would have to determine what these other factors are, what effect they have, how they might affect one another, and so on.

How can we arrive at such explanations? Since the subject of study is living, ongoing human society and culture, we cannot experiment by setting up condition (C) repeatedly and watching to see if situation (S) always results. An obvious alternative is to look at *what has happened* in order to figure out how the alleged causal processes worked in a particular case. But this would suggest historical analysis, which most functionalists disallowed. An alternative might be to look at a variety of cases in which condition (C) also is associated with situation (S).

With that strategy we have another problem. We would need to be certain that what seem to be examples of condition (C) in multiple cases actually represent identical conditions, at least with regard to their essential aspects. (And of course, determining just what those "essential aspects" are is no small problem in itself.) We would also have a comparable problem in determining that situation (S) in each case is also, in fact, identical in crucial respects to situation (S) in other cases.

On these counts, the functional approach has been vulnerable. As we recall, the rejection of historical explanation effectively ruled out the first option. Functionalists did not pursue causal processes operating through time. As to the comparative approach, the complexities of human life create major difficulties in carrying out rigorous comparisons of conditions and their results.

A ceremonial feast among Native American groups on the Pacific Coast might have significant similarities to a ceremonial feast in Papua New Guinea, but they differ in important ways as well. What is the importance of these similarities and differences—not to mention the differences in their overall cultural contexts? Are these feasts truly comparable examples of the same situation, or entirely different phenomena that happen to share a few superficial aspects in common?

Without the capacity to generate rigorous formal explanatory statements, what procedure was left to the functionalists? For the most part it was necessary to fall back on assumptions about underlying principles: A ritual exists because it serves a function. How do we know it serves a function? Because if it did not serve a function, it would not exist.

Most functional discussions were not that blatantly circular. In many cases researchers have been able to discuss functional results with some specificity. A given ritual might promote solidarity, or recirculate wealth, or reinforce essential political relationships. But this brings us to yet another problem. Why does *that particular* custom fulfill these functions? Could some other custom accomplish the same thing? This raises the issue of **functional equivalence** (Cancian 1968).

Why does a custom take the form it does rather than taking a different form? Even if we accept the idea that a custom exists because it fulfills some function, how do we deduce causation from that? If the function of a custom involves some universal human need, why would the custom *itself* not be universal? If the custom is not an inevitable result of some universal need, what caused that custom to take the form it has?

A possible answer to the latter question would be that this particular function is a result of the interaction of other customs, institutions, or values that in themselves exist because *they* fulfill some functions. Ultimately, if we go too far along this road, we find functions generating other functions. In either case—universal human needs or mutually generating functions—we have a serious problem with identifying **functional prerequisites.** The variety and dubious comparability of customs in different societies only compound this problem.

It might be acceptable to claim that at a certain level all humans share basic needs, which go beyond the simple needs for food, shelter, and reproduction. We could also probably agree that all human groups need some means of controlling conflict and distributing goods. The literature is filled with functional examples of how groups meet these needs. But we face the question of why they do it this way and not that way. How useful is it to assert that among the Navajo, witchcraft helps to channel social stress and avoid conflict, while among the Inuit, song duels achieve much the same thing? Both are interesting examples of particular cultural practices, but do they really take us much beyond simple description, embellished by an explanatory assertion?

As we have noted, the comparative approach is questionable because of the issue of true comparabilty among customs. An approach that takes into account the histories of these groups and the influences they might have experienced from other groups might yield better results; but as we know, functionalists ruled out such questions.

Functional approaches also have operated under the implicit assumption that customs and institutions generally have a positive effect. This type of effect has sometimes been referred to as **eufunction.** This position is all but inevitable if we accept the argument that a custom or institution exists because it meets some individual or social need. This would suggest that the needs within society are shared, and perhaps even a matter of consensus. The view tends to depict a social order in which internal differentiation is complementary rather than grounds for conflict. As we recall, this aspect is one basis for the criticism that functionalism leaves little room for conflict in its analysis, except as a problem to be overcome.

In the experience of most people, however, conflicts of interest are all too familiar. Practices that benefit one constituency may disadvantage, exploit, or even seriously harm others. Functional analysis was forced either to downplay such phenomena, to see them as temporary aberrations, or implicitly at least, to see them as a price to pay for the greater good of the social system. It is worth noting that Marxist analysis had no problem incorporating conflict as a normal part of social existence. As we know, conflict arising from internal contradictions, in that view, is a central force for change. In stressing social order, functional analysis was somewhat crippled in its ability to deal with either conflict or change.

Some functionalists did attempt to incorporate the matter of conflict, however. Geoffrey and Monica Wilson suggested a model of successive or punctuated equilibrium in which social structure underwent breakdown and restored its equilibrium for a time before subsequent breakdown, followed by new equilibrium (1945). Few other theorists employed this model extensively elsewhere, however.

In any case, complex state systems offer many examples of customs or institutions that function well for one segment but oppress others. One could point to examples from tax laws favoring corporations, to institutionalized racial oppression, to gender discrimination. The ethnographic evidence does not indicate that smaller societies are necessarily free from such inequities. Although most modern anthropologists would agree that early functionalists provided a great contribution in dispelling derogatory images of small non-Western societies, the tendency to portray them as idyllic and relatively conflict-free is also a distortion of their human realities.

Critics of functionalist approaches have also pointed to the tendency to conceive of societies as isolates with distinct boundaries. This has also been true of other theorists. In assuming this definition, we might keep in mind the context in which the early functionalists worked, when it was necessary to make the fundamental point that these groups *had* societies with complex political structures, rather than simply being disorganized "hordes."

With regard to the model of societies as isolated entities, Malinowski had worked with island societies whose boundaries were a matter of shoreline. Within the Trobriand Islands the people themselves had numerous imposed political boundaries that Malinowski did not make up but merely recorded. A central aspect of Malinowski's research, however, involved the complex political and economic relationships between the Trobrianders and people of other islands hundreds of miles into the Pacific, particularly in the context of the Kula ring. Malinowski's analysis positioned the Trobrianders in a vast, complex regional system of trade.

The concept "society" or "social system" does present problems, nonetheless. Like many other terms and concepts that appear frequently in functional analysis, they call for definition but to some extent, defy it. It is all very well to talk about society in the abstract, and in doing so, to examine its dynamics. Europeans and Americans after the Enlightenment had given considerable thought to the nature of society. They had engaged in lengthy debate over what constitutes a society, what is the nature of the ideal society, and so on—particularly in the context of nation-building and the restructuring of government. The idea had long been a part of the familiar intellectual repertoire. When it came to operationalizing the concept of society with regard to populations *without* state systems, some of the problems with the model of the politicially-bounded society became more apparent.

Nation-states do have boundaries, disputed as they might be at times. A person either is or is not a citizen of France or the United States. In the case of many smaller populations, these formal political features might be ambiguous—particularly in the many cases in which one's social identity is a matter of kinship.

One can identify a number of separate villages in a region, each with its own garden plots and beach rights. Are these distinct societies? What if people generally marry people from other villages? Does that give each partner rights in the spouse's village? And what about their children? All right, suppose we find that the people of these villages all speak the same language. But not everyone who speaks English is an English citizen. Nonetheless, let us assume that the people in these villages all seem to be part of a linked set of relationships. Maybe it would be best, therefore, to consider all of them members of the same society. But wait. Suppose it turns out that periodically, these villages are apt to go to war with one another. At times the people of one village might even chase the others off and confiscate their lands. Are these the actions one could expect within a single society? Is this civil war, or something else altogether? And to make matters even more confusing, suppose that over the years people have moved in from elsewhere and taken over empty lands, and people from the local region have moved off to places unknown.

These sorts of situations, which are common in many parts of the world, offer challenges to the tidy concept of society as a coherent entity. We run into more problems when we attempt to apply the idea of society to the many nomadic peoples of the world. Some of them maintain highly structured and formal relationships among their own groupings, despite their mobile existence. This tends to be especially true of people with herds of livestock who need to move great distances to exploit seasonal pasturage. To such people, rights of ownership, debt, and inheritance may be a crucial part of life, but they may live most of the time in scattered groups that are essentially autonomous.

For many hunting and gathering peoples in sparse areas, the extent of structured relationships may amount to specific ties between individuals that produce networks that are not only mobile, but unstable. These clusters of abstract ties may exist concurrently with local residential groupings but not correspond with them. The terms designated for such clusters often translate merely as "the people of such and such a place."

As we can see, this ambiguity about society has led to many problems. If customs function to meet the needs of society, in some cases we must ask "which society?" or even "what society?" If, on the other hand, we see custom as functioning to meet human needs, we might also ask in some cases "whose needs?" Periodically going to war and taking over neighbors' garden plots might serve the needs of the perpetrators, but we might be hardpressed to see much benefit to the losers.

We encounter similar difficulties with the concept of **social integration.** Functionalists have posited that the overall function of some customs and institutions has been to promote social integration, if only indirectly. Here again, though, we need to have a clearer idea of just what that means. How can we judge whether a given society is more or less integrated?

To some extent this hearkens back to the idea of social order. We could use a low frequency of overt conflict as one criterion. But how would this criterion apply to a society in which a large part of the population is in a state of slavery, and in which any hint at rebellion is certain to result in dire consequences? Would a society of that kind be better integrated than a society in which people regularly argue and air their disputes freely in public?

FUNCTION AND ADAPTATION

One of the main assumptions of the functionalist perspective has been that function is linked somehow to adaptation. Once again, we must be careful here. To many people nowadays, adaptation implies some sort of optimal articulation to the environment, particularly to its non-human aspects.

Radcliffe-Brown, as we know, saw function in terms of society at large. If he would use the term *adaptation* at all, Radcliffe-Brown's scope would remain within the societal realm. In that sense function had little to do with articulation to the natural environment, except for the general assumption that for a society to exist at all, the population obviously needed to survive physically.

Malinowski, as we know, anchored his concept of function in biological needs. But he was not particularly concerned about the broad ecological implications of various practices involved in the production of food or adaptations to particular environmental circumstances. His approach had more to do with the ways in which people were able to maintain social relationships compatible with the needs of survival and the ways in which people managed to cope emotionally and psychologically with the challenges of existence.

Once again, though, however we might wish to *interpret* adaptation, how should we *define* the term? How do we evaluate adaptation in an operational sense? How can we tell whether a society or population is more or less adapted?

For most of the early functionalists, adaptation was all but synonymous with existence. If a group exists, they must have adapted to whatever conditions they faced in the past. In some respects, this conclusion goes back to the basic functionalist premise that no custom or institution would continue unless it had a functional payoff. There was an implicit assumption that whatever unknown history led these groups to the present, any nonadaptive practices they once had must have disappeared. Those remaining practices, therefore, had to be functional and adaptive.

This argument was not especially satisfying for some critics, though. A few attempted to find more precise ways than simple survival to evaluate adaptation. As Francesca Cancian pointed out, most populations *do* survive, except for those few who have been subject to extreme assaults or other disasters (1968).

In keeping with the ideal of framing anthropology as a science, one possibility would be to consider adaptation in biological terms, such as reproductive success and population increase. In a human context, however, these criteria have their own problems. Some of the most rapid population increases seem to occur among the most impoverished societies with the highest rates of infant mortality and the lowest life expectancies—societies that suffer the most severe economic deprivation and political oppression. The wealthiest societies in the world, for the most part, seem far closer to stabilizing or even decreasing their populations. What does biological adaptation really mean in a human context?

Perhaps population stability is the criterion. In that case, we might look to some hunting and gathering societies whose populations have been constrained by the **carrying capacity** of the environment. If this is not adaptation, what is?

We also have the issue of long-term versus short-term adaptation. A society might enjoy a boom time of prosperity, a florescence of the arts, excellent cuisine, and so on, only to deplete its resources eventually and suffer the consequences. We have the example of Sumer in the Mesopotamian region, one of the earliest great civilizations, which apparently declined as a result of cumulative deposits of salt from the irrigation of its fields. Some people in the United States see other, more recent environmental dangers arising from practices such as the use of pesticides and chemical fertilizers that produce short-term gains at the expense of long-term sustainability.

Altogether, it seems indisputable that although the idea of function marked a radical advance in understanding the human experience in the wake of nineteenth-century evolutionism, like any new paradigm it eventually became an old paradigm. As scholars worked to improve upon it, many of its flaws became more apparent. The shortcomings of "old" functionalism were often the very things that underlay the advances that functionalism had offered when it was new.

The general premise of functionalism, the idea that things somehow fit together, was far from dead after midcentury, however. It may be ironic that Leslie White's revival of cultural evolutionism incorporated the idea of functional interrelationships as an important assumption. As we recall from the chapter on evolution, White saw cultural evolution in the broad terms of "Culture with a big C," linking various stages to levels of energy use. For each of these levels, White posited social and cultural developments associated with technology, social organization, and belief systems. Although White did not define himself as a functionalist, the functional interrelationships in his model are clear.

Julian Steward's concept of multilinear evolution also involved a concept of linkages between the basic levels of subsistence and other aspects of life. Focusing on the specifics of local ecology, Steward, unlike White, developed the idea of the "culture core"—that is, aspects of culture and social organization that directly articulate with the needs of subsistence. In this case, Steward saw the core including such adaptations as kinship organization and residence patterns, while other aspects of life—the arts, belief systems, and so on—were relatively independent and consequently less predictable. Steward's work was an important precursor of one of the most significant revivals of functional concepts in a synthesis that became known as **cultural ecology.**

It is ironic, perhaps, that even though current conventional wisdom generally attributes more theoretical impact to Radcliffe-Brown than Malinowski, cultural ecology probably shows greater affinity with Malinowski's approaches (though generally, with little acknowledgment). Radcliffe-Brown's form of functionalism had its own counterpart in sociology, with the approaches of Talcott Parsons (1937). By the late 1960s, though, the alleged positivist aspects of this approach had become passé. Beyond any political aspersions, fair or otherwise, many scholars found the abstraction of these models too far removed from human realities to sustain much continued interest.

The development of cultural ecology, however, gave new life to some old questions. To some degree this was a reflection of the climate of the times, when issues of human degradation of the environment in the United States had risen to the public consciousness. The hard-won concept that people in smaller societies have viable, sustainable social systems was compatible with the idea that their articulation with the non-human environment was worthy of study.

FUNCTIONALISM AND CULTURAL ECOLOGY

Some of the people who addressed cultural ecology were not only acquainted with the idea that small-scale societies are viable entities—an idea that by the 1960s was already an old one in anthropology as a result of the work of Boasians in the United States and functionalists in Britain—but many also were interested in strengthening the scientific legitimacy of anthropology. In that vein, they were acquainted with many of the recent developments in the biological sciences and particularly in *ecology*, the study of biological systems.

Two of the most prominent figures in this approach, **Andrew Vayda** and **Roy Rappaport,** were particularly influential in developing empirical studies of human adaptations to particular environments (see Vayda 1961). One important work was Rappaport's classic study of the Tsembaga Maring, a highland horticultural people of Papua New Guinea (1968).

Rappaport carried out a comprehensive study of Tsembaga subsistence, ranging from their knowledge of plants to their gardening techniques. More significantly, he managed to link the cycles of their gardening and the raising of pigs to the cycle of warfare with neighboring groups.

Rappaport showed that while gardening produced the vast bulk of the Tsembaga diet, pigs were an essential source of high-quality protein. The Tsembaga, like most peoples in that part of the world, prized pigs and raised them not only for direct consumption on infrequent occasions, but for social purposes such as marriage exchanges. For the Tsembaga, like most people of Papua New Guinea, pigs were wealth.

But the practice of pig raising has complications. To have too few pigs is not good. But having too many pigs can be worse. They mess up the place, they require extra work on the part of women who have primary responsibility for raising them, they make extra demands on the food supply, and they can even be a threat to small children. At a certain point, then, when the number of Tsembaga pigs became a liability—a point that Rappaport was able to calculate, based on the caloric costs of maintaining a critical number of pigs—women began to complain about it. The solution was a *kaiko*—a major, lengthy celebration in which pigs were exchanged, cooked, and eaten.

This ceremony consisted of many phases and could take a year or more to complete. By the end of it, the pig stock was pretty much depleted. But in the meantime, Rappaport noted, the Tsembaga generally carried out warfare with their neighbors. These wars could arise for numerous reasons—past grievances, disputes over marriage payments, and so on—but they often resulted in the acquisition of garden lands.

Rappaport drew connections among these apparently distinct phenomena. Put simply, when the Tsembaga prepared for the *kaiko*, they also prepared for war. War, of course, is a highly stressful activity. Stress increased nutritional needs. The pig feasts accommodated this by providing high-quality protein—a factor that is normally not a major part of the Tsembaga garden-based diet.

By the time the warfare and pig feasts ended, the pig herd was reduced to a manageable size and land had been redistributed, generally with the stronger and more numerous group in possession of some of the weaker or smaller group's garden plots. The adversaries agreed to a truce, which they symbolized by staking an emblem in a field between their territories. The truce stipulated that peace would prevail until the emblem rotted and fell to the ground—a period of time that coincided roughly with the time it took for the pig herd to grow once again to troublesome proportions.

Rappaport's analysis employed numerous functional insights. It went beyond earlier functional studies, however, in incorporating ecological aspects and linking the system of social activities to subsistence in a quantitative way. The study was subject to criticism, in fact, for being *too* functional—particularly for portraying the entire scenario as an overarching system without taking into account human decisions and planning. Rappaport answered these criticisms by pointing out the role of women in initiating the *kaiko*. Their increasing annoyance at caring for an excessive number of pigs initiated the cycle.

Maurice Godelier offers another critique of cultural ecology studies (1977) from a Marxist perspective. He claims that cultural ecologists, by dealing with what he calls the "visible" relationships among observable phenomena, oversimplify the situation. The true nature of the relations of production among the Tsembaga or any other group reside in the underlying arrangements arising from the material needs of life, including power disparities—between men and women, for example—that such overt actions as pig exchanges and intergroup conflict may disguise.

The cultural ecology approaches tend to separate economic from other aspects of life, even in the process of showing the ways in which they interact with one another. The articulation of two or more entities, after all, implies and requires their fundamental separateness. In the view of Godelier, the mode of production is not an aspect of life separable from other domains of existence, but pervades and determines them (1977:36–37).

The most important aspect of this study, though, may have been its success in integrating a comprehensive range of aspects of the life of a people, including the extrahuman aspects of ecology, in portraying an intricate adaptive system. Although the earlier models of functionalism are now out of fashion, it seems clear that many aspects of the idea of function have left a legacy deeply embedded in current anthropological thinking.

Despite the anomalies and the contradictions of human existence in any society—despite the ways in which people hurt one another or themselves and sometimes make abysmal errors—a basic legacy of functionalism has persisted. The core of that idea is that the lives of any living people represent attempts at solutions to issues with which we, as fellow humans, have always grappled.

FOOD FOR THOUGHT

Does function imply stability?

Some functionalists argue that a cultural practice will not persist unless it fulfills a function for that culture. There are numerous customs that exist or have existed, however, that have no apparent reason behind them.

What are some examples of them, and how might they be reconciled with a functionalist perspective?

Discuss both positive and negative aspects of social stability. How would you define social stability?

Malinowski saw that some practices are of social significance and contribute to an individual's social status but have no material purpose. Compare this situation to our own society. Do we have similar practices?

If Durkheim lived in our society today, do you think he would hold the same idea that the division of labor within a society is a result of social condensation rather than material gain?

How does Durkheim's concept of mechanical solidarity fit with the now well-known fact that smaller societies, such as hunter-gatherers or even small agricultural or pastoral societies, also show a high degree of division of labor, particularly along gender lines?

Chapter 6

THE IDEA OF RELATIVISM

The idea of relativism offers a disquieting proposition. At a basic level it recognizes that the world looks different to different people. This sounds like a commonsense observation. But it implies that our perceptions of the world have a lot to do with the nature of our minds. It suggests that the way we perceive the world is not a direct reflection of the way the world is. Conversely, it means that the world (or "reality") is not necessarily the way we perceive it.

If our minds are our "windows on the world," they filter, interpret, and distort the stimuli they receive. They can even create images or thoughts that may not have any basis in external reality at all. Our minds are not pristine standardized universal human equipment, except in the most general sense. They are products of varieties of individual experience.

One of the most important functions of the human brain is to change as a result of learning. Recent research has indicated that this literally involves physical changes with the development of new neural synapses. As a result, our minds, in addition to whatever innate capacities they may have, are the products of our particular experiences. The ways in which they process and assemble information at one point in time has a tremendous amount to do with the ways in which they deal with subsequent information.

If we take this process to extremes, as some have, it can imply a rather disconcerting free-floating mental existence that is only tenuously anchored to reality, if at all. In that view, "reality" is a dubious concept. On the other hand, the idea of relativism does not necessarily extend to such a conclusion.

Relativism has actually meant a number of different things and been used in different ways.

At the milder end of the spectrum, relativism can involve merely a recognition that people—especially people in different populations—see things differently and operate according to different rules. Taken a step further, it can be a basis for separating the attempt to understand these differences from the inclination to judge their worth.

In the classical writings of Herodotus and Thucydides, we find many fairly dispassionate observations about varieties of foreign customs and beliefs. Generally these ancient observers exercised restraint in judging those differences. They did occasionally offer their opinions about exotic customs, but generally they seemed more concerned with reporting than evaluating. As one scholar of the classics observed:

> But this is much to say that Herodotus is a true anthropologist—his business is not to moralise, but to observe. Nor is he really careless: his whole outlook shows a deep reverence for custom, which, even if distasteful or horrible, is not lightly to be altered. Only a madman, he thinks, would laugh at the habits of another race. (Sikes 1914; quoted in Montagu 1974:11)

This reluctance to judge the customs of other peoples went out of fashion in Europe during the next thousand years or so. Christian theology entailed a sense of absolute laws that precluded a neutral stance toward divergent customs. Exotic peoples, in that view, were not only different but were also erroneous in their ways, or worse.

The Enlightenment led to some departure from this attitude. Montaigne, writing a century or so earlier, had observed that "barbarian" ways of life were no less rational than those of Europeans, although his point seemed to be directed more toward criticizing his fellow Europeans than extolling the virtues of barbarians (1958). In keeping with the importance that Enlightenment thinkers placed on rational thought, they generally believed that experience, and education in particular, molded the human mind.

We generally credit John Locke with the idea that the mind is fundamentally an "empty cabinet" to be filled with knowledge gained through experience. Locke stressed the diversity this process had produced among humankind:

> Whether there be any such moral principles, wherein all men do agree, I appeal to any who have been but moderately conversant in the history of mankind, and looked abroad beyond the smoke of their own chimneys. Where is that practical truth that is universally received without doubt or question, as it must be if innate? (Locke 1894:66 [orig. 1690])

The thrust here was an argument against absolutism and the espousal of a relativistic perspective.

Some thinkers took the idea of human malleability to a more extreme degree. Jean Jaques Rousseau even suggested that education might have the power to turn apes into humans (1964 [orig. 1751]). Lord Monboddo argued this position forcefully (1774). As bizarre as these ideas might seem in light of present scientific knowledge, as Marvin Harris points out, "Monboddo's flights of fancy . . . were grounded in a very solid appreciation of the power of enculturation and the plasticity and indefiniteness of human nature . . . " (1968:16).

This recognition of human flexibility and the variety that exists as a result of it did not necessarily involve a total abstention from value judgments. One theme of the Enlightenment's intellectual milieu was a faith in rational thought. It seems safe to say that while Enlightenment thinkers might have enjoyed pointing out that Europeans were not necessarily more rational than "savages," they assumed that rationality itself was an absolute and desirable quality. We find little sense here that multiple, equivalent forms of rationality might exist.

We find no trace at all, moreover, of later views that reality itself is an illusion. The very bedrock of Enlightenment scientific endeavor was the assumption that human life is subject to the laws of nature. The primary means of understanding those laws was to be through careful and systematic observation, with the assumption that something exists to observe. As complex as the laws of nature might have seemed, it would hardly have occurred to the thinkers of the time to question whether a perceptible nature was there at all.

We find the same assumptions about absolute rationality in the work of nineteenth-century theorists like Edward Burnett Tylor. As we remember, Tylor saw cultural evolution as a matter of ever-increasing rationality. Once again, there is little sense here that rational thought is anything but an absolute standard. For Tylor and other evolutionists, the differences among societies involved the degree to which various peoples had mastered rational thinking.

One indication of a somewhat different perspective, however, appeared in the work of the German philosopher Immanuel Kant. The work of Kant reflects some of the insights of Locke and other Enlightenment thinkers. Kant, perhaps even more than Locke, grappled with the extent to which the human mind is a product of experience and learning, or conversely, how much it depends on "innate ideas." In refining this question, Kant concluded that although the mind is immensely malleable, certain basic concepts amount to universal aspects of human thought. These, he suggested, included concepts of time, space, and morality (1951 [orig. 1790]).

Kant's ideas had far-reaching impact in many fields, even to the extent of inspiring a "neo-Kantian" movement in Germany in the nineteenth century. It was in this fashion, according to Marvin Harris, that his ideas influenced the thinking of Franz Boas (Harris 1968:267).

Boas, we recall, was trained as a physical geographer. His conversion to anthropology occurred during his research expedition to the Arctic Ocean. During that time he spent many cold nights in camp with his Inuit guides

Franz Boas (1858–1942)

and companions, writing letters, keeping a journal, and reading. He was especially interested in reading Kant, "so that I shall not be completely uneducated when I return" (quoted in Stocking 1965:58). We can only speculate about the ways in which ideas developed in Boas's mind during that time, but there is no doubt that as Boas developed his concept of cultural relativism, the ideas of Kant were a part of his thinking.

We can see several themes contributing to the eventual development of relativism in anthropology, almost like creeks trickling into a river. One is a recognition that differences in customs do not necessarily result from ignorance but involve different ways of thinking and perceiving, which entails a recognition of the malleability of the human mind. It involved the realization that the mind is largely a product of experience. As we have noted, this realization had profound implications. If human perceptions are the result of the influence of experience, how is it possible to privilege one person's perception—even one's own—over another's?

Late in the twentieth century this aspect of relativism eventually would lead some thinkers to question the possibility that anyone can accurately perceive reality at all. For most of this century, though, the idea of **cultural relativism** in anthropology stopped far short of that point. For Boas, cultural relativism was an attitude that would help clear the way for understanding other cultures. Boas understood clearly the difficulty in entering the intellectual realms of other peoples. But as far as we know, he never doubted that he was dealing with reality. Cross-cultural views of reality might be elusive, but reality was not mere illusion.

THE RELATIVE MODESTY OF CULTURAL RELATIVISM

Boas wrote in 1887, "Civilization is not something absolute but . . . relative, and our ideas and conceptions are true only so far as our civilization goes" (Boas 1887, quoted in Stocking 1974:66. Also discussed in Cole 1999:132). In 1911 he wrote, "It is somewhat difficult for us to recognize that the value which we attribute to our own civilization is due to the fact that we participate in this civilization, and that it has been controlling all our actions since the time of our birth . . . " (1911).

Boas found the schemes of the cultural evolutionists unsatisfactory for a number of reasons. At a fundamental level he believed that for anthropology to have any scientific validity, it was essential to have precise, complete data relevant to the subject under study. For Boas this meant more than such things as family organization or the presence or absence of pottery or the bow and arrow. It meant comprehending the meanings of these and other things to the people who created them. It meant understanding the thought and emotion *behind* observable behavior.

As we know, Boas entered anthropology at a time when prevailing views held non-Western peoples in low regard. The ethnocentrism of dominant evolutionary theory might have been gratifying to its proponents, since it afforded them the illusion of superiority, but it was clear to Boas and some others that such assumptions contributed little to the scientific stature of the discipline. Aside from being self-affirming, they offered little insight into the human condition. A concern for scientific rigor, then, was an essential part of Boas's development of the concept of cultural relativism. It is worth a short digression to consider the interplay of these ideas.

BOAS AND THE FOUR FIELDS

We have discussed some of the intellectual influences on Boas's thinking and the climate of thought in which he began his career, but it would be an oversight to ignore some of the personal experiences that may have helped to shape Boas's perspectives. For one thing, Boas, a Jew born and educated in Germany and seeking a professional career in the United States at the turn of the twentieth century, had certainly experienced discrimination in his own

Franz Boas (second from left) as Military Cadet

life. He encountered such treatment even after he established his stature as one of the leading anthropologists of his time. We must conclude that for Boas, racial and ethnic bigotry was more than an abstract concept. It seems reasonable to suspect that such experiences gave energy to his lifelong opposition to racism, even though much of his battle against it took the form of scientific research.

A second aspect of Boas's thinking seems to have arisen from his time among the Inuit of the Arctic Coast. Boas himself described it as the experience that led him to anthropology. It seems to have been more than a cool intellectual decision to alter the direction of his research. As he told his students many years later, his "conversion" experience also involved a life-threatening episode.

As a young student fresh from Europe, Boas no doubt was familar with the prevailing view of Inuit (or "Eskimos") as "primitive" hunters surviving in a barren land remote from civilization. In the 1880s, few outsiders except trappers, traders, or missionaries had ventured into the area. To survive, Boas had to depend on the Inuit.

At one point, according to Boas, he found himself in serious trouble. Suffering from hypothermia, he fell unconscious and almost certainly would have died. He awoke later in an Inuit dwelling with people tending to him, slapping his hands, and working to restore his body temperature. Beyond a doubt, they had saved his life. As a result of this experience, Boas found it difficult to see these people as anything less than complex human beings with immense, intricate knowledge of their difficult environment. His subsequent work, *The Central Eskimo*, based on that time in the field, focused largely on Inuit intellectual command of the environment (1888; see also Muller-Wille 1998).

Since that time, numerous anthropological studies have addressed comparable issues. But once again we need to recall that in the 1880s, the preeminent anthropologists of the day were still speculating on "primitive society" from their comfortable libraries and well-furnished studies. Boas's field experience with the Central Canadian Inuit gave him far more intimate insight into the realities of these people, and for him, it made earlier ethnocentric depictions of "primitives" anachronistic. **Ethnocentrism** would, of course, survive long afterward in Euroamerican thought. But for Boas and his many students who established American anthropology, people in other societies could never again be relegated to simplistic caricatures of "savages."

Boas brought to anthropology a broad sense of the scope of human existence. In the nineteenth century, as we know, evolutionary theorists had sometimes blurred physical evolution with cultural development. Boas, on the other hand, had a clear sense of culture as a distinctly non-biological, extrasomatic aspect of human life. But he also believed that the physical or biological aspects of humanity were essential areas of study in their own right. In this view, culture and biology offered distinct but complementary fields of inquiry, both of which Boas pursued. He also saw the study of language as an essential field of inquiry in the attempt to understand the human experience. And he emphasized the importance of studying the human past, particularly the past of specific societies, through archaeology.

> The task of ethnology is the study of the total range of phenomena of social life. Language, customs, migrations, bodily characteristics are subjects of our studies. Thus its first and most immediate object is the study of the history of mankind; not that of civilized nations alone, but that of the whole of mankind, from its earliest traces found in the deposits of the ice age, up to modern time. (Boas 1940:627–628)

This approach to the past was consistent with Boas's view that each human group has its own history and therefore requires detailed study in its own right, and it represented a departure from the evolutionary schemes of the time. With regard to understanding the human past, Boas's views were consistent with painstaking archaeological investigations of *particular*

Boas Late in His Career

cases—a view more congenial to modern archaeological research—more than with sweeping generalizations about universal stages.

With this allocation of research attention, Boas set American anthropology on a course quite different from developments in Britain or France. American anthropology became a "four-field" discipline, incorporating ethnology, linguistics, physical anthropology, and archaeology. Subsequent anthropologists have disputed and challenged this idea of distinct but complementary approaches. The four-field model does, however, remain a widely accepted ideal in the discipline, often reflected in the academic requirements for students in anthropology departments. The four-field approach had the effect of distinguishing anthropology from other disciplines such as sociology, economics, or political science. None of them have embraced such a comprehensive scope incorporating the study of language, prehistory, and biological factors as standard aspects of the range of inquiry.

Boas himself made important contributions to most of these fields. Paradoxically, perhaps, considering his clear distinction between the cultural and physical aspects of humanness, his work in these fields involved important feedback between these two areas of research. As we have noted, Boas did not consider racial differences to be a valid explanatory factor in accounting for cultural differences. Ironically, some of his early work in physical anthropology with European immigrants to the United States provided support for this view in a rather unexpected way. He measured the head shapes of immigrants who had been born and grown up in Europe and compared them with the head shapes of these immigrants' children. Astonishingly, it turned out that the head shapes of children born in the United States differed significantly from those of their own European-born parents (Boas 1912).

Whatever the reasons for this phenomenon might have been, his findings made it clear that factors other than simple biological inheritance were at work. If such an obviously physical aspect as the shape of one's cranium could alter in a different environment, how likely was it that such complex behavioral patterns as temperament or "intelligence" could be biologically fixed?

One of the most significant aspects of this research, aside from the findings themselves, was the fact that Boas addressed the question of race from a scientific, empirical perspective. From what we know of Boas, there is little doubt that he considered racial and ethnic discrimination to be morally repugnant. But his approach to these issues did not rely on moralistic rhetoric. It focused on empirical data.

This theme of objective inquiry was entirely consistent with Boas's development of cultural relativism. Whether or not he felt that it was ethically desirable to approach other cultural systems without judging them, the key issue for anthropology was that the objectives of science made it necessary to *separate value judgments from observation.* The aim was to observe, record, and understand, not to evaluate. The emotional reactions of the observer, which inevitably arise from the observer's own cultural and personal experience, could only obscure and distort understanding.

As an aside, we might note that the general notion of relativism seems to have been an aspect of the broader intellectual climate at the time. Albert Einstein, who was twenty-one years old at the beginning of the twentieth century, developed his theory of relativity showing that even time itself was affected by speed. In the same era, post-impressionist painters renounced artistic realism. In different ways, the intellectual energies of the period challenged complacent absolutist assumptions about the nature of reality and conventional perceptions of it.

The Boasian version of cultural relativism has sometimes been subject to misunderstanding. The premise of cultural relativism is not to assume that each and every practice or custom anywhere in the world, no matter how apparently cruel or unjust, is "good." Such an assumption would not only be difficult to sustain; it would be absurd. More to the point, such a position would also contradict the basic idea of cultural relativism because it would amount to a value judgment, albeit a positive rather than a negative one.

CULTURAL VERSUS MORAL RELATIVISM

In that vein, it is important to draw a distinction here between cultural relativism as Boas developed the idea and moral relativism. *Moral relativism* would imply that morality is unanchored to any absolute standard. The implication of this perspective is far stronger than the simple idea that we should suspend value judgment in order to understand the observed phenomena. It would mean that one can never make such judgments, since all moral systems are suspect. To put another way, it is an assertion that no morality is privileged.

This is a philosophical question worthy of debate at length. The issue here, though, is that such a view has little to do with the Boasian version of cultural relativism. Boas himself held strong positions on racism and other issues that he felt were morally repulsive and violations of human rights. He often expressed these views in public forums and in print. In his thinking, the attempt to approach other cultural systems with dispassionate objectivity did not entail moral disengagement from the world around him.

> As an anthropologist I feel very strongly that it is possible to state certain fundamental truths which are common to all mankind, notwithstanding the form in which they occur in special societies. (Letter from Boas to the American Council of Learned Societies, February 17, 1941; quoted in Lewis 2001:451)

Boas was a vociferous advocate of causes associated with disadvantaged groups in the United States and Canada. "What I want to live and die for, is equal rights for all, equal possibilities to learn and work for rich and poor alike" (quoted in Cole 1983:37). Boas proposed a study to guide government policies for educational and economic development for Native Americans and African Americans. Early in the twentieth century he worked to establish a Black Studies curriculum at Columbia University, long before San Francisco State College established the first such program in 1968 (Lewis 2001:456). He was a strong opponent of government restrictions on the Native American potlatch in Canada and the religious use of peyote in the United States. He was a colleague and ally of W. E. B. DuBois and a mentor of Zora Neale Hurston. These, and many more examples from Boas's long career, offer ample evidence that his view of cultural relativism did not mean a lack of involvement in moral and ethical issues.

The issue of the relationship, if any, between scientific knowledge and moral judgment has long troubled social thinkers. Max Weber in the late nineteenth century saw a clear distinction between the two (see Giddens 1995:42; Weber 1949:110–111). Weber, in Prussia, had experienced the eruption of the Revolution of 1848, with its espousal of idealism and political freedoms. He had also lived through its defeat and the restoration of a strong central government under Otto von Bismark, the "Iron Chancellor." Most of Weber's work reflected an attempt to reconcile the social idealism that inspired the revolution and the social order that a strong central government provided, if just. Weber, provisionally at least, accepted the legitimacy of the state's monopoly of violence.

Franz Boas was the product of a family who were strongly affected by the idealism that lingered in the intellectual milieu of Germany in the late nineteenth century. As Boas himself put it, "The background of my early thinking was a German home in which the ideals of the Revolution of 1848 were a living force" (Boas 1938:201; quoted in Lewis 2001:451). In that sense he shared the same climate of ideas that Weber did. Unlike Weber, though, Boas was less prone to separate scientific knowledge from moral choices. During his professional life, Boas emphasized scientific knowledge to promote ethical causes. For Boas, it seems, the two were complementary aspects of human thought, not separate channels.

In another way, Boas was comparable to Weber in finding himself in a juxtaposition of two paradigms. For Weber, the paradigms were personal freedom versus social order. For Boas, as an anthropologist, the competing paradigms were the ideals of liberal German social thinking, as represented in the ideals of the mid nineteenth century, and the hierarchical, racist models of nineteenth-century evolutionist, social Darwinist assumptions. Rather than attempting to reconcile the two, Boas used the force of scientific reasoning and data to embrace one and combat the other.

Melville Herskovits, a student of Boas, expressed it in another way. With regard to evaluating behavior in cultures other than one's own, Herskovits asserted that "there is no way to play this game of making judgments across cultures except with loaded dice" (1958:270). On the other hand, cultural relativism is fully compatible with the recognition that within particular societies or cultural systems, rules and moral precepts exist and are important subjects of study. Indeed, the extent to which members of a society live up to their own standards is a legitimate question. As Herskovits put it, "There is no cultural relativist, as far as I know, who asserts that his doctrine is based on, describes, or implies behavioral anarchy" (1958:270).

When it came to assessing practices of one's own society, Herskovits, as a member of that society, stated:

> . . . it is something entirely different when we, as Americans, try to do something to correct "the racial caste system of the United States" of which we, as members of the society of whose culture this is a part, do not approve. (1951:30)

In a later publication, in response to assertions that tended to confuse moral and cultural relativism, he wrote:

> It should be pointed out that those who most strongly urged the uniqe historical position of each culture also insisted on the unity of Homo sapiens in opposing the doctrines of racial determinism. (1958:271)

Even Robert Redfield, a critic of cultural relativism, allowed that the concept "is not a doctrine of moral indifference" (1953:146).

THE INFLUENCE OF CULTURAL RELATIVISM
ON AMERICAN ANTHROPOLOGY

Cultural relativism became a fundamental philosophical position in American anthropology by the 1920s and 1930s. Many of Boas's students, major figures in their own right, contributed to the refinement of the concept. Alfred Louis Kroeber—Boas's first student to earn a doctorate in anthropology and a figure who, after Boas, became the "Grand Old Man" of American anthropology to many—expressed some of the major tenets of cultural relativism in 1949:

> The method of science is to begin with questions, not with answers, least of all with value judgments.
>
> Science is dispassionate inquiry and therefore cannot take over outright any ideologies "already formulated in everyday life," since these are themselves inevitably traditional and normally tinged with emotional prejudice.
>
> Sweeping all-or-none, black-or-white judgments are characteristic of totalitarian attitudes and have no place in science, whose very nature is inferential and judicial. (1949:219)

Alfred Louis Kroeber (1876–1960)

In the study of linguistics, Edward Sapir's work with Native American languages helped to free linguistics from the conventional idea that Latin and Greek should serve as a general model for all languages. Sapir showed that other languages involved profoundly different systems of logic and ways of dealing with reality. As Sapir put it, "other cultures involve different realities, not just the same reality with different labels attached" (1929). Sapir also argued that without language, thought was not possible. This assertion remains debatable; but in the context of the development of cultural relativism, it carried the idea that reality, rather than simply "being there" to be expressed neutrally through language, was processed through culturally variable categories of thought that in themselves are embedded in language.

Sapir's student Benjamin Lee Whorf carried this insight further, contrasting the thought categories of European languages (which he summarized as "Standard Average European" or "SAE") with Hopi, a Native American language of the Southwest. Whorf showed that concepts of even such universal aspects of reality as time, space, and matter vary radically between these linguistic systems (Whorf 1956).

As cultural relativism became a key concept in cultural anthropology, its implications led the discipline down a rather problematic avenue in some respects. A desire for scientific objectivity had led in the first place to the dispassionate observation of other cultures, which cultural relativism prescribed. But cultural relativism's emphasis on the uniqueness of each cultural system meant that in important ways, cultures were not comparable.

In the view of some thinkers, this posed a serious problem for the aims of developing anthropology as science. If we refer back to scientific ideas as old as the Enlightenment, dispassionate observation and accurate description were not enough to make anthropology scientific in that view. One needed to draw some conclusions from these observations—to come up with some generalizations or laws that would apply to more than one particular case.

Boas himself, despite his high hopes for scientific standards, soon abandoned the view that human phenomena could lend themselves to the kinds of explanation that applied to the natural or physical sciences of the day. He disavowed the idea of a "physicalist" model for anthropology (see, for example, Boas 1940:641–645). At the beginning of his career, he had hoped that given enough data, some general laws appropriate to this field of study might become apparent, but this hope dimmed as Boas confronted the complexity and variability of cultures.

Ruth Benedict, one of Boas's most prominent students, addressed this issue by emphasizing and perhaps even celebrating the uniqueness of cultural systems and discussing them in terms of their incommensurability. In her book *Patterns of Culture*, she discussed the overriding themes and values of four different groups (1932). In a sense, Benedict's work represents a rejection of scientific comparison among cultural systems except to contrast them, focusing instead on what she saw as internal consistencies between their collective patterns and the minds of individuals within these societies.

Cultural relativism also came heavily into play in the tension between cultural and biological explanation. By the 1920s, despite Boas's renunciation of racism, biological explanation retained a solid place in American popular thought and conventional wisdom. Margaret Mead, a student of both Boas and Benedict, contributed important insights into this discussion. As we recall from a previous chapter, much of Mead's early work argued for the formative influence of culture, and hence presented a case for cultural relativism to challenge the widely accepted ideas of biological explanation, especially with regard to the supposed fixity of behavior. To do so, as a true student of Boas, she used data from field research.

As we have seen, perhaps the most outspoken advocate of cultural relativism was Melville Herskovits. Cultural relativism has meant a variety of things, both to its opponents and its proponents. Herskovits pointed out that relativism challenges the idea of the ranking of cultures, which would impute superiority to some and inferiority to others. "To this question, American anthropologists, at least, have given a clear and unequivocal answer; in the vast majority, we are agreed that objective indices of cultural inferiority and superiority cannot be established" (1951:22).

Herskovits may have been overstating the point to some extent. Some anthropologists did, in fact, question the idea that value judgments are totally illegitimate. Most, perhaps all, at the time endorsed the idea of objective observation, which required the researcher to avoid allowing personal preferences to cloud his or her view, to the extent that this was possible. But some took exception to the implication that no opinions were permissible after the fact. Clyde Kluckhohn, for example, wrote:

> to understand "the meaning of a way of life to those who have it" is a significant and indeed a noble undertaking. To understand, however, does not necessarily mean to accept or even to remain content with description. (1948:11–12)

Herskovits had an answer for this, of course, pointing again to the effects of cultural conditioning on the observer's perceptions. "Can his judgments be so Olympian that they are not influenced by these standards? The inevitable basic questions enter: Whose good? Whose bad? Whose means? Whose ends?" (1951:271).

CHANGING ASPECTS OF RELATIVISM

We have seen that the general idea of relativism has taken on many forms and aspects over the years. At its simplest level, it merely involved a recognition that not only styles of life, but concepts of good, evil, rationality, or absurdity vary widely from place to place and even among the same population at

"Papa Franz" and a Group of Boasians at a Columbia University Anthropology Picnic, c. 1925

different periods of time. This view implied a rejection of absolutism. Very little, it seemed, was constant or uniform about the general human experience. For Boas and his students, this view involved a departure from the evolutionary assumptions of the nineteenth century, but even this rejection in itself was not absolute. More properly, it involved the insistence that any generalizations about human development require empirical demonstration. It was primarily a rejection of unproven assumptions, rather than a categorical rejection of evolution itself.

For many, the recognition of human cultural variability underscored their reluctance to judge one society by the standards of another, but as we have noted, this did not mean that cultural relativists were required to abandon their own sense of morality. It simply meant the recognition that these moral views were themselves products of their own cultures and would contribute little or nothing to understanding other cultural systems.

Among other things, this implied a general avoidance of interfering in any way with the people one was trying to understand. The idea was to learn from them, not to try to change them, even "for their own good." Moreover, the very idea that an outsider could determine what was best for another population struck many as arrogant.

On the other hand, however, the idea that anthropological insights should be of practical use has a long history in anthropology. Boas, as we discussed earlier, was deeply engaged in social issues throughout his career. Malinowski urged his students to address issues of practical importance to peoples who were undergoing rapid changes, generally in a colonial context.

Radcliffe-Brown, early in his career, held similar views (see, for example, Kelly 1985:125). Margaret Mead, Phileo Nash, Lloyd Warner, and many other American anthropologists offered their services to the government and various organizations.

In the 1950s one of the most famous and controversial practical or "applied" projects, known informally as the "Vicos Project," began under the auspices of Cornell University. The lease on a mountain hacienda in Peru was about to expire. The current administration of the hacienda had run it essentially under a feudal arrangement, and the population lived in a state of severe poverty. Anthropologist Alan Holmberg persuaded Cornell University to take over the lease to enable a team of anthropologists to help institute measures to improve the educational and economic situation of the people, hoping eventually to turn the community over to their control.

The project was controversial from the outset. Many were uneasy that Cornell would assume the role of hacienda manager. There was also some ambivalence about an anthropologist taking over the position of administrating such a community. The proponents, in the aftermath, viewed the project as a success; the economic and educational levels did improve, and the Vicosinos did enjoy greater freedom, at least initially. Others, however, claimed that the success was relatively limited, and that eventually a few Vicosino entrepreneurs were able to establish disproportionate control over the community. (For sources on this project, see Holmberg 1958; Vasquez 1964; Cochrane 1971:17–19.)

More recently, however, many anthropologists, including some with undergraduate degrees, have ventured into non-academic positions as consultants and staff members of a variety of organizations that range from HIV/AIDS education programs to marketing firms. In general, these endeavors tend to focus on practical and often short-term issues. It will be interesting to see whether such work causes further refinement of anthropological theory or generates its own.

The prevailing reluctance of many anthropologists to engage in directed projects has not arisen only from cultural relativism as such. It also sprang from a realization of the complexity and systemic nature of the cultures of even the smallest populations. A recognition of the systemic aspect of culture, which meant that the various aspects of any cultural system tend to be interrelated in intricate ways, implied that any alteration of one aspect could have unforeseen repercussions. Even the best intentions could result in unforseen catastrophes.

Not all social scientists have subscribed to this view to the same extent. Sociologists, who generally have worked within their own social system, have had little trouble in identifying such phenomena as poverty, crime, child abuse, and so on as social pathologies. Economists have had even clearer signposts involving wealth, resource distribution, and productivity, whether domestically or on an international scale. With regard to other cultural systems, economists have often paid little attention to cross-cultural differences in values and traditional practices except as problems to overcome in the interest of development. As well-intentioned as many such Third World development projects have been, the record is rife with examples of initiatives that have had disastrous local results.

Often the failure to understand the complexities of "traditional" systems or to consult with the local people has created problems (see, for example, Erasmus 1961; Bodley 1982). In that vein, we have seen forced relocation of villages from high country to fertile river banks, only to have their populations suffer from epidemics of malaria, bilharzia, or other water-associated diseases. Peasant farmers who formerly planted a wide variety of indigenous strains of rice, assuring them of at least some crop yield whatever the weather conditions, have faced starvation when agencies have persuaded them to plant a single "high yield" hybrid variety that failed. The full consequences of the increased use of pesticides and chemical fertilizers have yet to be calculated, but some of the problems they have created are already apparent.

Anthropologists have generally not been widely involved in such projects. Partly, no doubt, this is because they have not been invited, but there also has been some reluctance on their part. Late in the twentieth century, nonetheless, a subfield called "applied anthropology" developed. Generally this endeavor involved a sense that anthropology could help to resolve some issues that the local people themselves defined as problems, often acting as their advocates or as mediators. This activity has not as yet become a dominant aspect of the discipline. Many anthropologists have tended to view applied projects with some misgivings. One result has been that major development projects generally have relied on the advice of economists and political scientists rather than anthropologists (see Cochrane 1971).

In the 1960s a reaction to the tradition of non-involvement arose within anthropology. Some younger anthropologists in particular felt that the stance of cultural relativism had led to an unacceptable lack of involvement in the lives of the people with whom anthropologists had worked. In this view, the idea of dispassionate, value-free study was no longer adequate and, in the opinions of some, was immoral. In the world of the twentieth century, indigenous peoples all over the world had suffered at the hands of powerful interests. Anthropologists, according to some, had an ethical duty to come to their assistance.

This view arose most strongly during a time when issues ranging from civil rights and racism to the war in Vietnam were provoking violent outrage in many quarters of American society, with manifestations in Europe and other places as well. For anthropology, the discovery that a few anthropologists had acted as consultants and "counterinsurgency" experts for the military in Southeast Asia provoked extreme anger. To many anthropologists this appeared to be using anthropological knowledge to help oppress vulnerable indigenous populations. Resolutions condemning such activities were passed at the national meetings of the American Anthropological Association in the 1970s. All of this strengthened the opinions of those who argued that anthropology could not remain neutral in the face of injustice and oppression.

In practice, the issue of greater involvement was extremely complex. It was one thing to argue that anthropologists should use whatever resources they had to help the indigenous communities in which they worked. As most anthropologists with field experience know, however, very few communities are unanimous in their opinions on every important issue. Consequently, the pitfalls of becoming involved in the internal affairs of a community, and perhaps finding oneself aligned with one faction in opposition to others, remained troublesome.

Nonetheless, many anthropologists have subscribed to the idea that they should place themselves at the service of indigenous peoples and attempt to be of assistance on issues that seemed to be particularly clear-cut, such as land confiscation and forced relocation for development projects. Over the years this development has had significant results. Anthropologist David Maybury-Lewis and his colleagues, for example, founded the organization Cultural Survival, which took on the task of monitoring issues affecting indigenous peoples on a global scale, publicizing cases as a means of arousing political awareness and generating political pressure on their behalf.

RELATIVISM AT HOME AND ABROAD

Those developments brought to light other nuances of cultural relativism. Anthropologists had long accepted the idea that as researchers the appropriate stance toward other cultural systems was to attempt to understand their practices, not to evaluate or criticize them, no matter how repugnant they might seem. As we know, this neutrality did not involve universal approval of all human behavior everywhere. Also, as many anthropologists have recognized, the idea of striving for objective, clear-eyed understanding did not, and could not, prevent responses on a personal level to cruelties and atrocities. The balance entailed a complex interplay between the attempt to observe and record other ways of life in an effort to contribute to a broader understanding of the human experience, and to some extent, a strong discomfort with the idea of any outsider meddling in the lives of communities. If a society were to change, in the view of many, it should do so because of the actions, beliefs, and free choices of its own members.

When it came to the actions of powerful nation-states affecting smaller indigenous communities, the issue was different. Most anthropologists are members of these same nation-states. As "natives" of these larger communities, many anthropologists from Boas onward have felt that they had legitimate standing to criticize and attempt to change the policies of their own society without violating the principles of cultural relativism. As a result, anthropologists in the 1960s felt no discomfort in attempting to promote social change and reform and to try to put a stop to the injustices their own political system was perpetrating against indigenous peoples.

During the same general era, cultural relativism's posture of refraining from criticism of the customs and practices of other cultures suffered challenges from a different direction. A few anthropologists became impatient with what they saw as a fastidious refusal to criticize even the most repugnant customs. Chronic warfare, headhunting, cannibalism, wife beating, and so on seemed to be practices that almost anyone could agree were wrong, cruel, and unjust. Marvin Harris, critiquing his version of Boasian cultural relativism, wrote "The preposterous assumption here is that reliable descriptions of cannibalism and infanticide cannot be achieved by ethnographers who openly oppose these practices" (1968:163). In the current age, he went on, "it will become increasingly difficult to convince anyone that descriptions of poverty, exploitation, disease, and malnutrition are admissible only to the extent that they lack 'subjective pronouncements' " (1968:164).

A few anthropologists have been even more hostile to the general idea of relativism. One of the most extreme, perhaps, seems almost nostaligic for a return to nineteenth-century ethnocentric models. Robert Edgerton laments "our inability to test any proposition about the relative adequacy of a society. Our relativistic tradition in anthropology has been slow to yield to the idea that there could be such a thing as a deviant society, one that is contrary to human nature" (1978:470). Others might argue that rather than having been "slow to yield" to such a view, relativism has combatted it directly.

RELATIVISM'S IMPLICATIONS FOR DIFFERENT THEORETICAL APPROACHES

If we focus on such material factors as subsistence, population size, and calorie intake as causal factors to explain cultural patterns, we are dealing with things that are concrete and mostly indisputable. They are weighable, measurable, and countable. The number of calories in a basket of wheat is what it is, regardless of the belief system of the person who is carrying it. Materialism offers one aspect of absolutism in the study of culture.

This view was involved in the debate over the proper approach to understanding culture, as we noted in Chapter 3. Is it more useful to focus on information that any careful outside observers would agree on, such as the size of gardens or the number of houses in a village? Or does the most important information involve the way life appears to the people involved, the explanations and rationales they offer, and the meanings of things from their perspective?

As we noted earlier, the former approach, which offered objective, confirmable information that could lend itself to comparative generalizations, came to be known as an **etic** approach. The latter, known as an **emic** approach, offered a more intimate view of the lives of people, but because of its focus on the uniqueness of particular cultures, it is far less amenable to comparative generalization. The emic approach appears more compatible with cultural relativism, while an etic approach tends to be less so.

While the terms "emic" and "etic" have fallen out of fashion in most current writing, the different perspectives they represent continue to offer alternative approaches. In fact, few if any anthropologists have ever embraced one of these as a pure form to the exclusion of the other. Perhaps this is one reason why these terms that seem to imply mutually exclusive approaches have fallen out of general use.

In recent evolutionary models, which have generally tended toward the etic and materialist modes of inquiry, cultural relativism has been ignored more than directly challenged. Given the macroscopic nature of most cultural evolutionary models, judgments or evaluations of the worth or value of particular customs have rarely been an issue. One might say that these studies usually have focused on long-term processes rather than short-term descriptions of particular cultural systems, except to the extent that they have served as examples of stages. Perhaps the fact that much of this research has to do with events that occurred far in the past has a good deal to do with the generally dispassionate approach to it.

By and large, we might also note that within social and cultural anthropology in general, cultural relativism seems to have been mostly an American issue. In some respects, though, a certain degree of relativism was implicit in most of the approaches that developed in anthropology during the twentieth century. The influence of Durkheim carried with it a sense that human life responds to social forces beyond the control of individuals and has few moralistic implications, except to the degree that Durkheim attached a moral value to social order itself. Durkheim also addressed the uniqueness of the various forms that society could take and retain even through historic change.

Later forms of functionalism focused on the ways in which various customs or practices meet human needs or maintain the social order, with little acknowledgment of the possibility that some of them might not. This, of course, tended to give a positive slant to any value judgments that might leak through the skein of objectivity.

The powerful influence of Radcliffe-Brown tended to downplay the issue of culture in the work of many of the earlier British social anthropologists. His student E. E. Evans-Pritchard eventually took exception to structural functionalism's disdain for the study of belief systems and other aspects of culture. Evans-Pritchard's ethnographies tended to focus on the task of portraying intimate, accurate views of people's lives, attempting to depict the way life looks to them, rather than to evaluate those systems in terms of absolute values. We would probably be justified in saying that such anthropologists as Evans-Pritchard, Raymond Firth, and others were cultural relativists without making an issue of it.

In archaeology, even such data as evidence of human sacrifice or ancient massacres have rarely raised questions of relativism. Perhaps because of the span of time separating such events from the observer and fact that these represent bygone events rather than continuing practices, such discoveries tend to provoke research questions rather than outrage or moral dilemmas—except among groups whose ancestors might be involved, thereby raising questions of political sensitivity and public relations.

Archaeological research on particular sites or even regions, likewise, has tended to pose questions that have little to do with evaluating cultural practices. The most exciting developments in pre-Columbian Maya research, for example, have had to do with constructing a fuller picture of Maya life and political and economic processes on the basis of limited evidence. Although some researchers have allowed themselves to reflect on the wider philosophical meaning of the Maya experience (see, for example, Thompson 1954), there tends to be little discussion about whether the Maya should or should not have practiced human sacrifice.

Notwithstanding the questions, doubts, and debates within anthropology, however, it is worth noting that cultural relativism has never become a major issue in most other disciplines. As later controversies over multiculturalism have shown, the idea that other cultures are worthy of a place in the general high school and college curricula was difficult for some people in the humanities and the social sciences to accept. For many of those whose major subjects of study have always been the nation-states of the Euroamerican sphere, people in small "Fourth World," indigenous societies have remained "primitives." As subjects of interest, they are not so much targets of criticism as irrelevant anachronisms. As for the general media, late in 1999 *The New York Times* referred to peoples of the Brazilian rainforest as "Stone Age people" (Schemo 1999). For many scholars of Western civilization, such communities continue to be of marginal interest.

Nonetheless, in assessing the role of relativism in anthropological thinking, Clifford Geertz points out that through exploring the range of human existence, anthropologists

> . . . have been the first to insist on a number of things: that the world does not divide into the pious and the superstitious; that there are sculptures in jungles and paintings in deserts; that political order is possible without centralized power and principled justice without codified rules; that the norms of reason were not fixed in Greece, the evolution of morality not consummated in England. Most important, we were the first to insist that we see the lives of others through lenses of our own grinding and that they look back on ours through ones of their own. (1984:275)

POSTMODERNISM

In the 1980s cultural relativism as most anthropologists had understood the term underwent a bizarre challenge from a direction that few could have foreseen in Boas's time. Relativism became a basis for attacking anthropology itself, and for good measure, history and other disciplines as well. Among other things, this attack involved extending relativism to an extreme form, in essence "pumping it up" to take the shape of what some saw as an intellectual monster (see Perry 2000).

This development did not arise in anthropology, although a few anthropologists eventually embraced it. It seems to have arisen from post-structuralism, which we discussed in the chapter on structure, and extended that perspective to a range of fields, from architecture to popular culture. From the perspective of anthropology, the literary mode was most significant.

For postmodernist critics of anthropology, the term "modern" came to be associated with the approaches of anthropologists from the late nineteenth century through the 1970s, and in some cases, beyond. Most of these earlier anthropologists, whatever their theoretical persuasions, had worked under the assumption that the most useful and appropriate way to develop an understanding of reality, including social and cultural reality, was through direct observation. The term "modern" in that sense referred to the development of these ideas in the Enlightenment as a departure from theological explanation. This perspective encompassed the position known as **positivism**—the idea that reality operates according to discoverable laws.

In literary criticism and art, *modernism* has a more distinct meaning. The historian Carl Schorske (1998) notes that modernism denoted an emphatic dissociation from the past.

> The very word "modernism" has come to distinguish our lives and times from what had gone before, from history as a whole, as such. Modern architecture, modern music, modern science—all have defined themselves not so much out of the past, indeed scarcely against the past, but detached from it in a new, autonomous cultural space. (1998:304)

As we recall, some post-structuralists took the position that for an observer to impute structure to social phenomena was to impose constraints, regularities, and external rules on social relationships. Some postmodernists went far beyond questioning structure itself and challenged the very idea that an observer could describe *any reality* with truth or accuracy. As Jean-Francois Lyotard puts it, "I define postmodernism as an incredulity toward metanarratives" (1986:xxiv). In the view of many postmodernists, for an outsider to describe the beliefs and customs of a different community was to impose a foreign version of reality. Much of the argument in this vein invoked references to oppression, control, the extension of hegemony over the powerless, and so on.

As with other discussions involving relativism, the strength of this assertion has varied among its proponents. At the "weak" end of the continuum, one could argue that it is difficult, if not impossible, for anyone to understand and to convey the perspective of anyone else fully and accurately, even leaving aside for the moment whether one has nefarious motives for attempting to do so.

Most anthropologists would agree with this, especially those who have tried it. This is one reason why so many ethnographies have included ample quotations from local people in the attempt to convey the people's perspectives as much as possible "in their own words." It is also why field workers repeatedly check their understanding of the information with the people in the community and seek their corrections.

There are some serious problems with this method, of course. Usually the local people offering their views on their own culture and society are not speaking in the language in which the researcher eventually writes and publishes the ethnography. This means that translation is necessary. To publish a book for an American readership filled with untranslated quotes in Hindi would make little sense if the purpose is to acquaint the reader with life in a community in rural India. But as Saussure pointed out many years ago and most people knew anyway, direct and accurate translation is extremely difficult. Some loss or distortion of meaning is inevitable.

Saussure wrote that "language is a system of interdependent terms in which the value of each term results solely from the simultaneous presence of the others . . . " (1959:114). He asserted that ideas do not exist prior to language or independently of it. The ideas through which humans categorize and engage reality are the products and consequences of language. The linguistic unit, or *sign*, consists of two components: the *signifier*, or "sound-image," and the *signified*, or the concept to which the signifier refers.

The relationship between signifier and signified, as we saw in Chapter 4 in our discussion of Derrida's ideas, is entirely arbitrary. There is no intrinsic relationship between any signifier and signified. Any sound-image can be linked with any concept, although once established, signs are not subject to change through individual whim. The meaning or "value" of any sign does not reside in the sign itself but derives from its contrastive or comparative relationships to other signs within the same system of signs.

Given the arbitrary nature of signs and their diverse possibilities of meaning and value within the field of other signs in the same language, signs are not easily translatable across language boundaries. Saussure offers the example of the French "*mouton*," for which the conventional English translation is "sheep." But when the term refers to food, one dines on mutton, not on sheep. Hence the meaning of the terms, though similar, does not entirely coincide (1959:115–116).

With regard to perceptions of reality, "only the associations sanctioned by that language appear to us to conform to reality, and we disregard whatever others might be imagined" (Saussure 1959:65). For many postmodernists this explanation has seemed to imply a cognitive universe in which signifier and signified frolic and drift in an ethereal realm unconnected to earthly reality. There is little reason to think that Saussure himself held such a view, however. As Paul Atkinson notes:

> The post-Saussurean recognition that the linguistic sign is "arbitrary" does not condemn us to the view that we have lost everything in a sea of whimsical or random semioses . . . the fact that linguistic signs derive their meaning from their relations with other signs—paradigmatic and syntagmatic—does not strip them of their referential function. (1990:176)

Some postmodernists, though, appear to have seized upon the relationships among signifiers while tending to ignore Saussure's discussion of the relationship between signifiers and signified.

The major revelation of the deconstructionists was that descriptive statements (or "texts"), being products of humans immersed in specific cultural, social, and political milieux and enmeshed among their own signifiers, can never be objective or accurate accounts of reality. Any text requires deconstructing. The layers of nuances arising from the author's biases, slants, and special interests (however unconscious they might be) require a peeling away to reveal the hidden agenda.

But there is a problem here. The deconstructor, being in the same situation as the author of the text (though perhaps in a different boat), cannot be a reliable authority either. The process of deconstructing any text creates another text that requires deconstruction. Logically, the concept seems to create a hall of mirrors in which "reality" is elusive and perhaps irretrievable.

This concept could also implicitly relegate those who adopt such an approach to the role of critiquing the work of positivists and other miscreants rather than producing their own fresh, insightful analyses of real-world phenomena.

One could also object that even double-checking with one's local consultants is no guarantee of accuracy. Typically, the researcher is from a large, wealthy, and powerful industrialized society, while the community he or she is studying may be historically, or even currently, oppressed. Will the local people talk freely? Is some subtle intimidation involved, causing people in the community to say what they think the researcher wants to hear?

Most anthropologists who have worked in the field would probably be comfortable in asserting that this was not the case in their research. Certainly there are many instances in which people in the community have withheld information or given the wrong information intentionally. Often this has arisen in cases in which the local consultant feels that the researcher is not worthy or entitled to learn certain things, or perhaps decides that it would be entertaining to mislead a curious guest (see, for example, Chagnon 1992:25).

The problem of accuracy remains daunting. But the validity of information has always been one of the central concerns of ethnographic fieldwork. There are few solutions to it beyond care, consultation, cross-checking, and good luck. Though unresolved, the problem is hardly new.

At the "strong" end of the postmodernist relativist position, however, the difficulties are even greater. As we have noted earlier, this view would hold that since our perceptions of reality are entirely a result of conditioning, we cannot be sure that reality exists at all outside our perceptions of it. In its most extreme form, as we noted, this can take the form of a philosophical position known as *solipsism*. As I imagine that I write this, for all I know there is no one else in the universe but me. On the other hand, you, the reader, may only be imagining the page in front of you. Maybe what you think I have written is only a figment of your imagination. We could probably avoid all further need for discussion by going down that road (what road?).

Let us assume for the moment, though, that something we call "reality" does exist independently of our perceptions. Suppose that such phenomena as the speed of light, the force of gravity, molecular structures, and the temperature at which water boils would be the same even if no human beings had ever existed. Provisionally, let us assume that these and other aspects of reality are not the products of human imagination.

This is not the same thing as saying that we fully understand all of these phenomena. Indeed, one might argue that a large part of human intellectual endeavor has been to figure such things out rather than invent them. True, we humans have invented many erroneous explanations for phenomena, such as the attribution of fire to phlogiston, or explaining conception by imagining a tiny homunculus inside the sperm cell. We have discarded these historic explanations, as we will many others that we presently accept. We have not abandoned them merely because they have gone out of fashion, but because they have not stood up under further testing against new evidence (or reality). Even if the principle of gravity has been difficult to understand over the centuries, though, a falling coconut can bruise a head nowadays just as severely as it did a thousand years ago.

In anthropology, of course, for the most part we are not dealing with such questions as whether we can predict that a drip from a faucet into the sink will fall with a splat rather than rise and fly away. We are dealing with people, and when that happens, we inevitably have interaction. To some degree or other, most people are sensitive to other people in their presence. Whether this provokes curiosity, irritation, attraction, or any other of a possible range of responses, the response itself complicates the interaction. It is more complicated than an observer dispassionately watching a falling coconut or a drip in the sink.

Interaction means that part of the general problem of humans trying to understand each other is that they also react to each other in a variety of ways, some of them difficult to predict, and many of them even unconscious.

This introduces a good deal of static into communication and observation. It is likely to affect the perceptions of any human observing human events.

Returning to the issue of the extent to which cultural conditioning affects our perceptions of reality, we might also point out that the people the researcher is trying to understand are just as subject to their own conditioning, and their perceptions of reality may well be just as inaccurate as the observer's. In an important respect, however, this takes us past the problem. The question for anthropology in general is not so much a matter of what reality "really is." That, more properly, is a matter for natural scientists and philosophers. For the anthropologist, the question is what reality is for the people she or he is trying to understand. This does, however, require an assumption that those people are really there.

Perhaps the central challenge postmodernism has offered to anthropology, as we have noted, is the assertion that the effort to understand other cultures is not only doomed to failure, but in many cases it constitutes a reprehensible attempt to impose one's own reality on others. A related charge has had to do with the fact that an ethnographer living in a community with other human beings is bound to experience and observe a complex range of multiple events and incidents. The task of ethnography has always been to "make sense" of these chaotic bits of data and to present them in a way that would enable a reader who is unfamiliar with that community to understand something about it. This means going beyond simply recording who did what how many times a day. It means summarizing events, perceiving patterns or regularities, and describing them in a comprehensible way.

The task of gathering complex information into a coherent and accurate report does inevitably involve forming composites of disparate events, deciding on emphasis or omission, and choosing ways to interpret ambiguous situations. Mary Louise Pratt writes that the narrative form of ethnography "mediates a contradiction within the discipline between personal and scientific authority" (1986:32). In other words, the ethnographer needs to find a way to convey information effectively and credibly, resting on the "authority" derived from having been there and done the work.

There is no doubt that conveying social or cultural information effectively in a form understandable to others generally requires one to summarize a mass of detail to depict a perceived pattern. Let us take an example from the Apache. When I was doing fieldwork in Arizona many years ago, an elderly Apache woman asked me, "Do owls speak to you in English?" When I responded that they do not, she told me, "They speak in Apache real plain. One time an owl said to me, 'I'm your grandfather.' Another time I dreamed I saw an owl among the chickens. It said, 'You're going to cry.' A few weeks later, my little niece died."

A couple of days later a young woman told me of a time when she dreamed that an owl had told her that her father would soon die. In her dream she pleaded with the owl, and it said, "All right, if you all pray real hard, he'll be hurt, but he won't die." A month or so after that, she said, her father was involved in a car accident, but he survived.

Small children sometimes scared one another by claiming to hear an owl. Some Apache parents during that time were upset by the logo of a national scholastic testing service, which was a stylized owl. On the night when the elderly woman told me about owls, she concluded by saying, "We shouldn't be talking about owls. They hear everything we say."

Ethnographic accounts of Chiricahua Apache, based on observations in the 1930s, give us more indications that the Apache associate owls with ghosts of deceased relatives, and that they consider them harbingers of death (see, for example, Opler 1941:30, 229–239). In John Bourke's account of a military campaign in the Sierra Madres in 1883, Apache scouts became upset when a packer kept an owl for a pet. They demanded that he release it (1886). On the other hand, an elderly Plains Apache man told me a few years ago that he was not afraid of owls. With some relish, he said that when he was young he used to shoot them every chance he had.

Considering such information, is it valid for us to conclude that the Apache associate owls with death and view them with dread? To approach accuracy in one way, we might try to gauge which and how many Apache individuals share such a belief, and how strongly they believe it. But this would miss another aspect of Apache "reality." Individuals have shared this belief and transmitted it among themselves over generations. As such, it amounts to a supra-individual phenomenon, existing independently of particular persons who might or might not hold it. It is, in other words, a feature of Apache culture. Even the elderly Plains Apache man's divergent stance, shooting owls and discussing it as he did many years later, acknowledges the belief, even in denying its power.

Does it amount to a hegemonic imposition of an "observer's model" to speak of this shared idea about owls as a cultural feature, or is it just a matter of drawing a reasonable conclusion from multiple events? Does the generalization rest primarily on the "authority" of the ethnographer, or does whatever authority the account may have arise from the gathering of evidence "on the ground," "at the scene," "in the field," and even in the library?

This aspect of anthropological fieldwork became another basis for challenging the validity of ethnography. As Mary Louise Pratt puts it, ethnographic writing involves "strategic choices" on the part of the ethnographer as to which information to include, which to ignore, and which to emphasize (Pratt 1986). One postmodernist historian has referred to ethnographies as "fictions" (Clifford 1988). In this vein, some writers took up the idea that ethnographies are merely "stories," and since ethnographies are "stories," "texts," and "fiction," the argument goes, they are not to be "privileged" over any other stories. The "authority" of the ethnographer based on having "been there" is specious.

This position, of course, has devastating implications for the attempt to understand other cultural systems. Followed to its logical conclusion, it would seem that any fiction is potentially as valid or invalid as any other. In this view, one has no need to have "been there" to write about a particular community. Why not imagine a story in the comfort of one's own study, fortified with a glass of sherry? Why not, in fact, make up a fictional culture?

We can see the inspiration of literary criticism in these arguments. The terms "fiction," "stories," "text," and "authority" certainly have weighty connotations. If we choose an alternative term for "authority," perhaps we should substitute "credibility." Few, if any, anthropologists have claimed to "speak for" the people with whom they have worked, although many have attempted to give voice to what they have learned from them. A central question in the postmodernist debates seems to be whether being on the scene and listening directly to the people of a community confers any more credibility than simply making up stories without even having seen the people who are the subjects of one's text.

THE MANY FACES OF RELATIVISM

As we have seen, relativism involves a bundle of issues. Can humans in different communities understand one another at a deep level, even with long mutual collaboration? Do some issues, such as those involving human rights, transcend cultural boundaries? Are some versions of reality more accurate than others?

In lieu of resolving these issues, we might close with a further question. As we have noted, some critics have asserted that the attempt to understand and describe other cultural systems amounts to an attempt to control and oppress the people of these communities. If so, we might ask what would be a preferable alternative? One possibility would be to ignore all cultures in the world but one's own. But although this might be an appealing prospect to some, most of us would consider this an unsatisfying and ultimately, perhaps, a dangerous course.

Should cultural description be the sole prerogative of people who are members of the community? This might be feasible in many cases, since we now have a body of ethnographic works written by people who have described their own cultures as anthropologists. To mention a few, Beatrice Medicine has written about her own Lakota culture, Epeli Hau'ofa about Tonga, Sir Peter Buck about the Maori, Francis Mading Deng about his Dinka community, Victor Uchendu about the Igbo, and Alfonso Ortiz about San Juan Pueblo. There are many others as well. We could also include the example of the anthropologist Jules Henry, who wrote a critical study of American society (1963).

On the other hand, we also must confront the fact that people of many indigenous communities have not produced or published ethnographies. In numerous cases, elders have died with the knowledge they possessed, which means that it has been lost forever. For some of these communities, ethnographers from the outside have recorded a legacy of information from the ancestors with whom they worked. We could cite the example of Franz Boas and his extensive work among the Kwakwala speakers of the Pacific Coast of North America. His published work has become a rich source of information for the present generation on their own heritage. For that matter, we could add the work of the nineteenth-century French historian Alexis de Toqueville in the United States, whose insights and observations continue to provide a fascinating addition to the ample historical record we have of our own past (1835).

Oppression and control of indigenous peoples have taken many forms over many centuries—most of them involving violence. Among the most pernicious, aside from overt force, has been the misrepresentation of other societies and cultures. Distortion of indigenous realities has been among the most common tools of oppression. In this vein, we must ask ourselves whether one "story" is, in fact, as good as another. Perhaps the comments of Ziaddin Sardar, a professor of policy science, get to the point:

> Postmodernism does not mark a break, a discontinuity from oppressive modernity; rather, it represents an underlying continuity of thought and actions about Other cultures, which formed the bedrock of colonialism, was the foundation of modernity and is now housed in postmodernism. Colonialism signified the physical occupation of the territory of Others, the non-Western cultures. Modernity signaled their mental occupation. Postmodernism now moves in to take possession of their total reality. (1998:20)

FOOD FOR THOUGHT

Does cultural relativism preclude the possibility of fully understanding other cultural systems?

If the ethnographer is a member of the group being studied, can he or she come to the truth or just a higher degree of accuracy compared to an ethnographer from outside the culture?

If you were an anthropologist living with an indigenous group in the Brazilian Amazon and a proposed hydroelectric dam was to flood their territory, would you stand by and observe how the village reacts to the dam, or would you take an active role in helping the village to control the future of their territory?

How do anthropologists explain warfare? Many people believe it is wrong, but most societies have engaged in it. If everyone does it, does that make it right?

What do you think about the idea that some cultures may be so-called "deviant societies"? Can you think of any particular cultural heritage that seems to stand out in some way as being "contrary to human nature"?

Geertz claims in his article on the Balinese cockfight that he managed to stay "invisible" to the people engaged in what he was observing. Is it possible for a cultural anthropologist working in the field to achieve nearly complete "non-existence?"

What is there about contemporary academics that has allowed faculty to teach subjects on cultures they have no real knowledge about? Is it a manifestation of universities dealing with other cultures in a superficial way?

Chapter 7

EPILOGUE

LOOKING BACK

The five key concepts we have discussed here do not, of course, capture all of the various strands and nuances of anthropological thinking. For many of us, one of the appeals of the discipline of anthropology is that it has always been "all over the map," literally and figuratively. Notwithstanding the importance of the concepts of structure, social order, and shared beliefs, some have found comfort in the relatively unbridled nature of inquiry and the near anarchy among its adherents. As we have seen, the history of anthropological thinking has been rife with challenges to the prevailing opinions of the time.

On the other hand, at this stage in anthropology's development, certain ideas have not only survived the test of scrutiny so far but have received affirmation from further research. Five of these ideas come to mind.

1. **Patterns of human behavior are learned, not inherent.** Although this may seem obvious to anthropologists, these same anthropologists may feel somewhat disheartened at the extent to which this fact has failed to penetrate popular thinking. For one thing, it means that cultural differences among human populations are not due to biological differences.

2. **"Race" is not appropriate, or useful, or valid as a biological concept.** The reason is not merely the connotations the term has acquired over the

centuries. More important than this, genetic research has demonstrated that human populations have no clear genetic boundaries. Genetic criteria do not support the idea of human "races" as distinct groupings, since gene frequencies overlap and blur in chaotic, clinal fashion throughout the globe.

3. **Human social and cultural patterns "make sense."** This is not an assumption of human infallibility; it is merely a recognition that, contrary to much nineteenth-century thinking, no human society practices a hodgpodge of irrational customs. This premise found its most formal expression in the various versions of functionalism, but it is also a central aspect of cultural relativism.

4. **Human social and cultural phenomena are systemically interrelated and immensely complex, even in the smallest societies.** This view rests implicitly on a recognition that existing customs represent the results of development, adaptation, or trial and error in specific local contexts, and that all human populations have equally long histories. It constitutes a rejection of the concept of "primitive" societies as simplistic, undeveloped, or inadequately formed ways of life.

5. **The complexities of human cultural and social phenomena warrant the close study of specific cases rather than broad generalizations.** Although anthropologists have not abandoned the search for general principles, they share a general recognition that valid principles can only be based on solid empirical evidence from the close study of real cases. This position represents a rejection of earlier ethnocentric and racist models based on assumptions regarding "savage" or "primitive" society as a generic category. The inception of fieldwork that provided detailed and first-hand information on small societies did much to humanize academic perceptions of small, kinship-organized communities.

UNSETTLED ISSUES

These several points of general agreement do not mean that anthropology has reached a stifling state of consensus. Many issues remain contentious. By the 1970s, for example, the anthropology of sex and gender became a major concern within the discipline in consonance with the feminist movement and the growth of attention to women's issues in the wider society. Many anthropologists expressed concerns that the perspectives and lives of women had not received sufficient attention in traditional ethnography.

To some extent this seems paradoxical, since many of the foremost anthropologists during the first part of the twentieth century have been women, and by the 1980s, more than half of the cultural anthropologists in the United States were women. Nonetheless, there was widespread agreement that anthropology had not adequately addressed some of the important issues relating to gender. Major issues centered on defining the criteria for relative gender status and roles in a variety of cultural settings, perceiving causes and regularities based on ethnographic evidence, and exploring the notion of "male dominance."

Tangential to these debates within anthropology, some feminist scholars also posited a prehistoric matriarchal past—a view that anthropologists had discredited in the nineteenth century. Although arguments of this sort often suggested the aura of anthropology, they have generally had little anthropological evidence to support their theoretical positions.

Many other issues remain points of contention. Materialists and idealists still disagree on the critical factors to explain culture—even if they can agree on what "explanation" means. Anthropologists also continue to disagree on the issue of relativism. Should anthropologists take stands on what appear to be major *moral* issues? So far, most agreement has focused on instances of powerful interests or nation-states oppressing indigenous peoples. When it comes to troublesome issues involving apparent cases of oppression or abuse *within* indigenous societies, the questions have remained divisive or have been ignored.

We also should acknowledge that, although anthropologists have for some time considered old ideas of "race" as a dead issue, racism continues to be a factor in modern life. Perhaps there is no more important task for anthropology now than to readdress this subject and present the case to the public more effectively.

APPROPRIATION OF THE CULTURE CONCEPT

Another issue, related in some ways, is the appropriation of the concept of culture in some segments of the media and the subversion of its original meaning. When the popular media deal with issues involving indigenous peoples, sooner or later the idea of "culture" usually comes up. But it is ironic that sometimes culture is used as a more acceptable euphemism for the term "race."

As we discussed in the chapter on culture, the term shares the same root as the term *cultivate*. In its original meaning, it asserts the human acquisition of behavior through learning and experience. It began as a conceptual *rebuttal* to the idea of the biological fixity of human behavior, the idea of inherent human differences. Culture's implications are that human behavior tends to be malleable, situationally adaptive, and instrumental. In popular journalism and public discussions, "culture" now often refers to some essential element that profoundly differentiates one human population from another. It implies a level of identity that is deep-seated, shadowy, essentially fixed, mysterious to outsiders, and most of all, inherently irrational. Why do such and such a people make the choices they do, believe as they do, act as they do? It's their culture. Need we say more?

We see this use of the term more and more in public discourse. It often evokes images of "ancient tribal hatreds," superstitions, and generally, rather odd and inscrutable ways of looking at things that few in the "civilized" world can ever really understand. In some ways it resembles a return to discredited nineteenth-century views of "savages."

This view, of course, inverts the original meaning of the term. It also posits "culture" as a prime mover, a not-necessarily rational determinant of human action, rather than as an adaptive mechanism or a product of human creativity. Basically, it denies human beings credit for rational, strategic thought.

What does this imply with regard to public perceptions of indigenous peoples? Among other things, it obfuscates such fundamental issues as sovereignty and the capacity for such people to exert control over their own lives and resources, under a smoke cloud of alleged cultural imperatives.

We know of hundreds of historic indigenous struggles against state systems and multinational powers over the past several centuries. In many cases, the parties to these struggles have had distinct cultural traditions and identities. But rarely have people taken up arms merely to preserve their culture. Not that culture is not important. It often serves as a unifying element. But in that sense, culture is only an instrument in the struggle; it is not what the struggle is about. Usually the struggle is about far more universal, basic issues: land appropriation, resource control, dislocation, and other forms of injustice and oppression that, in fact, are not so culturally mysterious after all. To attribute such unrest to mere attempts to preserve culture for some romantic reason is to caricature it, and to some extent, to discredit it.

We might consider a few examples. The Apache of the Southwestern United States managed to hold off defeat for over three hundred years, engaging Spanish, Mexicans, Angloamericans, and various other Native American peoples. In that sense, they were quite successful for a long time. If one were able to discuss this issue with Apache individuals of the early nineteenth century, we suspect that the idea that they were fighting to preserve or defend Apache culture probably would have made no sense to them. They were fighting because settlers were encroaching on their lands, depleting their food supply, attacking their encampments, enslaving their children, and generally disrupting their lives. Their concerns, in other words, were practical and not particularly mysterious, even to those who knew very little else about them (see Perry 1991, 1993).

We might also look at the so-called "Caste Wars" of Yucatan in the early nineteenth century, when the Yucatec Maya ostensibly rebelled against Mexican rule. Superficially, once again, one could see this as an attempt to reassert traditional Maya culture. But much of the symbolism that the rebels used to unite their forces was strongly and clearly Christian. A major element in that outbreak had to do with land confiscation, debt peonage, and forced labor. Not only that, but it began at the instigation of competing Mestizo interest groups, even though it was the Maya who suffered most of the casualties.

More recently, Mayan people in the impoverished Mexican state of Chiapas rose up in the 1990s to assert their rights and express their grievances, adopting the name *Ejercito Zapatista de liberacion nacional* (EZLN—the Zapatista Army of National Liberation). Some writers have described it as a Mayan cultural uprising; but clearly that is a gross oversimplification and probably reflects an inclination to exoticize the movement. As many others have pointed out, as disenfranchised agricultural people in the region, the Zapatistas had plenty of material grievances that required few esoteric cultural explanations. They had been intimidated by gangs hired by the landowners, driven off their lands, and sometimes murdered (Collier 1994a, 1994b).

It is true that much of the Mayan cultural mystique associated with the early years of this movement was a direct result of leadership strategies, particularly on the part of secretive Subcomandante Marcos, who issued a position statement couched in Maya imagery and metaphor, although Marcos himself is not ethnically Maya. We might also note that many local Maya people seem to have opposed the Zapatista movement.

The name Zapata is not Maya but refers to a Nahuatl-speaking mestizo from Morelos—a hero of the Mexican Revolution ably portrayed by Marlon Brando in the film *Viva Zapata*. Most significantly, perhaps, it seems clear that much of the impetus behind the Zapatista movement arose from the aggregation of displaced Maya in refugee centers who, as a result, developed a sense of common purpose that transcended their previous local cultural and narrower sense of identity.

By no means does this diminish the EZLN as a significant movement of indigenous peoples. It merely calls attention to the fact that the movement is far more complex than a simple "assertion of cultural identity." In fact, if anything, it may represent a growing trend among many indigenous peoples to *override* their specific cultural identities in recognition of common purpose in the face of transnational assaults on them and their resources. The issue in many cases seems to have more to do with economic and political power disparities than with cultural nuance.

The issue of culture arose in another interesting and rather famous case, this time in Queensland in northern Australia (Williams 1986). In the 1970s the Yolngu, an aboriginal people, sued commercial interests to regain the rights to their lands, which they argued had been unfairly appropriated from them. Their arguments were couched in their longstanding cultural precepts involving the inextricable bond between the land and the people who believed themselves to belong to it. They encountered difficulty in expressing their views in the Australian court, but their position fundamentally was that their bond to the land was ancient and beyond question.

The cultural issue that became most significant in this case was on the Australian side, since the judge insisted that the case rested on whether the Yolngu could prove "ownership" in a sense that was consonant with the centuries-old concept of ownership recognized in British law—a concept owing much to the writings of John Locke. In Locke's view, ownership arises from investing labor in the land—an investment that is most evident in farming.

The Yolngu, of course, being hunters and foragers, had not plowed the land or planted crops. Moreover, they readily admitted in court that although certain people had special rights to particular places by virtue of their kinship and place of birth, these people readily gave permission for other people to travel through, hunt, gather plants, and live there. Most important, perhaps, in the view of Yolngu and other Australian peoples, the people arose from the land and remained associated with it in a sense that merged past events and locality to produce a timeless and intrinsic bond between humans and places. They saw themselves as an aspect of the territory. To alter the terrain by farming or mining it—even if such activities had been feasible for the Yolngu—would have consititued unthinkable desecration.

From the point of view of British and Australian legal codes, which entailed exclusive rights to land as an aspect of property ownership, this argument was not acceptable. As a result, despite the general recognition that the Yolngu had inhabited the land in question "from time immemorial" and had not willingly surrendered it, the court ruled that they had not demonstrated proper "ownership" of it.

This decision was soon reversed and gave rise to a series of reforms in the Australian government's recognition of aboriginal land rights. Nonetheless, we might note that what this case was all about, at the most fundamental level, was who had rights to land. Cultural differences complicated the process, impeding communication and mutual understanding, but it was not "about" culture. It was about land rights.

We can all think of many other examples. Were the East Timorese struggling with the Indonesian government from the 1970s through the 1990s, suffering over 200,000 deaths, to assert their culture or to gain freedom from rule by an oppressive state?

The concept of culture also is often used in a pseudo-sympathetic fashion, as a means of accounting for purported "deficiencies" of indigenous communities. Allusions to alleged inherent factionalism in some Native American communities are one example. We often hear of "tribal factions" and comments that "they can't seem to get their act together." In "mainstream" communities, however, political disagreements are not only common but are likely to be interpreted as "democracy in action."

Perhaps even more pernicious, observers often refer to economic problems in indigenous communities as manifestations of culture. The San Carlos Apache of Arizona, for example, have had a chronic unemployment rate of about 75 percent. One sometimes hears the view that this is a result of their cultural background—that somehow, people with a heritage of hunting and raiding are not quite "ready" to take a productive part in the modern work force.

If this is true, how do we account for the fact that at the turn of the last century, Apaches constituted the major work force in the Southwest (Adams 1971)? They built roads, harvested crops, dug ditches, and in fact, eagerly sought any work available and enjoyed almost full employment. In the 1920s, however, other groups came into the Southwest—mainly Eastern European immigrants and Mexicans—and the Apaches lost their jobs. There has been very little work available for them ever since, even though they have doggedly tried to institute a range of enterprises on the reservation.

On the other hand, we do know that in many cases indigenous cultural patterns have been targeted by state systems. In Australia, Canada, and the United States, indigenous children were forced into boarding schools where their cultural identities faced a frontal assault. The story of Native American children being beaten for speaking in their own languages has been told many times, but it cannot be told often enough. Nor should we ever forget that mortality rates of children in some of these schools approached 30 percent (Dickason 1992:336).

This kind of oppression should remind us that, although culture may not be the fundamental reason for indigenous resistance, it is significant enough for elites to feel that they need to attack it. To grasp why this is so, we might step back and consider the wider arena in which indigenous groups find themselves.

The very term "indigenous peoples" implies something about their situation with regard to the wider context. Before the presence of state systems, these populations for the most part existed as autonomous societies. They certainly interacted with surrounding peoples, not always in a friendly way. But in general, they were able to call their own shots. Once incorporated into a state system, however, this autonomy was reduced, and they found themselves in a different situation altogether.

As the political scientist Nikos Poulantzas and other Marxist scholars have pointed out, a state is more than the apparatus of governance (1980). A state, by its nature, constitutes an arena of interest groups, most of them in competition with one another. In the United States, for example, we might think of the military power structure, the farm lobby, the Christian Right, the National Educational Association, the oil lobby, the gun lobby, and so on. Some of these interest groups are clearly far more powerful than others and far more likely, therefore, to get what they want.

A small indigenous population incorporated into a state—historically almost always by force—finds itself another of many interest groups in this competitive arena, whether its members want to be or not, and usually a relatively weak one. The only hope for such a group to defend its interests, if there is much hope, is at least to remain a group. This is where culture plays a crucial role. Common cultural identity can act as a powerful cohesive force in allowing such a group to continue. Conversely, to eliminate this cohesive factor and transform an indigenous group into scattered individuals who disappear into the general population is effectively to eradicate the population as an entity capable of defending its own interests—which in the vast majority of cases historically has involved the control of resources. This, for the most part, has been the aim of assimilationist programs to "bring people into the mainstream" or to promote "equal citizenship for all." It has also been one reason why many indigenous peoples have fought to retain their own cultural integrity and distinctness. Cultural identity is far more than a romantic, sentimental attachment to a "traditional way of life." Culture has strategic implications on both sides.

This brings us, finally, to another distortion of the culture concept—the idea of "traditional" indigenous culture being essentially stable, preserved from ancient times. This distortion is a weapon with more than one lethal edge. One is the myth of "culture loss," which arises from the idea that the "true" culture of an indigenous people was their culture immediately preceding their "discovery" by European invaders. If one were to accept that premise, then any change from that "pristine" configuration would constitute a loss of that "true" culture. In one sense, this premise amounts to yet one more way of conjuring the disappearance of indigenous peoples.

The absurdity of this presumption is not far below the surface, since culture has always been a dynamic abstraction. We discussed the concept of adaptation in the chapter on function; whatever its aspects, adaptation, including cultural adaptation, means *change*. Yet the static view of indigenous culture has had some important material consequences for many indigenous groups. Every few years, for example, some political leader in the U. S. Congress calls for the abrogation of treaties with Native American populations on the grounds that they no longer live the way their ancestors did. A prominent midwestern politician allegedly stated, with regard to treaty rights of a Native American population of his state, "If they want treaties, let them go back to birchbark canoes." One can only wonder what his reaction would be if one were to propose that the U. S. Constitution no longer applies to Americans because we no longer wear powdered wigs, three-cornered hats, and knee breeches that show a well-turned calf.

The tendency to see "traditional" culture as stable has also been used to oppose adaptive responses on the part of many indigenous peoples. Somehow, for example, to many observers it appears deeply inappropriate for Native American communities to engage in resource-generating activities in a contemporary context. Casinos, whatever one may think of them, offer one example. We might also look at the Mescalero Apache of New Mexico with their expensive four-star ski resort, the White Mountain Apache with their forest management and trophy elk herd, and other groups with mineral extraction or timber operations on their lands. These enterprises might vary in their success, wisdom, and ecological soundness, but they represent human choices that amount to dynamic readjustments of culture, not necessarily culture loss.

This is not to say that culture loss does not happen. If we want to persist in using that term, we could say that Cree children destroying their nervous systems by sniffing gasoline indicates culture loss. High crime and suicide rates among Australian aboriginal teenagers represent culture loss. On the other hand, what about a young Cheyenne woman who is a partner in a Denver law firm, keeps in touch with her many relatives, and represents her community in the legal system? Does this represent a loss of Cheyenne culture, or its persistence in a contemporary context?

The concept of culture remains a vital tool in our attempts to understand the struggles of indigenous peoples. But some have misused the term to obscure the true nature of the struggle. It is a peculiar abuse to use the concept to discredit innovative strategies for dealing with those issues merely because they are innovative. The concept seems in danger of being distorted to become a tool, as the discredited concept of race has been a tool, to exoticize, essentialize, and relegate the lives and realities of indigenous peoples to an unbridgeable distance from our own.

BEYOND THE FENCE

As anthropological ideas have developed over the past century or so, the discipline has borrowed from, and contributed to, a range of sister disciplines. Anthropology, in fact, has developed into the most interdisciplinary of disciplines. Much of this mixture derives from the early Boasian conception of anthropology as a field of inquiry that encompasses the totality of the human experience.

This scope narrowed considerably in France and England under the influence of Durkheim and, later, Radcliffe-Brown. It took a far broader trajectory in the United States under the influence of Boas who, as we know, encouraged the study of culture, language, the archaeological record, and human biology as important and complementary aspects of the discipline.

Since that time the range of subfields or focal areas has proliferated. We have seen vigorous research in psychological, economic, political, biological, medical, legal, and even mathematical anthropology. We should also note ethnohistory, ethnomusicology, and ethnobotany. Most of these fields, in fact, have their own organizations within the American Anthropological Association. With this proliferation, some anthropologists now worry that the Boasian "four fields" seem to have exploded into fragments of increasingly disparate disciplines. To some, anthropology seems to be at risk of losing its unity as a coherent field of study.

Perhaps anthropology's main strength remains what it has always been: It incorporates the attempt to understand humanity in the broadest sense. Cultures and regional populations—whether we focus on political, economic, artistic, religious, or psychological aspects of life—are examples of the broad human experience rather than isolated objects of study in themselves.

Unlike many other scholars, anthropologists have not been content to focus on their own societies. Indeed, they have suffered criticism for paying insufficient attention to that fertile area of inquiry. To many who have chosen anthropology as their lifelong field of endeavor, to focus only on one's own society is comparable to a botanist focusing only on her own backyard. There is certainly much to learn there—probably more than one could learn in a lifetime. But how much more lies beyond the fence?

FOOD FOR THOUGHT

The "four-fields" model in anthropology has become standard in the United States. Are there some negative aspects of this?

What effect has the Human Genome Project had for or against the theories of sociobiology?

Has the "advancement of technology" in a given society in the past been a direct result of the needs of the people in that society? If so, have we moved away from that progress by advancing technology past our needs?

If one were to argue that human society does not exist on a continuum with animal species but is fundamentally different, where would one draw the distinction?

Why do disciplines such as history, government, economics, and psychology seem to adamantly refuse to acknowledge culture, such an integral part of human life, in their research? Or do they?

GLOSSARY OF KEY TERMS AND NAMES

Acephalous. Used with reference to societies without a centralized government (literally, "headless").

Affinal relatives. Relatives by marriage ("in-laws").

Anarchism. A philosophy that opposes formal government.

Animism. Proposed by Edward Burnett Tylor as the earliest phase in the evolution of religion, animism involves the attribution of life or "souls" to inanimate objects.

Apollonian. A term used by Ruth Benedict that she borrowed from Friedrich Neitszche to describe a controlled, nonviolent personality type.

Asiatic mode of production. An idea developed by Karl Marx as a variant form of the mode of production. Characterized by a strong central regime developed as a means of controlling and regulating access to scarce resources such as water. (See also Feudal mode of production.)

Asymmetric marriage system. A system of nonreciprocal marriage exchange between unilineal descent groups that results from a rule of mother's brother's daughter/father's sister's son marriage.

Bands. As used by Elman Service, a group characterized by egalitarian social structure, lack of overall political organization, and loose political boundaries.

Barnett, Homer G. Author of *Innovation: The Basis of Culture Change.* Emphasized innovation as a recombination of existing elements.

Basic personality. Concept developed by Abram Kardiner and Ralph Linton at Columbia University; used in exploration of the ways in which child-rearing patterns affect adult personality. ("Basic Personality Structure" is sometimes referred to as BPS.) See also Primary institution and Secondary institution.

Benedict, Ruth (1887–1948). A student of Boas and a pioneer in culture and personality studies; utilized a configurationalist approach to cultures, emphasizing the uniqueness of particular cultural systems and the internal consistency between personality and culture. Author of *Patterns of Culture*.

Bilateral kinship. A kinship system in which relatives on the father's side and the mother's side are considered equivalent.

Bint 'amm marriage. A form of marriage known among some noble tribes in the Arabian peninsula. Preferred marriage is between a man and his father's brother's daughter.

Biological determinism. The idea that biological factors mold or determine behavior.

Boas, Franz (1858–1942). Sometimes considered the founder of American anthropology. Associated with "historical particularism," the development of cultural relativism, and the "four-fields" model of anthropology.

Boserup, Esther. Geographer best known for revising older ideas of the "invention" model of agriculture, demonstrating the significance of population pressure.

Carrying capacity. Sometimes used in an ecological sense, referring to the extent to which the resource base of a given region can support a human population.

Clans. Unilineal descent groups whose members may not be aware of specific relationships among themselves.

Classificatory kinship terms. Kin terms that apply to a category of relatives beyond specific kin, often on the basis of descent group membership (e.g., all members of one's own clan may be called by sibling terms).

Clines, clinal. In biology, a tapering distribution of traits from a center of intensity, generally without distinct boundaries.

Cognitive mazeway. Developed by Anthony F. C. Wallace in his discussion of the ways in which cognitive structures of individuals respond to institutional change.

Collateral relatives. Nonlineal relatives on each side (e.g., aunts, uncles, and cousins).

Commodity value. A concept used by Karl Marx referring to the value of an item on the market, as opposed to its use value.

Communitas. A concept developed by Victor Turner referring to the collective state of social cohesion often associated with a state of *liminality*.

Comparative method. As used by Tylor and others, the equation of contemporary cultures with cultures of the past.

Complex marriage system. A marriage system that specifies whom one cannot marry, usually on the basis of demonstrable kin ties.

Complexity. As used by Spencer and others, refers to the internal differentiation of the component parts of an entity (e.g., social complexity increases with the differentiation of institutions).

Comte, Auguste (1798–1857). Proponent of "positive philosophy"; considered by some to be the founder of sociology.

Configuration. Developed by Benedict and others; refers to a model of culture that emphasizes internal consistency but in unique patterns or configurations.

Cross cousins. Cousins who are children of one's mother's brothers or father's sisters.

Cultural ecology. A field of inquiry that focuses on the ways in which cultural systems work to meet material needs. Often associated with the pioneering work of Andrew Vayda and Roy Rappaport.

Cultural relativism. As developed by Boas and others, the idea that one should avoid value judgments in attempting to understand other cultural systems.

Culture core. A concept developed by Julian Steward; those aspects of a culture that arise in adaptive response to particular environmental situations.

Darwin, Charles (1809–1882). Produced major arguments for the biological evolution of species; developed the idea of natural selection.

Deductive. The scientific method that stresses hypothesis testing.

Delayed exchange. A type of marriage system in which marriage exchange between clans or lineages is one-directional in a given generation but reverses in the following generation, giving rise to eventual balanced reciprocity. Associated with rules that specify father's sister's daughter/ mother's brother's son marriage.

Diffusion. Refers to the tendency of cultural traits or features to spread from one culture to another.

Dionysian. A term Benedict borrowed from Friedrich Neitszche to describe a personality type that seeks excess and tends toward violence; employed in her book *Patterns of Culture*.

Distinctive features. A basis for distinguishing one speech sound from all others on the basis of phonetic characteristics; expressed in terms of + or −.

Divison of labor. Social divisions associated with task responsibility (e.g., gender-based division of labor).

Dualism. The idea that behind apparent or observable reality, a deeper or underlying reality exists; associated with Plato's concept of "ideal forms."

DuBois, Cora (1903–1991).   A student of Franz Boas; best known for her study *The People of Alor*, which pioneered the use of psychological projective tests to determine *modal personality*.

Durkheim, Emile (1858–1917).   French sociologist often referred to as the founder of functionalism; associated with a superorganic concept of social structure.

Emergent phenomenon.   A phenomenon that develops different properties under certain conditions, as the change of liquid water to ice.

Emic.   An approach to the study of culture that stresses a perspective from within the society; based on the term *phoneme*.

Enlightenment.   Sometimes known as the Age of Reason; generally associated with Western Europe in the eighteenth century. A departure from theological explanation to the pursuit of science through rational thought, observation, and experiment.

Epiphenomenon. (pl. epiphenomena)   An unforeseen or unintended consequence of some other development or phenomenon.

Eskimo terminology.   A terminology that distinguishes siblings from cousins and does not differentiate cousins from one another.

Essentialism.   A view that posits deep, inherent differences among phenomena. In the study of cultures, it would stress profound and incommensurable differences between cultures.

Ethnocentrism.   The view that one's own cultural system is superior to others.

Ethnography.   Cultural description.

Ethology.   The study of animal behavior.

Etic.   An approach to the study of cultures and societies that stresses measurable, observable data on which multiple objective observers would agree. Based on the term *phonetic*.

Eufunction.   A phenomenon whose function is beneficial.

Exogamous.   Marrying outside some specified group such as a clan, lineage, or moiety.

Extrasomatic.   Meaning "outside the body"; refers to the idea that culture is distinct from biology.

Feudal mode of production.   A notion developed by Karl Marx, which he saw as a phase preceding the development of capitalism in Europe.

Fieldwork.   The study of cultures or societies through first-hand observation.

Fortes, Meyer.   British social anthropologist best known for his work with the Tallensi. With Evans-Pritchard, co-edited *African Systems of Kinship and Marriage*.

Frazer, Sir James (1854–1941).   Sometimes referred to as "the father of anthropology"; one of the most prominent anthropologists in England at the end of the nineteenth century; associated with unilinear evolution; author of the massive work *The Golden Bough*.

Function. In anthropology, the purported effect (usually assumed to be positive) of a social phenomemon on the lives of people in a society or on the overall social structure.

Functional equivalence. With regard to alternative customs, institutions, or social practices, a situation in which both or several fulfill the same function.

Functional prerequisites. The conditions necessary for particular social phenomena to exist.

Geertz, Clifford R. (1926–). A major proponent of "interpretive" approaches to cultural description.

General evolution. A term proposed by Marshall Sahlins and Elman R. Service to contrast the broad cultural evolutionism of Leslie White with Julian Steward's model of multilinear evolution.

Hawaiian terminology. A terminology that groups siblings and cousins in the same category.

Hegemony. The extension of power. Used either to refer to power based on force or, in the ideas of Antonio Gramsci, power based on acceptance by the population.

Herodotus (c. 484 B.C. to c. 425 B.C.). Greek traveler and historian who described the customs of various populations in the Mediterranean region.

Herrnstein, Richard. Prominent proponent of the idea that intelligence is biologically determined to a significant degree. With Charles Murray, co-author of *The Bell Curve.*

Historical particularism. Associated with Franz Boas and his students early in twentieth-century American anthropology. Stresses the close study of particular cultures, with great attention to unique detail and avoidance of premature generalization beyond the specific case.

Hypothesis. A statement or assertion, often pertaining to causal relationships, subject to testing and possible refutation.

Ideology. In general, the prevailing belief system of a society. As used by Karl Marx, a prevailing view of reality promoted by the elite class to disguise exploitative relationships.

Image of limited good. A notion developed by George Foster with regard to peasant communities, it assumes that one person's good fortune is balanced by the misfortune of others.

Inductive. A scientific method emphasizing the gathering of data prior to developing theoretical assumptions.

Iroquois cousin terminology. A terminology that differentiates cross cousins from parallel cousins and equates parallel cousins with siblings.

Jakobson, Roman (1896–1982). A leading founder of structural linguistics; a major influence on Claude Levi-Strauss in his development of structural models.

Khaldun, Abu Zayd 'Abd Ar-rahman (1332–1406).   Arab scholar born in Spain who traveled throughout much of the Mediterranean region and studied differences among populations, emphasizing the effects of nomadic versus urbanized ways of life.

Kardiner, Abram (1891–1981).   Trained in psychiatry; in collaboration with Ralph Linton, developed the concept of *basic personality*.

Kroeber, Alfred Louis (1876–1960).   Earned the first doctorate in anthropology in the United States as a student of Franz Boas; major proponent of a humanistic approach to the study of culture.

Kropotkin, Prince Peter.   Well-known anarchist at the beginning of the twentieth century. Emphasized the competitive value of cooperation; probably had some influence on the early thinking of Radcliffe-Brown.

Laissez fair.   "Hands off" policy; generally associated with unregulated competition, as among business firms; compatible with a philosophy of "survival of the fittest" associated with social Darwinism.

Langue.   A term most associated with Fernand de Saussure; refers to the formal structure of language, as opposed to discrete acts of speech, or *parole*.

Law of evolutionary potential.   Developed by Elman R. Service; states that relatively undeveloped societies may enjoy some advantage over more advanced societies because they are able to adopt state-of-the-art technology.

Leveling mechanisms.   A term generally referring to customs, practices, and beliefs that inhibit the development of extreme disparities of power and wealth within a community.

Levels of sociocultural integration.   Julian Steward's term referring to levels of cultural and social evolution.

Levi-Strauss, Claude (1908–).   Developed modern French structuralism.

Lewontin, Richard (1929–).   Geneticist who demonstrated that genetic variance among individuals within a population exceeds variance between populations.

Liminality.   A concept developed by Victor Turner; often associated with transition between social statuses. A condition of being "in-between," to some extent outside the social structure.

Lineage.   A unilineal descent group that consists of people descended through one line (either the mother's or the father's) from a common ancestor, and who can demonstrate specific kin ties among themselves.

Lineal relatives.   Relatives in a single line of descent (e.g., parents, children, and grandchildren).

Linton, Ralph (1893–1953).   Developed the concepts of role and status; worked with Abram Kardiner to develop the concept of *basic personality*.

Maine, Sir Henry James Sumner (1822–1888).   British legal scholar who spent time in India and incorporated this experience in writing a comparative analysis of law. Generally known for his distinction between relationships based on principles of "status" versus "contract" as aspects of social evolution.

Malinowski, Bronislaw (1884–1942).   Considered one of the founders of British social anthropology and a major proponent of fieldwork. Associated with functionalism based on his theory of needs.

Malthus, Thomas (1766–1835).   Nineteenth-century scholar who predicted eventual catastrophe based on the fact that population increases geometrically, while the food supply increases arithmetically.

Mauss, Marcel (1872–1950).   French student and colleague of Emile Durkheim who developed the principle of reciprocity as a key element in sociocultural systems.

Matrilineal clans.   Clans whose membership is based on descent through the mother's line.

Mead, Margaret (1901–1978).   The best-known American anthropologist of the mid twentieth century. A student of Franz Boas, she was best known for her work in the South Pacific, which emphasized the importance of culture rather than biology in matters of socialization and gender.

Means of production.   A concept developed by Karl Marx referring to the methods and equipment necessary for production such as factories, the ownership or control of which has important implications for relationships among classes.

Mechanical models.   Discussed by Levi-Strauss as a model of social phenomena depicting rules and principles of social phenomena (such as marriage systems) rather than actual behavior.

Mechanical solidarity.   A term Emile Durkheim used to refer to social cohesion in societies with a low degree of social differentiation; solidarity based on similarity.

Modal personality.   A concept used by Cora DuBois and Anthony F.C. Wallace based on the attempt to depict personality traits in a statistical fashion through the results of projective tests.

Mode of production.   Developed by Karl Marx. Refers to the manner in which a society meets its material needs; has a determining effect on other aspects of life. (See also Means of production, Relations of production.)

Models.   Depictions of phenomena through expression of significant relationships among their components. (See also Mechanical models, Statistical models.)

Monism.   Generally in opposition to *dualism*; the view that reality consists entirely of what humans are able to sense; a denial that another, abstract level of reality underlies the sensible realm.

Monogenesis.   In the context of debates over human origins, the position that all humans are descended from a single divine creation.

Morgan, Lewis Henry (1818–1881).   One of the major figures of nineteenth-century unilinear evolution; focused on the development of the family through a series of stages.

Multilinear evolution. Developed by Julian Steward to accommodate principles of cultural evolution with specific differences in local ecology.

Murray, Charles. Major late twentieth-century proponent of biological determinism and the inheritance of intelligence. With Richard Herrnstein, co-author of *The Bell Curve.*

Mystification. A term sometimes used by Marxists referring to prevailing beliefs or deceptive views of reality that disguise exploitative relationships.

Nomothetic. A term favored by Marvin Harris (based on the root *nomo*, meaning law). In anthropology, a nomothetic statement would apply to multiple cases, ideally expressing a causal relationship.

Organic analogy. The idea that society has the characteristics of a living organism.

Organic solidarity. A term used by Emile Durkheim to refer to social cohesion in societies with a high degree of social differentiation. Solidarity based on complementarity.

Oriental despotism. A concept used by Karl Wittfogel and Julian Steward, based on Marx's "Asiatic mode of production"; associated with strong central governments developed to control access to resources, typically irrigation water.

Parallel cousins. People whose parents include siblings of the same sex (e.g., the mother's sister's children or the father's brother's children).

Parole. Associated with the work of Fernand de Saussure; refers to discrete acts of speech, as opposed to the formal structure of language.

Phenomenology. An approach associated with the ideas of Edmund Husserl; emphasizes the primary importance of immediate sensory information, as opposed to projected theoretical frameworks.

Phonemics. The study of the smallest units of sound that have some significance in a language.

Phonetics. The study of the distinctive features of minimal units of sound.

Pike, Kenneth (1912–). Linguist associated with suggesting the terms *emic* and *etic* from the linguistic approaches known as "phon*emic*s," the study of the ways in which sounds function in a language, and "phon*etic*s," the ways in which sounds are produced physically.

Polygenesis. In the context of debates about human origins, the idea that different human populations are descendants of separate divine creations.

Positive philosophy. A philosophical position espoused by Auguste Comte and later theorists holding that reality is discernible through observation and that it operates according to discoverable laws.

Positivism. Based on the assumption that reality, including society, operates according to discoverable laws. (**Positivists:** those allegedly holding such a view.)

Primary institution. Associated with Linton's and Kardiner's model of *basic personality*; involves practices and customs associated with child rearing and early childhood experience.

Primitive promiscuity. In the nineteenth century, a supposition that the earliest human societies lacked rules regulating sexual behavior, resulting in generalized sexual access.

Psychic unity. Generally associated with nineteenth-century evolutionary models; the idea that the human mind everywhere tends to find similar solutions to comparable problems.

Psychological functionalism. A view associated primarily with Bronislaw Malinowski that practices, beliefs, and customs function to meet psychological and emotional needs, such as the alleviation of anxiety.

Radcliffe-Brown, A.R (1881–1955). Considered the founder of structural functionalism; one of the major figures of British social anthropology during the first half of the twentieth century.

Rappaport, Roy (1926–1997). One of the major figures in developing the subfield of cultural ecology in the second half of the twentieth century. Author of *Pigs for the Ancestors*, which demonstrated a functional relationship between pig raising and warfare in highland New Guinea.

Reciprocal altruism. In sociobiology, the idea that an animal that sacrifices itself to warn others about a predator does so because this action will allow more of its kin to survive, thereby ensuring the survival of more of the genes it shares with them.

Reciprocity. Developed by Marcel Mauss, the principle that equivalence in exchange, or lack of it, has important implications for social relationships.

Reification. The "fallacy of misplaced concreteness," or treating an abstraction as if it were a concrete entity or phenomenon.

Relations of production. A concept developed by Karl Marx; refers to the social arrangements in a society that develop as a consequence of its mode of production.

Rites of passage. A term used by Arnold Van Gennep to describe rituals that effect a change in social status.

Sapir, Edward (1884–1939). A student of Franz Boas and a major figure in American linguistics in the first part of the twentieth century. A proponent of cultural and linguistic relativism.

Saussure, Ferdnand de (1857–1913). A linguist with major influence on structuralism and post-structuralism; drew the distinction between *langue* and *parole*; pointed out the arbitrary relationship between signifiers and signified and the fact that meaning arises from relationships and contrasts among signifiers.

Secondary institution. Associated with the concept of *basic personality* developed by Abram Kardiner and Ralph Linton; secondary (or "adult") institutions are manifestations of basic personality traits developed in childhood as a result of primary institutions.

Service, Elman R. (1915–1996). A student of Leslie White; developed the "law of evolutionary potential" and discussed differences between band, tribe, and chiefdom levels of social evolution.

Skepticism. A view stemming from classical Greek philosophy and adopted by many post-structuralists and postmodernists that disputes the reliability of narrative, or in some cases, of sensory reality.

Social condensation. Used by Durkheim to refer to the differentiation of social or economic roles to reduce social stress.

Social Darwinism. The idea that human societies, like the rest of nature, are engaged in a competitive struggle for existence.

Social integration. A concept that stresses the degree of cohesion or complementary relationships in a community. Bears some relationship to Durkheim's concept of solidarity.

Sociobiology. The idea that human behavior, like the behavior of other species, is determined largely by the imperative of passing on a maximum of one's genes.

Solipsism. The view that only the existence of the self is knowable, and that sensory perceptions of reality are illusions.

Specific evolution. Developed by Marshall Sahlins, Elman R. Service, and their colleagues to distinguish the general evolution of Leslie White from the multilinear evolution of Julian Steward.

Spencer, Herbert (1820–1903). Generally recognized as the originator of *social Darwinism*. Spencer argued that society is a part of nature and evolves according to natural laws, generally involving progress from the simple to the complex. Credited with the development of the organic analogy and the concept of society as the *superorganic*.

Stages. In the context of nineteenth-century evolutionary models, levels of evolutionary progress.

States. Often referred to as "complex societies" on the basis of their internal heterogeneity; also associated with large population size, market systems, social stratification, writing, and monumental architecture.

Statistical models. Used by Levi-Strauss; refers to models of social phenomena (such as marriage systems) that depict actual behavior.

Steward, Julian (1902–1972). A student of Kroeber; developed the concept of multilineal evolution to incorporate specific issues of cultural ecology in the analysis of social evolution.

Structural functionalism. An approach generally associated with A.R. Radcliffe-Brown and his followers; emphasizes the primacy of the social structure in functional analysis.

Superorganic. With reference to culture or society, the idea that these phenomena exist above the organic level of reality (e.g., the rules of individual psychology cannot explain society or culture).

Surplus value. A concept developed by Karl Marx referring to the difference between commodity value of an item on the market and the wages paid to the worker whose labor produced it.

Symbol. An object, graphic shape, or sound with an ascribed, agreed-upon meaning.

Synchronic. Regarding the study of social, cultural, or linguistic phenomena, an analysis focusing on aspects other than change through time.

System. A field or set of relationships whose component aspects mutually influence one another.

Systematic bias. Underlying or *a priori* assumptions that may cause multiple observers of the same or similar phenomena to arrive at similar misinterpretations.

Teleology. The sense that change occurs according to some predetermined direction or toward some ultimate aim.

Thick description. A term used by Clifford Geertz referring to ethnographic description that goes beyond, or beneath, superficial observation and explores the symbolic significance of action and performance.

Totality. With regard to social or cultural issues, generally a principle that has effects on all aspects of the culture or society.

Tribes. Generally applied to indigenous populations; increasingly controversial term because the concept imputes characteristics such as boundaries and internal social cohesion that may not be warranted.

Tylor, Edward Burnett (1932–1917). Prominent British unilinear evolutionist who developed the concept of animism as the earliest phase of religion; credited with an early, classic definition of culture.

Unilineal descent groups. Groups who attribute their commonality to descent from one line (the mother's or the father's) from a single ancestor.

Unilinear evolution. The idea that cultures or societies develop along a single path.

Use value. A concept developed by Karl Marx that refers to the intrinsic value of an item, as differentiated from its commodity or market value.

Vayda, Andrew (1931–). Noted for the development of cultural ecology as a major subfield during the second half of the twentieth century.

Wallace, Alfred Russell (1823–1913). A contemporary of Darwin's, he developed a model of biological evolution independently during the same period.

Wallace, Anthony F.C. (1923–). A major figure in culture and personality studies, his use of the concept of modal personality did much to turn the direction of research away from older models.

Weltanschauung. The German word from which the English term *world view* derives.

White, Leslie A. (1900–1975). Responsible for a revival of interest in cultural evolution in the twentieth century. Credited nineteenth-century theorists for many of his ideas, but incorporated the criterion of energy use to distinguish stages.

Wilson, Edward O. (1929–). An entomologist world-renowned for his work with social insects; attempted to extend the model of instinctive behavior to humans.

Wittfogel, Karl (1896–1988). A scholar influenced by the work of Marx who developed the model of irrigation as a basis for strong centralized governments; a major influence on Julian Steward.

Wolf, Eric R. (1923–1999). A major figure in anthropology in the last half of the twentieth century who urged the increased use of history and insights from other disciplines, particularly in showing global relationships among indigenous peoples and state systems.

World systems theory. A model developed by Immanuel Wallerstein depicting the extension of a global division of labor between powerful *core* and *peripheral* regions.

World view. A summary concept incorporating the body of knowledge, belief, and explanatory principles held by people in a particular cultural system or society.

REFERENCES

Adams, William Y. 1971. "The Development of San Carlos Apache Wage Labor to 1954," in Keith H. Basso and Morris E. Opler, eds., *Apachean Culture History and Ethnology*, pp. 116–128. Tucson: University of Arizona Press.

Ardrey, Robert. 1970 [orig. 1961]. *African Genesis: A Personal Investigation into the Animal Origins and Nature of Man*. New York: Atheneum.

Asad, Talal, ed., 1973. *Anthropology and the Colonial Encounter*. Atlantic Highlands, NJ: Humanities Press.

Atkinson, Paul. 1990. *The Ethnographic Imagination: Textual Constructions of Reality*. New York: Routledge.

Barnett, Homer G. 1953. *Innovation: The Basis of Culture Change*. New York: McGraw-Hill.

Barnouw, Victor. 1973. *Culture and Personality*. Homewood, IL: Dorsey Press.

Barth, Fredrik. 2001. "Rethinking the Object of Anthropology," in Robert Borofsky, et al., "WHEN: A Conversation about Culture," *American Anthropologist* 103(2): 432–446.

Bateson, Gregory. 1972. *Steps to an Ecology of Mind*. London: Paladin.

Bellah, Robert N. 1964. "Religion and Evolution," *American Sociological Review* 29: 358–374.

Benedict, Ruth. 1932. *Patterns of Culture*. New York: Houghton-Mifflin.

Berger, Peter. 1969. *The Social Reality of Religion*. London: Faber.

Berlin, Brent, and Paul Kay. 1969. *Basic Color Terms: Their Universality and Evolution*. Berkeley: University of California Press.

Blok, Anton. 1989. "The Symbolic Vocabulary of Public Executions," in June Starr and Jane F. Collier, eds., *History and Power in the Study of Law*, pp. 31–54. Ithaca: Cornell University Press.

Boas, Franz. 1887. "Museums of Ethnology and Their Classifications," *Science* 9:587–589.

———. 1888. *The Central Eskimo.* Report of the Bureau of Ethnology, 1884–1885, pp. 399–669. Washington: Smithsonian Institution.

———. 1894. "The Half-Blood Indian, An Anthropometric Study," *Popular Science Monthly* 45:461–470.

———. 1896. "The Limitations of the Comparative Method in Anthropology," *Science* 4:901–908.

———. 1897. *The Social Organization and the Secret Societies of the Kwakiutl Indians.* Report of the U.S. National Museum, 1895. Washington.

———. 1911. *The Mind of Primitive Man.* New York: Macmillan.

———. 1912. *Abstract of the Report on Changes in Bodily Form of Descendants of Immigrants.* The Immigration Commission. Washington: Government Printing Office.

———. 1938. "An Anthropologist's Credo," *The Nation* 147:201–204.

———. 1940. *Race, Language, and Culture.* New York: Macmillan.

Boaz, Noel, and Alan J. Almquist. 2002. *Biological Anthropology: A Synthetic Approach to Evolution.* Upper Saddle River, NJ: Prentice Hall.

Bodley, John. 1982. *Victims of Progress.* Palo Alto, CA: Mayfield.

Bohannan, Paul, and Mark Glazer, eds. 1988. *High Points in Anthropology,* 2d ed. New York: Knopf.

Bordieu, Pierre. 1990. *The Logic of Practice,* Richard Nice, trans. Stanford: Stanford University Press.

Borofsky, Robert, et al. 2001. "WHEN: A Conversation about Culture," *American Anthropologist* 103(2):432–446.

Boserup, Esther. 1965. *The Conditions of Agricultural Growth: The Economics of Agrarian Change under Population Pressure.* Chicago: Aldine.

Bourke, John. 1886. *An Apache Campaign in the Sierra Madres. An Account of an Expedition in Pursuit of the Hostile Chiricahua Apaches in the Spring of 1883.* New York: Charles Scribner's Sons.

Braudel, Fernand. 1979. *The Perspective of the World,* vol. III, *Civilization and Capitalism.* New York: Harper & Row.

Brinton, Daniel G. 1896. "The Aims of Anthropology," *Proceedings of the 44th Meeting of American Academy for the Advancement of Science* 1–17.

Cancian, Francesca. 1968. "Functional Analysis: Varieties of Functional Analysis," in David L. Sills, ed., *International Encyclopedia of the Social Sciences,* pp. 29–43. New York: Macmillan and Free Press.

Carneiro, Robert L., ed. 1967. *The Evolution of Society: Selections from Herbert Spencer's Principles of Sociology.* Chicago: University of Chicago Press.

Chagnon, Napoleon. 1992. *Yanomamo,* 4th ed. Fort Worth: Harcourt Brace Jovanovich.

Clifford, James. 1988. *The Predicament of Culture: Twentieth Century Ethnography.* Berkeley: University of California Press.

Cochrane, D. Glynn. 1971. *Development Anthropology.* New York: Oxford University Press.

Codere, Helen. 1950. *Fighting with Property.* Monographs of the American Ethnological Society, 18. New York: J.J. Augustin.

———. 1956. "The Amiable Side of Kwakiutl Life," *American Anthropologist* 58:334–351.

———. 1957. "Kwakiutl Society: Rank without Class," *American Anthropologist* 59: 473–485.

———. 1959. "The Understanding of the Kwakiutl," in Walter Goldschmidt, ed., *The Anthropology of Franz Boas*. American Anthropological Association Memoir 89: 61–75.

Codrington, R.H. 1891. *The Melanesians, Studies in Their Anthropology and Folk-Lore*. Oxford: Oxford University Press.

Cole, Douglas. 1983. " 'The Value of a Person Lies in His *Herzenbildung*': Franz Boas's Baffin Island Letter Diary," in George W. Stocking, Jr., ed., *Observers Observed: Essays on Ethnographic Fieldwork*, pp. 13–52. Madison: University of Wisconsin Press.

———. 1999. *Franz Boas: The Early Years, 1858–1906*. Seattle: University of Washington Press.

Collier, George.1994a. *Basta! Land and the Zapatista Rebellion in Chiapas*. Oakland: Institute for Food and Development Policy.

———. 1994b "The Roots of Rebellion in Chiapas," *Cultural Survival Quarterly* 18(1):14–18.

Comte, Auguste. 1896. *The Positive Philosophy*. Harriet Martinequ, trans. London: G. Bell.

Conklin, Harold C. 1955. "Hanunoo Color Categories," *Southwestern Journal of Anthropology* 11:339–344.

Coon, Carleton S. 1962. *The Origin of Races*. New York: Knopf.

Cote, James E. 1998. "Much Ado about Nothing: The 'Fateful Hoaxing' of Margaret Mead," *The Skeptical Inquirer* 22(6):29–34.

D'Andrade, Roy. 2000. "Moral Models in Anthropology," in Jon McGee and Richard L. Warms, eds., *Anthropological Theory: An Introductory History*, pp. 351–368. Mountain View, CA: Mayfield. (Orig. in *Current Anthropology* 36(3):399–408, 1995.)

Darwin, Charles. 1858. *Origin of Species*. New York: New American Library.

———. 1876. *The Descent of Man and Selection in Relation to Sex*. New York: D. Appleton.

Dawkins, Richard. 1989. *The Selfish Gene*. Oxford: Oxford University Press.

Derrida, Jaques. 1967. *Of Grammatology*. Baltimore: Johns Hopkins University Press.

———. 1982 [orig. 1972]. *Margins of Philosophy*. Chicago: University of Chicago Press.

Descartes, Rene. 1960. *Discourse on Method and Other Writings*, Arthur Wollaston, trans. Hammondsmouth: Penguin Books.

Dickason, Olive P. 1992. *Canada's First Nations: A History of Founding Peoples from Earliest Times*. Toronto: McClellan and Stewart.

Douglas, Mary. 1966. *Purity and Danger: An Analysis of the Concepts of Pollution and Taboo*. London: Routledge and Kegan Paul.

———. 1970. *Natural Symbols: Explanation and Cosmology*. New York: Pantheon.

DuBois, Cora. 1944. *The People of Alor: A Social-Psychological Study of an East Indian Island*. Minneapolis: University of Minnesota Press.

Durkheim, Emile. 1915 [orig. 1912]. *The Elementary Forms of the Religious Life*. London: Allen & Unwin.

———. 1933 [orig. 1893]. *The Division of Labor in Society*. New York: Macmillan.

———. 1938 [orig. 1895]. *The Rules of the Sociological Method*. New York: Free Press.

Durkheim, Emile, and Marcel Mauss. 1970 [orig. 1903]. *Primitive Classification*. London: Routledge.

Edgerton, Robert. 1978. "The Study of Deviance, Marginal Man and Everyman," in George Spindler, ed., *The Making of Psychological Anthropology*, pp. 444–471. Berkeley: University of California Press.

Elias, Norbert. 1994. *The Civilizing Process*. Cambridge, MA: Blackwell.

Erasmus, Charles J. 1961. *Man Takes Control*. Minneapolis: University of Minnesota Press.

Evans, Richard J. 1999. *In Defense of History*. New York: W. W. Norton.

Evans-Pritchard, E. E. 1937. *Witchcraft, Oracles and Magic among the Azande*. Oxford: Clarendon Press.

———. 1940. *The Nuer: A Description of the Modes of Livelihood and Political Institutions of a Nilotic People*. Oxford: Clarendon Press.

———. 1949. *The Sanussi of Cyrenaica*. London: Oxford University Press.

———. 1950. "Social Anthropology Past and Present," *Man* 198:118–124.

———. 1962. *Social Anthropology and Other Essays*. New York: Free Press.

Fadhlan, Ibn. 1948. "The Vikings Abroad and at Home," in Carleton Coon, ed., *A Reader in General Anthropology*, pp. 410–416. New York: Henry Holt.

Fernandez-Armesto, Felipe. 1995. *Millennium: A History of the Last Thousand Years*. New York: Scribner.

Fortes, Meyer. 1945. *The Dynamics of Kinship among the Tallensi*. London: Oxford University Press.

———. 1949. *The Web of Kinship among the Tallensi*. London: Oxford University Press.

Foster, George. 1965. "Peasant Society and the Image of Limited Good," *American Anthropologist* 67:293–314.

Foucault, Michel. 1972. *The Archaeology of Knowledge*. London: Harper Colophon.

———. 1973. *The Order of Things*. New York: Vintage.

———. 1976. *Madmen and Civilization: A History of Insanity in the Age of Reason*. New York: Vintage/Random House.

Frake, Charles. 1961. "The Diagnosis of Disease among the Subanum of Mindanao," *American Anthropologist* 63:113–132.

———. 1962. "The Ethnographic Study of Cognitive Systems," in Thomas Gladwin and William G. Sturtevant, eds., *Anthropology and Human Behavior*, pp. 72–85. Washington: Anthropological Society of Washington.

Frank, Andre Gunder. 1972. "Introduction," in *Dependence and Underdevelopment: Latin America's Political Economy*. James D. Cockroft, Andre G. Frank, and Dale L. Johnson, eds. Garden City, NY: Doubleday, pp. ix–xxix.

———. 1975. *On Capitalist Underdevelopment*. Bombay: Oxford University Press.

Frazer, James G. 1958 [orig. 1890]. *The Golden Bough*. New York: Macmillan.

Freeman, Derek. 1983. *The Making and Unmaking of an Anthropological Myth*. Cambridge: Harvard University Press.

Fried, Morton. 1967. *The Evolution of Political Society*. New York: Random House.

Geertz, Clifford. 1965. "The Impact of the Concept of Culture on the Concept of Man," in John R. Platt, ed., *New Views of the Nature of Man*. Chicago: University of Chicago Press.

———. 1973. *The Interpretation of Cultures*. New York: Basic Books.

———. 1984. "Distinguished Lecture: Anti-Anti-Relativism. . . ." *American Anthropologist* 86:263–278.

Giddens, Anthony. 1995. *Politics, Sociology and Social Theory: Encounters with Classical and Contemporary Social Thought*. Stanford: Stanford University Press.

Godelier, Maurice. 1977. *Perspectives in Marxist Anthropology*. Cambridge: Cambridge University Press.

Goldman, Irving. 1975. *The Mouth of Heaven: An Introduction to Kwakiutl Religious Thought*. New York: Wiley.

Goldschmidt, Walter. 2001. "Historical Essay: A Perspective on Anthropology," *American Anthropologist* 102(4):789–807.

Goody, Jack. 1995. *The Expansive Moment: The Rise of Social Anthropology in Britain and Africa*. New York: Cambridge University Press.

Graebner, F. 1911. *Die Methode der Ethnologie*. Heidelberg: C. Winter.

Graves, Joseph L., Jr. 2001. *The Emperor's New Clothes: Biological Theories of Race at the Millennium*. New Brunswick, NJ: Rutgers University Press.

Harris, Marvin. 1968. *The Rise of Anthropological Theory*. New York: Thomas Y. Crowell.

Hegel, G.W.F. 1910. *The Phenomenology of Mind*, J.J.B. Balillie, trans. London: Allen & Unwin.

———. 1956 [orig. 1837]. *The Philosophy of History*, J. Sibree, trans. New York: Dover.

Henry, Jules. 1963. *Culture Against Man*. New York: Vintage.

Herodotus. 1998. *The Histories*, Robin Waterfield, trans. New York: Oxford University Press.

Herrnstein, Richard J., and James Q. Wilson. 1985. "Are Criminals Made or Born?" *New York Times Magazine*, August 4.

Herskovits, Melville. 1951. "Tender and Tough-Minded Anthropology and the Study of Values in Culture," *Southwestern Journal of Anthropology* 7:22–31.

———. 1958. "Some Further Comments on Cultural Relativism," *American Anthropologist* 60:266–273.

Hobbes, Thomas. 1958 [orig. 1642]. *Leviathan*. New York: Liberal Arts Press.

Hoebel, E. Adamson. 1954. *The Law of Primitive Man: A Study in Comparative Legal Dynamics*. Cambridge: Harvard University Press.

Holmberg, Alan R. 1958. "The Research and Development Approach to the Study of Change," *Human Organization* 17(1):12–16.

Homans, George C., and David M. Schneider. 1955. *Marriage, Authority and Final Causes*. New York: Free Press.

Horkheimer, Max, and Theodor W. Adorno. 1972. *Dialectic of Enlightenment*. New York: Herder and Herder.

Hughes, Robert. 1986. *The Fatal Shore: The Epic of Australia's Founding*. New York: Vintage Books.

Husserl, Edmund. 1931. *Ideas: General Introduction to Pure Phenomenology*. New York: Macmillan.

———. 1970. *Crisis of European Sciences and Transcendental Phenomenology: An Introduction to Phenomenological Philosophy*. Evanston: Northwestern University Press.

Hymes, Dell, ed. 1969. *Reinventing Anthropology*. New York: Pantheon.

Jackson, Michael, ed. 1996. *Things as They Are*. Bloomington: Indiana University Press.

Jakobson, Roman. 1971. *Selected Writings, I: Phonological Studies*. Stephen Rudy, ed. The Haque: Mouton.

Kant, Immanuel. 1951 [orig. 1790]. *A Critique of Judgment*, H. Bernard, trans. New York: Hafner.

Kardiner, Abram, ed. 1945. *The Individual and His Society*. New York: Columbia University Press.

Kardiner, Abram, Ralph Linton, J. West, et al. 1945. *The Psychological Frontiers of Society*. New York: Columbia University Press.

Keesing, Roger. 1987. "Anthropology: An Interpretive Quest," *Current Anthropology* 28:161–175.

Kelly, Lawrence. 1985. "Why Applied Anthropology Developed when It Did: A Commentary on People, Money, and Changing Times, 1930–1945," in June Helm, ed., *Social Contexts of American Anthropology, 1840–1984, Proceedings of the American Ethnological Society*. New York: American Anthropological Society.

Kenyatta, Jomo. 1953. *Facing Mount Kenya: The Tribal Life of the Gikuyu*. London: Heinemann.

Khaldun, Ibn. 1958. *The Muqaddimah: An Introduction to History*, Franz Rosenthal, trans. New York: Pantheon.

Kluckhohn, Clyde C. 1948. "Comments" in *Saturday Review of Literature*, September 18, pp. 11–12.

Kroeber, Alfred L. 1915. "The Eighteen Professions," *American Anthropologist* 17:283–289.

———. 1917. "The Superorganic," *American Anthropologist* 19:163–213.

———. 1923. *Anthropology*. New York: Harcourt Brace.

———. 1939. *Cultural and Natural Areas of Native North America*. University of California Publications in American Archaeology and Ethnology 38.

———. 1949. An Authoritarian Panacea," *American Anthropologist* 51:318–320.

Kroeber, Alfred L., and Clyde C. Kluckhohn. 1963. *Culture: A Critical Review of Concepts and Definitions*. New York: Vintage Books.

Kropotkin, Peter. 1919 [orig. 1901]. *Mutual Aid: A Factor of Evolution*. London: Heinemann.

Kuhn, Thomas. 1962. *The Structure of Scientific Revolutions*. Chicago: University of Chicago Press.

Kuper, Adam. 1983. *Anthropology and Anthropologists*. New York: Routledge.

Lakatos, Imre, and Alan Musgrave, eds. 1970. *Criticism and the Growth of Knowledge*. London and New York: Cambridge University Press.

Leach, Edmund. 1954. *Political Systems of Highland Burma: A Study of Kachin Social Structure*. Boston: Beacon Press.

Lerner, David. 1964. *The Passing of Traditional Society: Modernizing the Middle East*. New York: Free Press.

Lett, Robert. 1987. *An Introduction to Theory in Anthropology*. Cambridge: Cambridge University Press.

Levi-Strauss, Claude. 1953. "Social Structure," in A. Kroeber, *Anthropology Today*, pp. 524–553. Chicago: University of Chicago Press.

———. 1961. *Tristes Tropiques*, J. Russel, trans. New York: Criterion Books.

———. 1963. *Structural Anthropology*, C. Jacobson, trans. New York: Basic Books.

———. 1966. *The Savage Mind*. Chicago: University of Chicago Press.

———. 1969a [orig. 1949]. *The Elementary Structures of Kinship*. Boston: Beacon Press.

———. 1969b. *The Raw and the Cooked*. New York: Harper & Row.

———. 1973. *From Honey to Ashes*. Chicago: University of Chicago Press.

Levy-Bruhl, Lucien. 1923. *Primitive Mentality*. New York: Macmillan.

———. 1926 [orig. 1910]. *How Natives Think*. London: Allen & Unwin.

Lewis, Herbert. 2001. "The Passion of Franz Boas," *American Anthropologist* 103(2):447–467.

Lewis, Oscar. 1951. *Life in a Mexican Village: Tepoztlan Restudied*. Urbana: University of Illinois Press.

Lewontin, Richard C. 1972. "The Apportionment of Human Diversity," in T. Dobzhansky, ed., *Evolutionary Biology*, vol. 6, pp. 381–398. New York: Plenum.

Lewontin, Richard, S. P. R. Rose, and L. J. Kamin. 1984. *Not in Our Genes.* New York: Pantheon.

Li An-che. 1937. "Zuni: Some Observations and Queries," *American Anthropologist* 39:62–77.

Lindesmith, A. R., and A. L. Strauss. 1950. "Critique of Culture-Personality Writings," *American Sociological Review* 15:587–600.

Locke, John. 1894 [orig. 1690]. *An Essay Concerning Human Understanding.* Oxford: Clarendon Press.

Lorenz, Konrad. 1970 [orig. 1966]. *On Aggression*, Marjorie Kerr Wilson, trans. New York: Bantam Books.

Lucretius. 1951. *On the Nature of Things*, Ronald Latham, trans. Baltimore, MD: Penguin Books.

Lyotard, Jean-Francois. 1986. *The Post-Modern Condition: A Report on Knowledge.* Manchester: Manchester University Press.

Maine, Henry S. 1861. *Ancient Law.* London: J. Murray.

Malinowski, Bronislaw. 1922. *Argonauts of the Western Pacific.* New York: Dutton.

———. 1935. *Coral Gardens and Their Magic.* New York: American Book.

———. 1939. "The Group and the Individual in Functional Analysis," *American Journal of Sociology* 44:938–964.

———. 1944. *A Scientific Theory of Culture.* Chapel Hill: University of North Carolina Press.

———. 1948. *Magic, Science, and Religion and Other Essays.* Garden City: Doubleday.

Malthus, Thomas. 1960 [orig. 1798]. *On Population.* New York: Modern Library.

Marx, Karl. 1973 [written 1857–1858, orig. published 1939–1941]. *Grundrisse*, Martin Nicolous, trans. Hammondsworth: Penguin.

———. 1977 [orig. 1867]. *Capital: A Critique of Political Economy*, Ben Fowkes, trans. New York: Vintage Books.

Mauss, Marcel. 1954 [orig. 1924]. *The Gift.* New York: Free Press.

McGee, Jon, and Richard L. Warms, eds. 2000. *Anthropological Theory: An Introductory History*, 2d ed. Mountain View, CA: Mayfield.

Mead, Margaret. 1928. *Coming of Age in Samoa.* New York: Morrow.

———. 1930. *Growing Up in New Guinea.* New York: Blue Ribbon.

———. 1935. *Sex and Temperament in Three Primitive Societies.* New York: Morrow.

Mill, John Stuart. 1923 [orig. 1848]. *Principles of Political Economy.* London: Longmans and Green.

Monboddo, J. B., Lord. 1774. *On the Origin and Progress of Language*, vol. 1. Edinburgh: J. Balfour and T. Cadell.

Montagu, Ashley. 1974. *Frontiers of Anthropology.* New York: Capricorn Books.

———. 1997 [orig. 1945]. *Man's Most Dangerous Myth: The Fallacy of Race*, 6th ed. Walnut Creek, CA: Altamira.

Montaigne, Michel de. 1958. *Essays*, J. M. Cohen, trans. London: Penguin Books.

Morgan, Lewis Henry. 1851. *The League of the Ho-de-no-sau-nee, or Iroquois.* Rochester: Sage and Broa.

———. 1870. *Systems of Consanguinity and Affinity of the Human Family.* Washington: Smithsonian Institution.

———. 1963 [orig. 1877]. *Ancient Society.* Eleanor Leacock, ed. New York: Meridian Books World Publishing.

Morris, Desmond. 1967. *The Naked Ape: A Zoologist's Study of the Human Animal.* New York: McGraw-Hill.

Muller-Wille, Ludger, ed. 1998. *Franz Boas among the Inuit of Baffin Island, 1883–1884, Journals and Letters,* William Barr, trans. Toronto: University of Toronto Press.

Murray, Charles A., and Richard J. Herrnstein. 1994. *The Bell Curve: Intelligence and Class Structure in American Life.* New York: Free Press.

Nader, Laura. 1965. "The Anthropological Study of Law," *American Anthropologist* 67(6, pt. 2):3–32.

Nagel, E. 1948. "The Development of Modern Science," in J. L. Blau, J. Buchler, and G. T. Matthews, eds., *Chapters in Western Civilization.* New York: Columbia University Press.

Nanda, Serena. 1999. *Neither Man nor Woman: The Hijras of India.* Belmont, CA: Wadsworth.

Needham, Rodney. 1962. *Structure and Sentiment.* Chicago: University of Chicago Press.

———. 1964. "Explanatory Notes on Prescriptive Alliance and the Purum," *American Anthropologist* 66:1377–1385.

Nietzsche, Friedrich. 1968. *The Will to Power.* W. Kaufmann, ed. New York: Random House.

Opler, Morris E. 1941. *An Apache Life-Way: The Economic, Social, and Religious Institutions of the Chiricahua Indians.* Chicago: University of Chicago Press.

Pagden, Anthony. 1982. *The Fall of Natural Man: The American Indian and the Origins of Comparative Ethnology.* Cambridge: Cambridge University Press.

Parsons, Talcott. 1937. *The Structure of Social Action.* New York: Free Press.

Peel, J.D.Y. 1972. *Herbert Spencer on Social Evolution.* Chicago: University of Chicago Press.

Perry, Richard J. 1978. "Radcliffe-Brown and Kropotkin: The Heritage of Anarchism in British Social Anthropology," *Kroeber Anthropological Society Papers* 51 and 52:61–65.

———. 1980. "Sociobiology: Science in the Service of Ideology," *Ethics* 91:125–137.

———. 1991. *Western Apache Heritage: People of the Mountain Corridor.* Austin: University of Texas Press.

———. 1993. *Apache Reservation: Indigenous Peoples and the American State.* Austin: University of Texas Press.

———. 1996. *From Time Immemorial: Indigenous Peoples and State Systems.* Austin: University of Texas Press.

———. 2000. "Attack on the Straw Men: Postmodern Critiques of Anthropology and Vice Versa," in Neil L. Waters, ed., *Beyond the Area Studies Wars: Toward a New International Studies,* pp. 109–136. Hanover, NH: Middlebury College Press.

Perry, W. J. 1923. *Children of the Sun.* London: Methuen.

Piddocke, Stuart. 1965. "The Potlatch System of the Southern Kwakiutl: A New Perspective," *Southwestern Journal of Anthropology* 21(3):244–264.

Pike, Kenneth. 1954. *Language in Relation to a Unified Theory of the Structure of Human Behavior,* vol. 1. Glendale, IL: Summer Institute of Lingistics.

Pomponio, Alice. 2000. *Seagulls Don't Fly into the Bush: Cultural Identity and Development in Melanesia.* Prospect Heights, IL: Waveland.

Popper, Karl. 1957. *The Poverty of Historicism.* Boston: Beacon Press.

———. 1966. *The Open Society and Its Enemies.* London: Hutchinson.

Poulantzas, Nikos. 1980. *State, Power, Socialism*. London: Verso.

Pratt, Mary L. 1986. "Fieldwork in Common Places," in James Clifford and George Marcus, eds., *Writing Culture*, pp. 27–50. Cambridge: Harvard University Press.

Quetelet, Adolphe. 1842. *A Treatise on Man and the Development of His Faculties*. Edinburgh: William and Robert Chambers.

Radcliffe-Brown, A.R. 1924. "The Mother's Brother in South Africa," *South African Journal of Science* 21:542–555.

———. 1935. "On the Concept of Function in Social Science," *American Anthropologist* 37:394–402.

———. 1947. "Evolution, Social or Cultural," *American Anthropologist* 49:78–83.

———. 1948. *A Natural Science of Society*. New York: Free Press.

———. 1949a. "Functionalism: A Protest," *American Anthropologist* 51:320–323.

———. 1949b. "White's View of a Science of Culture," *American Anthropologist* 51:503–512.

———. 1950. "Introduction," in A.R. Radcliffe-Brown and C. Daryll Forde, eds., *African Systems of Kindship and Marriage*, pp. 1–85. London: Oxford University Press.

———. 1952a. "Historical Note on British Social Anthropology," *American Anthropologist* 54:275–277.

———. 1952b. *Structure and Function in Primitive Society*. London: Oxford University Press.

———. 1958. *Method in Social Anthropology*. Chicago: University of Chicago Press.

Rappaport, Roy. 1968. *Pigs for the Ancestors: Ritual in the Ecology of a New Guinea People*. New Haven: Yale University Press.

Rattray, R. S. 1923. *Ashanti*. Oxford: Clarendon.

———. 1929. *Ashanti Law and Constitution*. Oxford: Clarendon.

Redfield, Robert. 1930. *Tepoztlan, A Mexican Village*. Chicago: University of Chicago Press.

———. 1941. *The Folk Culture of Yucatan*. Chicago: University of Chicago Press.

———. 1953. *The Primitive World and Its Transformations*. Chicago: University of Chicago Press.

Rosaldo, Renato. 1993. "After Objectivism," in Simon During, ed., *The Cultural Studies Reader*, pp. 104–117. New York: Routledge.

Rousseau, Jean Jaques. 1938 [orig. 1762]. *The Social Contract*, G.D.H. Cole, trans. New York: Dutton.

———. 1964 [orig. 1751]. "Discourse on the Origin and Foundation of Inequality among Men," in *The First and Second Discourses*, R. and J. Masters, trans. New York: St. Martin's.

Rushton, J. Philippe. 1980. *Altruism, Socialization, and Society*. Englewood Cliffs, NJ: Prentice Hall.

Sahlins, Marshall D. 1969. "Economic Anthropology and Anthropological Economics," *Social Science Information* 8(5):13–33.

———. 2000. *Culture and Practice: Selected Essays*. New York: Zone Books.

Sahlins, Marshall D., and Elman R. Service, eds. 1960. *Evolution and Culture*. Ann Arbor: University of Michigan Press.

Sapir, Edward. 1917. "Do We Need a Superorganic?" *American Anthropologist* 19:441–447.

———. 1921. *Language*. New York: Harcourt Brace.

————. 1929. "The Status of Linguistics as a Science," *Language* 5(4):207–214.

Sardar, Ziauddin. 1998. *Postmodernism and the Other: The New Imperialism of Western Culture*. London: Pluto Press.

Saussure, Fernand de. 1959. *Course in General Linguistics*. New York: McGraw-Hill.

Schemo, Diana Jean. 1999. "The Last Tribal Battle," *The New York Times Magazine*, October 31, pp. 70–77.

Schmidt, Wilhelm. 1939. *The Culture Historical Method of Ethnology*, S.A. Sieber, trans. New York: Fortuny's.

Schoolcraft, Henry Rowe. 1851. *Personal Memoirs of a Residence of Thirty Years with the Indian Tribes*. Philadelphia: J. Lippincott.

Schorske, Carl. 1998. *Thinking with History: Explorations in the Passage to Modernity*. Princeton: Princeton University Press.

Service, Elman R. 1960. "The Law of Evolutionary Potential," in Marshall D. Sahlins and Elman R. Service, eds., *Evolution and Culture*, pp. 93–122. Ann Arbor: University of Michigan Press.

————. 1962. *Primitive Social Organization*. New York: Random House.

Shankman, Paul. 1996. "The History of Samoan Sexual Conduct and the Mead-Freeman Controversy," *American Anthropologist* 98(3):555–567.

————. 2001. "Requiem for a Controversy: Whatever Happened to Margaret Mead?" *Skeptic* 9(1):48–53.

Sikes, E.E. 1914. *The Anthropology of the Greeks*. London: David Nutt.

Smith, Grafton Elliott. 1928. *In the Beginning: The Origins of Civilization*. New York: Morrow.

————. 1932. *The Diffusion of Culture*. London: Watts.

Smith, William Stanhope. 1810. *An Essay on the Causes of the Variety of Complexion and Figure of the Human Species*. New Brunswick, NJ: J. Simpson & Co.

Spencer, Herbert. 1885. *Principles of Sociology*. New York: Appleton-Century-Crofts.

————. 1988. "The Evolution of Society," in Paul Bohannan and Mark Glazer, eds., *High Points in Anthropology*, 2d ed. New York: Alfred A Knopf.

Spencer, W. Baldwin, and F. Gillin. 1968 [orig. 1899]. *The Native Tribes of Central Australia*. New York: Macmillan.

Stanton, William. 1960. *The Leopard's Spots: Scientific Attitudes toward Race in America, 1815–59*. Chicago: University of Chicago Press.

Starr, June, and Jane F. Collier, eds. 1989. *History and Power in the Study of Law*. Ithaca: Cornell University Press.

Steward, Julian, 1955. *Theory of Culture Change: The Methodology of Multilinear Evolution*. Urbana: University of Illinois Press.

Stocking, George. 1965. "From Physics to Ethnology: Franz Boas' Arctic Expedition as a Problem in the Historiography of the Behavioral Sciences," *Journal of the History of the Behavioral Sciences* 1:53–66.

————, ed. 1974. *The Shaping of American Anthropology 1883–1911: A Franz Boas Reader*. New York: Basic Books.

————. 1992. *The Ethnographer's Magic and Other Essays in the History of Anthropology*. Madison: University of Wisconsin Press.

Sumner, William Graham, and A. Keller. 1927. *The Science of Society*. New Haven: Yale University Press.

Tacitus. 1948 [orig. A.D. 98]. *Tacitus on Britain and Germany*. London: Penguin.

Tattersal, Ian. 1999. *The Last Neanderthal*. Boulder, CO: Westview.

Templeton, Alan R. 1998. "Human Races: A Genetic and Evolutionary Perspective," *American Anthropologist* 100(3):632–650.

Thompson, J. Eric S. 1954. *The Rise and Fall of Maya Civilization*. Norman: University of Oklahoma Press.

Tocqueville, Alexis de. 2000 [orig. 1835]. *Democracy in America*. Harvey C. Mansfield and Delba Winthrop, trans. Chicago: University of Chicago Press.

Todorov, Tzvetan. 1987. *The Conquest of America*. New York: Harper & Row.

Turner, Victor. 1967. *The Forest of Symbols*. Ithaca: Cornell University Press.

———. 1982. *The Ritual Process*. Ithaca: Cornell University Press.

Tylor, Edward Burnett. 1889. "A Method of Investigating the Development of Institutions: Applied to Laws of Marriage and Descent," *Journal of the Royal Anthropological Institute* 18:245–269.

———. 1916 [orig. 1881]. *Anthropology: An Introduction to the Study of Man and Civilization*. New York: D. Appleton.

———. 1958 [orig. 1871]. *Primitive Culture: Researches into the Development of Mythology, Philosophy, Religion, Language, Art, and Custom*. London: J. Murray.

Van Gennep, Arnold. 1960 [orig. 1909]. *The Rites of Passage*. London: Routledge and Kegan Paul.

Vasquez, Mario. 1964. "Changes in the Social Stratification of an Andean Hacienda," in Dwight B. Heath and Richard N. Adams, eds., *Contemporary Cultures and Societies of Latin America*, pp. 405–433. New York: Random House.

Vayda, Andrew. 1961. "Expansion and Warfare among Swidden Agriculturalists," *American Anthropologist* 63:346–358.

de Waal Malefijt, Annemarie. 1974. *Images of Man: A History of Anthropological Thought*. New York: Knopf.

Wallace, Alfred Russell. 1905. *My Life*. London: Chapman and Hall.

Wallace, Anthony F. C. 1952. "The Modal Personality of the Tuscarora Indians as Revealed by the Rorschach Test," *Bureau of American Ethnology Bulletin* 150. Washington, DC.

———. 1956. "Revitalization Movements," *American Anthropologist* 58:264–281.

———. 1970. *Culture and Personality*. New York: Random House.

Wallerstein, Immanuel. 1974. *The Modern World System: Capitalist Agriculture and the Origins of the European World Economy in the Sixteenth Century*. New York: Academic Press.

———. 1984. *The Politics of the World Economy: The States, the Movements, and the Civilizations*. Cambridge: Cambridge University Press.

Weber, Max. 1949. *The Methodology of the Social Sciences*. Glencoe, IL: Free Press.

Webster, Elsie May. 1984. *The Moon Man: A Biography of Nikolai Miklouho-Maclay*. Berkeley: University of California Press.

White, Leslie A. 1945. "Diffusion versus Evolution: An Anti-Evolutionist Fallacy," *American Anthropologist* 47:339–356.

———. 1949. *The Science of Culture: A Study of Man and Civilization*. New York: Farrar, Strauss and Company.

———. 1959. *The Evolution of Culture*. New York: McGraw-Hill.

———. 1988. "Energy and the Evolution of Culture," in Paul Bohannan and Mark Glazer, eds., *High Points in Anthropology*, pp. 337–355. New York: Knopf.

Whorf, Benjamin Lee. 1956. *Language, Thought, and Reality*. New York: John Wiley & Sons.

Williams, Eric. 1984. *From Columbus to Castro: The History of the Caribbean, 1492–1969.* New York: Vintage Books.

Williams, F. E. 1923. "The Vailala Madness and the Destruction of Native Ceremonies in the Gulf District," *Territory of Papua, Anthropological Report No. 4.*

———. 1930. *Orokaiva Society.* London.

———. 1936. *Papuans of the Trans-Fly.* Oxford.

Williams, Nancy. 1986. *The Yolngu and Their Land: A System of Land Tenure and the Fight for Its Recognition.* Berkeley: University of California Press.

Williams, Raymond. 1958. *Culture and Society: 1780–1950.* New York: Columbia University Press.

———. 1981. *Culture: The Sociology of Culture.* New York: Schocken Books.

Wilson, Edward O. 1975. *Sociobiology: The New Synthesis.* Cambridge: Harvard University Press.

———. 1998. *Concilience: The Unity of Knowledge.* New York: Knopf.

Wilson, Geoffrey, and Monica Hunter Wilson. 1945. *The Analysis of Social Change.* Cambridge: Cambridge University Press.

Wilson, James Q., and Richard J. Herrnstein. 1985. *Crime and Human Nature.* New York: Simon & Schuster.

Witherspoon, Gary. 1977. *Language and Art in the Navajo Universe.* Ann Arbor: University of Michigan Press.

Wittfogel, Karl. 1953. "The Ruling Bureaucracy of Oriental Despotism: A Phenomenon that Paralized Marx," *The Review of Politics* 15:350–359.

Wolf, Eric R. 1957. "Closed Corporate Peasant Communities in Mesoamerica and Java," *Southwestern Journal of Anthropology* 13:1–18.

———. 1966. *Peasants.* Englewood Cliffs, NJ: Prentice Hall.

———. 1969. *Peasant Wars of the Twentieth Century.* New York: Harper & Row.

———. 1982. *Europe and the People without History.* Berkeley: University of California Press.

Wolpoff, M. H., J. Hawks, D. W. Frayer, and K. Huntly. 2002. "Modern Human Ancestry at the Periphery: A Test of the Replacement Theory," *Science* 291:293–297.

Worsley, Peter. 1984. *The Three Worlds: Culture and World Development.* Chicago: University of Chicago Press.

Zolbrod, Paul G. 1984. *Dine Bahane: The Navajo Creation Story.* Albuquerque: University of New Mexico Press.

PHOTO CREDITS

INDEX